Still Moving

Still Moving

Linda Durham

Mobius Pathways Press
Santa Fe, New Mexico

Still Moving is based not only on memory but also on decades of journals filled with stories of real events, real places, and real people whose names have not been changed. The author has made every effort to tell stories truthfully and to contact living persons mentioned. All references in this memoir to various ethnic and cultural groups are made with the highest respect for the dignity and plurality of peoples of all races, genders, and creeds. Where the author relates childhood stereotypical perceptions about the ethnic group that self-identifies as Gypsy, she references positive attributes that she admired and to which she was attracted. Childhood views gave way to adult awareness of the cruelty of racial and social injustice and deepened the author's commitment to value all life and to serve as an advocate for the environment, peace, and justice. The author and publisher welcome any corrections that should be incorporated in future reprints or editions of this book.

Paperback: ISBN 978-0-578-72293-1

E-book: ISBN 978-0-578-75748-3

LCCN: 2020916707

First paperback printing October 2020

Printed and bound in the United States of America

Front cover original cast-glass sculpture copyright © 2004 Christine Cathie, Auckland, NZ, reproduced by permission

Back cover photograph copyright © 2014 Jennifer Esperanza

Book design: Janine Lehmann Design, Santa Fe, NM

Mobius Pathways Press
Santa Fe, NM 87506

info@MobiusPathwaysPress.com

MobiusPathwaysPress.com

For my father, who encouraged me to think outside the box and color outside the lines.

Love is most nearly itself
When here and now cease to matter.
Old [wo]men ought to be explorers
Here and there does not matter
We must be still and still moving
Into another intensity
For a further union, a deeper communion
Through the dark cold and empty desolation,
The wave cry, the wind cry, the vast waters
Of the petrel and the porpoise.
In my end is my beginning.

–T. S. Eliot, extract from "Four Quartets: East Coker"

Contents

Introduction: Memoir As Mountain

"Get the newspaper, scissors, tape, and a pencil," Everett Graves gently ordered his little chatterbox, who had bounded down the stairs to greet him from the seemingly endless confinement to her room. Behind its closed door, she had felt rejected and confused by her mother's harsh banishment. That was until an extraordinary thing happened, and she nearly jumped out of her Mary Janes in her eagerness to reveal it to the most-trusted soul she knew.

In the living room of their cramped Philadelphia row house, this intuitive father—like Thoth, the Egyptian god of writing, magic, and wisdom—translated his four-year-old daughter's afternoon insights into a tangible object. He snipped a long, thin strip from the evening paper. With one end in his left hand and the other in his right, he made a quick and twisty abracadabra motion, brought the ends together, and secured them with tape. Then he drew tiny dashes along the endless length of that floppy loop until his last dash met the first, and the dashes began again to travel the one-sided path.

The Mobius strip my father made for me more than seven decades ago became the magical and moving symbol of the opposing forces in my never-static, unorientable life. It beckoned me forward—and back—tapped my shoulder into wakefulness and turned me upside down and inside out. Like a constant companion, that simple form guided me to those exquisite experiential intersections where disparate energies met, collided, battled, and were resolved, or dissolved.

When I was young, I had no idea how to transform the pre-shaped narratives of who others wanted me to be into authentic manifestations of my ever-unfolding self. It took trial and error and time to acquire the knowledge, skills, and courage to push back against the psychological, professional, cultural, and gender labels that attached to me.

Who would we be if the world never gave us a label? Labels attach early and follow us like shadows. Narcissism is my shadow. But wait. We are all far more than our shadows. We are complex, conscious, multidimensional beings whose stories reflect our fears, foibles, failures, and fractured lives.

For me, the deep symbolism of the Mobius strip is expressed clearly and exquisitely in its kinship to the dichotomous yin yang. Personalities are never all this or all that, all light or all shadow. We find ourselves somewhere along the continuum of creativity that defies naming. Labels imply boundaries. They distance us from ourselves and others.

Like the harsh clinical definition of a narcissist, I have (sometimes) exaggerated my abilities, talents, and accomplishments. Indeed, I've feigned confidence and given others room to assume that I could do something before I knew how to do it. Yet, it has been those displays of optimism that offered me a road map to follow so I could step and stumble into my true life personally and professionally. The eager explorer says, "Onward," followed by, "Oh, my God, how?"

If I hold that I am the center of my own universe, then I must further acknowledge that the center is always shifting. Do I strive to conquer, excel, and rise above? Yes, I have lived with a dread of being ordinary. I remain protective of my own uniqueness and successes. Ironically, whatever admiration I've earned has turned to embarrassment. Bigger and more powerful than those narcissistic traits to which I seemed attached, however, was the connection to my early childhood be-wild-er-ment.

Never-ending wonder filled me with admiration and deep empathy for the people I've encountered in the far and near cultural corners of our shared world. Especially artists. Not only those who make art as their profession or obsession but also those who lead creative, artful lives. We have shared our profound truths with one another as friends, acquaintances, and strangers who, in varied physical or emotional circumstances, found the strength to glean meaning from despair.

As I pulled the elements of *Still Moving* from fifty or sixty journals, scribbled notes, favorite quotes, photographs, and yellowing newspaper and magazine clippings, the map of interconnected themes took on definition. When I extended my hand to bridge the distance between other and me, lonely streets became only streets. Strangers became friends. Taking longer and shorter detours in my quest to reach There from Here, I lost and found myself over and again. In tame and wild places on five continents, I recorded coordinates and signposts of the sacred, mundane, magical, and profane—reminiscences that called out to be reclaimed across time.

We may think our past is behind us. Yet, sometimes it's blatantly in our face. Moments, seemingly lost, become inextricably intertwined with consciousness in the Here and Now. That's why the incorrigible habits of my unstructured life defied storytelling in chronological order, disordering my memory's Nows and Thens. Spiritual and psychological growth is not like an architectural structure that builds on a foundation. Sometimes we erect walls where they shouldn't be or needn't be when they bear no load. And, sometimes, the most forward-thinking course is to tear them down, leaving us nowhere to hide.

Once I overcame the fear of disrobing in plain sight, I stripped down to the barest emotions—revealing, behind the scars from clashes between dreams and perceived reality, a core of naked courage. Falling to bouts of abject loneliness, I succumbed to the need for forgiveness—of myself and others. All along, my constant comfort was Wonder. Through continuous exploration, I pulled threads from the tapestry of history—the world's and mine—and wove them, twisted them, braided them into my own story.

In the unfolding, each story became a step in my journey through daring encounters with self-revelation. Always searching, I learned that imagination—creating something that doesn't exist—and perception—acknowledging something that does exist—are linked. Like the two ends of the magical Mobius strip, turned and brought together, the brain's seemingly disparate parts share territory that triggers both processes. A neuroscientist described it this way: imagination is like running perception in reverse. I wonder if the opposite is also true: perception is like running imagination in reverse.

In my failures, have I succeeded? In my successes, have I—still and somehow—failed? Success and failure: How is it that one becomes the other? Paradox: lost and found!

For many years, my speeding train of thought, vision, desire, and intention barely slowed at the usual stations of wifehood, motherhood, and careerhood. It raced headlong toward a global platform where my emotional, physical, intellectual, and spiritual leanings and directions shifted. There, I disembarked and merged with my surroundings. The men, women, and children I met in Myanmar, Cambodia, Iraq, Gaza, Haiti, Madagascar, and other parts of the world where our global families live, work, struggle, create, and dream, brought me to tears of joy and sadness. Again and again, I carried home the gifts and burdens of my worldwide family. Their memory adorns my surroundings. They live in my work, in my heart, and in the nearly seven decades of dialogues in my journals with my self.

Still Moving is not a travelogue of exotic places and beautiful faces and information on where to catch a bus to Lesotho or how to slay the handless monkeys under the jungle bed. It explores the most elusive question of all—the why of our interconnectedness.

While laboring through the pains and joys of birthing *Still Moving*, I discovered that this memoir birthed me and revealed me to myself. I have whitewashed nothing. I trust that I have assembled meaningful stories to entertain, inform, soothe, or inspire you. Heady, existential questions still linger. What are the big lessons winnowed from life in the fast lane, the loner and lonely lanes, the curiosity lane? What did the detours, off-ramps, and even the twilight zone contribute to an understanding of my journey? How do we come to terms with the difference between who we are now and who we would become if we cut whatever ties, cords, and reins constrain us? Answers evolve—depending upon prevailing winds. Unseasonable storms. Persistent drought. Heat waves.

Those answers are subtle. I don't pretend to tell you how to respond to the inevitable or how to find alternate routes around roadblocks and rock slides. But I share with you my atlas-in-progress and invite you to discover your own map and to imagine and create your unique itinerary.

Banishment to my room by my mother those many years ago both affirmed my active inner life and portended an outer life suitable to my imaginings—a wild, unorthodox, adventuresome journey as a mystic gypsy, an accidental angel, and a peripatetic pilgrim.

In all of my manifestations—from worst to best—I recognized my revealed self as a microcosm in the macrocosm, a veritable manifestival, full of opportunities to go out and out and then return. Time after time, I ventured out looking for something, only to return with something else, something I didn't initially seek or know existed. Always, I sense that I have not gone far enough or that I have come back too soon. Much too soon.

Each planned or spontaneous sojourn contributed detail and color to my personal map, painting it with empathy, awe, and connection: connection to the Madagascar baobabs via a rough, eighteen-hour odyssey with everyday people who made room for an out-of-her-element foreigner; connection to a shriveled old woman in the dark, rainy wetness behind a remote truck stop with whom I shared the urgency to pee; connection to a private driver and interpreter—a soul brother from another mother, country, and culture—but from the same heart of God; and connection to the heartsick old man in a plaid bathrobe and slippers who was slowly, painfully losing his beauty queen wife to Alzheimer's.

Stop. Look. Listen. Pay attention. Notice, feel, see, hear, sense, discover. Witness the Universe sharing its messages of truth and comfort with you. Life's signposts are everywhere.

This once starry-eyed, theatre-crazed teenager and former New York Playboy Bunny, who had abandoned the addictive glamour of Manhattan, the intoxication of the counter-culture, and the false comforts of conventional family life in pursuit of the unknown, even found direction in the manufacturer's label "Anchor" in the sink in a nameless hotel in a forgotten town on my way back to forward.

Across borders, beyond so-called language, social, cultural, and political barriers, I have always found connection. Other is us: we are inseparable. Always, we can see opposites becoming one as we travel along a Mobius strip. We can seek those alchemical moments of accidental or purposeful encounters in which to discover new worlds, fresh ideas, and love after loss.

An essential first step may be reconnecting to ourselves. Let's not believe that the image in the mirror is us. When that mirror breaks and our flawed perception of the real crashes in sharp splinters on the floor, we can be cut deeply while picking up the pieces of our shattered lives. When shattered, I choose to survey the landscapes of my experiences and examine them through the transit of my remembrances.

Who are we when we've lost those things that we thought defined us? For years, I accepted the composed person I saw in the mirror—the one reflected by friends, associates, and even strangers. I became intoxicated by the power, intrigue, beauty, and energy of the art world. Collaboratively with my talented staff, I earned a place in the league of prominent and respected fine-art galleries in one of the nation's leading art centers. The future looked bright. Morning after morning, I awoke bright-eyed and bushy-tailed, ready to embrace whatever task or opportunity greeted me. My optimistic self-belief seemed unwavering. It never occurred to me that what went up and up could come tumbling down. Up seemed limitless. When those gallery doors shuttered once and for all in 2011, I found myself trapped inside a vanished dream, alone, in the shadows. Forever. I faced an unexpected and unacceptable reality: I was a failure.

The dark sea of perplexity and fear into which I had plunged seemed fathomless. Where were the rafts I had always climbed aboard? How could I rescue myself this time? Would I remain paralyzed, lost in a nebulous nowhere? Or could I drown my fears and chart my course by the stars?

Sail with me on this journey to places where time is irrelevant. We'll encounter the spaces between predilection and disinclination, where the ordinary meets the extraordinary, where fear may be the embryo of courage that, when hatched, is destined to become a magnificent bird of paradise.

Every day, our miraculous bodies conduct a freshly composed symphony: destruction and re-creation orchestrate in harmony. Daily, I build upon the one great journey that is mine in this lifetime, as I make tracks along the Mobius strip where, now and then, as the *I Ching* reveals, "retreat furthers."

Our battered suitcases were piled on the sidewalk again; we had longer ways to go. But no matter, the road is life.

–Jack Kerouac, *On the Road*

With my children, Rocky and Daisy, and Toronto, the cat, at the
Canyon Road Gallery, Santa Fe, NM, 1985 (Painting by Richard Hogan)
COURTESY OF VALERIE SANTAGTO

Linda Durham, Girl Art Dealer, Is Dead

My photograph, in profile, filled the cover of the March 2–8, 2011, issue of the *Santa Fe Reporter*.

SANTA FE LOSES LINDA DURHAM CONTEMPORARY ART— BUT NOT LINDA DURHAM

There it was. In eleven words and fifty-six characters. Inside, a lengthy interview and thirteen full-color illustrations summed up the beginning, middle, and end of Linda Durham, Girl Art Dealer, and her "Creative Life." This unanticipated and unwelcome turn of events carved out my heart and stripped me naked in front of my community.

> Durham and her gallery have been a force in Santa Fe's creative community since she first happened on her career and developed a habit of representing New Mexico and its artists locally and internationally. Now, after 33 years in business, Durham will close her gallery on March 4.
>
> That Durham's enterprise has survived for so long, but is coming to an end now, is a testament both to her talent and commitment, as well as the reach of the nation's shifting economic sands.
>
> "I never made a great deal of money, but I made enough to keep the gallery going and growing. I invested all the profits into advertising, art fairs, PR, design—because the gallery was my passion."

It's over! It's definitely over. My gallery, my obsession, my alter ego is now history. I have run out of steam, money, and time. I have lost my platform, my disguise, my raison d'être. I don't know where I will go from here.

–Journal, April 2011

More than a passion and more than a job, the gallery became my primary vehicle for communication. It was a full-time preoccupation. The art, artists, staff, and creative program made it a stellar place to experience original, authentic work. Everyone was welcome. On opening nights, friends rendezvoused, collectors collected, ideas percolated, and lively dialogues reverberated around the space. Through the decades, gallery-goers of all stripes attended elegant, innovative, and provocative events at one or more of our seven locations.

I "birthed" that improbable gallery in 1978. I raised it, day by day, year by year. I fed it with dynamic art, high energy, spontaneity, and optimism—my seat-of-the-pants formula for growth and success.

And it did succeed. It was groundbreaking. Linda Durham Contemporary Art helped launch an innovative contemporary art market in Santa Fe. Not only was it the first gallery to focus almost exclusively on abstract and non-representational art, but it also opened doors of opportunity and recognition for the vital New Mexico art scene through our participation in top-tier international art fairs.

For decades the gallery exhibited the paintings, photography, and sculpture of scores of accomplished New Mexico-based artists at respected expositions in Spain, Germany, and Scotland, as well as art fairs in Chicago, Los Angeles, San Francisco, Seattle, New York, and Miami. *Artforum, Art in America, ARTnews, Newsweek*, and *The New York Times* touted its bravado. Influencers in the art world took notice.

I thought my splendor in the grass would last forever. I never imagined the death of my dream. The gallery and I were a continuum. Yin and yang. Interconnected and interdependent. We exemplified polarity and paradox—the complementary nature of opposites. Clearly, I had miscalculated. The art market had changed. It was time to remove my rose-colored glasses and take a bare-faced look in the mirror.

My father worked for RCA Victor for thirty-five years. At retirement, management gave him a watch. My thirty-three-year gallery tenure was almost as long. But no one gave me a watch—at least not a timepiece. As I was sweeping out the final gallery detritus and preparing to surrender my keys, artist friend Matthew Chase-Daniel stopped by and gave me an antique "gold" pocket watch. In place of the working mechanism were hundreds of tiny seeds. Seeds of timelessness.

Linda Durham Contemporary Art closed, with finality, on March 4th. It will "march forth" no more.

—Journal, April 2011

Where Far Becomes Near and Near Becomes Far

Maybe it's not possible to start over. Perhaps one can only start again. And again. I had been living in a self-imposed dead zone, where my energy for continuing—let alone completing—had been captured in a snare of self-doubt, fear, indecision, and plain old ennui. Was I bored with my life? Unsure of direction? Was I afraid of ridicule, pity, dismissal, ordinariness? Did I doubt my ability to live up to my expectations?

Who am I? Who am I, really? Cut it out, Linda. Who am I?

I have countless answers to the question of who am I. Woman. Storyteller. Artist. Friend. Explorer. Writer. Mother. Wanderer. Abandoner.

Abandoner? Sadly, yes. Not just of relationships, ideas, passions, responsibilities, projects, and locations—but also of myself.

I claim to others—and to myself—that I long to start over. Go back to school. Study music and mathematics. Finish my book. Start a new business. Nurture plants and animals. Run away. Discard, sell, give away, leave everything behind. Leave everyone behind.

Why does the "start over, begin again" idea trail me and lead me?

It's the Mobius Strip Tease! And it's my father's fault.

As a rambunctious, willful, and chatterbox child, I was much too much for my stay-at-home and chronically depressed mother, whose mind always seemed elsewhere and who frequently wanted me to be elsewhere.

In 1947, in our small row house in Philadelphia, after lunch on an otherwise ordinary day, my mother ushered me upstairs to my bedroom. She pointed her finger at me and, with her you-better-do-what-I-tell you-or-else look, she commanded, "Stay in your room. Take a nap or play quietly. Do not come downstairs until your father comes home."

I don't know why she was so gruff with me. Maybe I ate the last banana without permission. Having delivered her instructions, she closed the door on her four-year-old daughter and went downstairs.

Feeling rejected, bored, and confused, but not tired, I sat on the floor with my

Raggedy Ann doll and a puzzle box and scattered pieces on the braided rag rug. I undressed and dressed Raggedy Ann. I pouted. I looked around the room. Minutes dissolved.

Something strange is happening. Things look blurry. My room is moving. I hug Raggedy Ann, rub my eyes, and blink. The edges and corners of the room are vanishing. The walls and door curve inward. My bed is tipping, and the bureau is leaning toward me. The room is now round—like a big see-through ball or bubble. I am sitting very still on the inside bottom of the bubble. I only move my eyes. The walls of the bubble begin to peel away, like giant flower petals. Opening. I am dizzy, but not scared. Now, without moving, I am sitting on the outside top of the round room. I don't want to let go of Raggedy Ann....

When my father came home from work, I bounded downstairs, eager to share that afternoon experience with him. He was always a patient and attentive audience for my daily recounting of ideas and adventures, as well as for my spontaneous performances of made-up songs, dances, and plays.

"You know what I know?" I looked up at him in complete trust.

My father cocked his head in a familiar, exaggerated, listening-to-me look.

"What do you know?"

"I know that the inside is the outside, and the outside is the inside."

He listened as I described my experience inside and outside of my bedroom bubble, and as I shared my theory of how opposites meet. I told him that there is a place where far becomes near and near becomes far. Excitedly, I explained that when light gets very, very bright, it begins to turn into dark, and then the dark gets darker and darker until it becomes light again.

I bubbled over with my hours-old understanding of how big becomes small and up turns into down. "If we go past all the stars," I said, not taking my eyes off my audience, "and if we keep on going and going and going, we will come back to here, to the beginning."

He smiled at my animated effort to explain newly encountered wonders of my expanding world. For a moment, my father was quiet and very still. Thinking, *what do I tell this child*, no doubt.

It is after dinner. My father asks me to get the newspaper, a pair of scissors, a pencil, and some tape. We sit on the living room floor of our rented row house. I watch as my father cuts a long, narrow strip from the morning paper. He holds the ends of the strip between his thumbs and index fingers. In a showman-like style, he stretches out his arms, and in a quick and magical twist, he brings the ends of the paper strip together and connects them with tape. Presto! I stare at the floppy loop of newspaper.

"This is a Mobius strip. It has only one side," he says. He dangles the loopy construction from the end of his finger, then places the floppy loop on the green plastic hassock. He picks up the pencil.

"If you were to walk on a Mobius strip," he says, making small pencil marks on the paper, "and, if you kept walking and walking in the same direction," he continues making tiny dashes—like miniature footprints, along the strip—dash, dash, dash, "you...would... end...up...back...where...you...started."

I watched in amazement as the little walking pencil dashes magically went all the way around and came back to the very first dash. Over the next few days, I cut up and taped together dozens of newspaper Mobius strips. Then I connected them into Mobius paper chains.

> In mathematical terms, the Möbius strip is a one-sided non-orientable surface obtained by cutting a closed band into a single strip, giving one of the two ends a half twist, and then reattaching the two ends. Like the cylinder, it is not a true surface, but rather a surface with boundary.

From that simple demonstration, a powerful image lodged somewhere behind my eyes. I still see the Mobius multiverses practically every day. The magical Mobius shape continues to illustrate an important aspect of my private sense of the world. It is the memory of that night with my father and the experience of seeing the neverendingness of something tangible in my narrow world that began to define my expanding spiritual universe.

Somewhere along the continuum, the end yearns to embrace the beginning, as the beginning reaches toward its non-end. If I look ahead, my path beckons. If I glance over my shoulder, I encounter a version of myself—a part of the continuum. Moving. Still.

That is where and when it all began, my fascination with connections, with circles and cycles, with beginnings, endings, and more beginnings. The years and myriad adventures sustained my vision of the mystery of the way things are at those junctions where opposites connect. My child's theory has matured into this woman's ever-searching philosophy.

Everything meets everything. Somewhere. This I choose to believe. In all things, there is connectedness. I envision a point where all manner of opposites intersect, collide, and explode. The persistent "same/opposite" notion that trails me, accompanies me, and leads me has its roots in that afternoon vision. It is at those intersections where great energy occurs. Where stillness moves. Where fear exhibits bravery. Where anger dissolves into peace. Where emptiness is filled.

Where "One" becomes "The Other." Where life meets death and death gives rise to life.

To make a Mobius strip, we simply secure the end to the beginning. After that, it's all middles.

In 1988, multiple myeloma killed my father. My mother said I could have his chess pieces—the familiar, small wooden objects that he kept in an old tin tobacco canister and which he used to best me at the game over and over again for more than a decade. My father taught me to play chess around the age of eight or nine, and we played throughout my high school years.

The chessboard rests on the green plastic hassock. My father leans forward in his brown tweed overstuffed chair and puts his elbow on his knee and cups his chin in his hand. I sit cross-legged on the floor and study the board. My father studies me. I cannot see ahead. I move a pawn, a knight, my queen....He immobilizes my king. Checkmate. I think I'll win this time. I don't. I never do. I feign disappointment. A quiet, mischievous smile spreads over my father's craggy face, and we drop the chess pieces back in the SAIL (extra mild Cavendish) pipe tobacco can, each making a little plunking sound.

When I came home for Thanksgiving after my first semester as a theatre major at Ithaca College, we pulled out the board and chess pieces. He in his chair, I on the floor. I won. We never played again. Sometimes there is not even a fine line between winning and losing.

Those small, ordinary chess pieces and an old gray suede jacket are the only possessions belonging to my father that came to me. I vowed to keep the jacket forever. I wore it sometimes. It was only slightly too large for me. Somewhere along the way, I lost track of the jacket. The chess pieces? They're still in the tobacco tin, in a cabinet with other games I never play.

An Internship

The first test-tube baby is born. Saigon has fallen. Elvis Presley has died. I am living with my husband Hobart "Bart" Durham, Jr., and our two young children in a historic hacienda on the east side of Santa Fe. It is 1977.

—From multiple journal entries

Often, on my walk to and from the neighborhood grocery store, the Plaza, or the State Capitol, I passed a rambling adobe art gallery. Friends had mentioned the remarkable treasures displayed inside and the charismatic man who built the business: Forrest Fenn. One afternoon, curiosity got the best of me.

I wandered among the rooms of eclectic paintings, sculpture, jewelry, and Native American weavings and artifacts. Somewhere in the midst of my wonder, I overheard a gallery associate describe a collection of newly acquired rare books to a spellbound older couple decked out in their wild Western regalia—expensive cowboy boots and beaded suede jackets with lots of fringe. The associate glanced my way and gestured toward a back hallway. I took her cue. A few steps from the main gallery, I discovered a small, inviting room with bookshelves that rose from the tan carpeted floor to a marvelous ceiling of patchworked squares made from remnants of Navajo rugs.

Sentinels of art history lined half the shelves. Cartons of books, stacked atop each other like miniature high-rises, covered the desk and floor. A parrot squawked from its cage in the corner. Leaning against the doorjamb, I took a deep breath and imagined myself spending time with those rare books in the company of the talkative Amazonian yellow-headed parrot. A smoldering desire to escape my lackluster homemaker life ignited. I felt a searing urge to experience more of this enticing place.

In the main gallery, a ruggedly handsome, square-jawed man, dressed in a crisp cowboy shirt and blue jeans embroidered on the right thigh with a colorful Indian symbol, strode through massive carved doors leading from an inner office.

He headed straight to me, smiled naturally, and extended his hand. "Forrest Fenn," he said, holding on to my fingers, squeezing them slightly.

Forrest's legendary charm charmed me. He insisted on giving me a personal tour of the gallery, including a visit to a bank-sized, walk-in vault with shelf upon shelf of Zuni, Hopi, and Pueblo treasures, exotic jewelry, old guns, magnificent textiles, and cowboy memorabilia. It was dizzying. A wave of emotion at the splendor and fineness of it washed over me—like Daisy Buchanan must have felt when Gatsby showed her the piles of monogrammed silk and linen shirts in the bedroom of his estate, and she "bent her head into the shirts and began to cry"—from the surprise and beauty of the moment.

I wanted to work there.

"I notice you recently acquired a collection of old art books," I said, recovering and voicing an idea as it burst upon me. "My husband and I are great book lovers." I ad-libbed nervously, gesturing in the direction of the room with the books, boxes, and parrot. "We have a small private book business, specializing in rare and out of print books."

Forrest escorted me back to the library.

"It would be exciting to work with this collection," I heard myself say as I picked up and caressed a volume of George Catlin prints. "I wish you were looking for a librarian. I'd love to work with these books."

Forrest telephoned the next afternoon and described a small research project he thought might interest me. It did. For a week, I paged through twenty or thirty late 19th- and early 20th-century bound volumes of *Harper's*, *Scribner's*, and *Century* magazines searching for a reproduction of a particular Frederick Remington illustration. In the process, I catalogued the Remington illustrations in every volume. None matched the drawing in Forrest's possession.

When I finished the project, Forrest called me into his office. "I've gotten used to having you around." He offered me a job and gave me a title. I went home as his new Director of Research at four dollars and fifty cents an hour. I promised to stay for a year. He promised to teach me the business.

Over those next months, all I wanted to do was immerse myself in the art and gallery business—in the "game." An addictive and dangerous game. It surprised me that I was so willing to shift attention from my marriage, my home life, and even compromise aspects of my soul for access to and membership in that new world.

"It doesn't matter who you are," Fenn told a *People* magazine reporter nine years later, in 1986. "It only matters who they think you are. It's true in Hollywood, in politics, and it's true with a painting."

He had never spoken those exact words to me. Or maybe he did.

Hello, my name is Linda. And I'm a research art librarian at Fenn Galleries. Hello, Linda.

Midway through my tenure at the gallery, Forrest showed me an early 20th-century painting—a roiling ocean under a full moon—that an elderly woman was planning to sell.

"This is a Ryder," Forrest said. "R-Y-D-E-R. Get some information on it."

I had never heard of Ryder. I took the ornately framed painting to my office and began my research. Works by the troubled late 19th-century painter Albert Pinkham Ryder captured the interest of collectors and forgers alike. Especially popular, and most frequently forged, were Ryder's distinctive moonlit seascapes. At the time, the Brooklyn Museum had the foremost experts on Ryder's work.

I spoke with several people in the American painting department about differentiating authentic Ryder works from the many fakes. One curator explained that Ryder didn't limit his technique to layering paints and glazes; he also added assorted unorthodox materials, such as grease or candlewax. A museum technician suggested that I have the painting X-rayed to determine the existence or absence of Ryder's characteristic extensive underpainting. Armed with the proper X-ray settings, I shepherded the moonlit seascape to the Santa Fe Imaging Lab. The X-ray results showed only a thin layer of paint. No wax, no hidden glazes.

I prepared my notes and proudly presented my formal report to Forrest, believing I would save him from buying a forgery. He studied it just long enough to grasp the conclusion, then slapped his hand on the desk.

"Damn it, Linda! You spent all that time and *my* money proving the painting is a fake? With the same effort, you could have proved it was authentic!"

That afternoon I discovered that, in segments of the art world, there is a thin—sometimes invisible—line between real and fake.

My knowledge grew exponentially that year with Forrest. I learned that loyalty mattered to Forrest more than anything. I learned that it almost always takes money to make real money and that actual, perceived, and intangible are vastly different kinds of values. I learned that everyone in the art business knows everyone else: dealers, collectors, museum directors, and auction officials. I learned that savvy dealers who dislike and distrust one another could wheel and deal their way through complex compacts as though they were close colleagues.

I learned that old, apparently unsigned, paintings could be shipped to Montana, or the Dakotas, to be cleaned and, magically—through the wonder of alchemy—the signature of a famous artist could appear. I learned that naiveté is dangerous—except in those rare instances when it's an asset.

Most disconcertingly, I learned that the world of artists, paintings, exhibitions, dealers, and consultants had a profound and intoxicating effect on me.

On the last day of my Fenn year—researching, socializing, and soaking up information and gossip about art, business, and art and business people—I drew up a proposal "for the better utilization of my time and talents." I ended the bulleted list of my responsibilities and accomplishments with a request for a two-dollar-an-hour salary increase.

Forrest was out of town. In his absence, gallery director John Rivenburgh, a former Chicago ad man, scrutinized my carefully crafted proposition. When he reached the part about my raise, he laughed.

I resigned that afternoon.

A New York art dealer with whom I had collaborated on ghost-writing the Albert Bierstadt and Ralph Blakelock catalogs for a Fenn Gallery exhibition suggested, practically in passing, that I might want to open my own gallery now that I was no longer working for Forrest.

My own gallery? It hadn't occurred to me. Nevertheless, minutes after the idea floated through my head, I wondered how I could start my own gallery. How would I find art? How would I find money once I found art? Where would I begin?

Showing valuable works by well-known dead artists like Nicolai Fechin, Leon Gaspard, Thomas Moran, the Taos Founders, and the Hudson River School painters was beyond my wildest financial imaginings. From New York to L.A., fistfuls of knowledgeable art dealers controlled those markets—dealing and double-dealing in that specialized field. No, I didn't want to compete—didn't know how to compete—with a bunch of heavyweights in an arena where I was barely a flyweight.

My non-plan idea bumped up against the no-money reality of my situation. There were obstacles to be addressed and overcome. If I were to have a gallery, it would have to be started on a shoestring, and it would have to showcase something other than works by famous dead painters and sculptors.

What if I could show consigned work by living, dedicated artists who were already friends, or friends of friends? An idea started to take shape. I envisioned a traveling exhibition of New Mexico-based painters and sculptors. A show in a metropolis. A show that would introduce New Mexico art to people I didn't know, people in big cities I had never visited. Perhaps I could organize and "travel" an international exhibition. The fantasy-in-waiting excited me.

New Mexico in Toronto

I chose Toronto as the perfect city to host my virgin venture into the international art exhibition world. Travel to Ontario, Canada, would be less complicated and far less expensive than organizing a trans-Atlantic or trans-Pacific exhibition, though I felt the tug of those "go big or stay home" delusions of grandeur. For my barely envisioned, first-ever art endeavor, Toronto would be just fine. A slight problem. I had never been to Toronto, and I didn't know anyone who lived or worked there. An insignificant deterrent, I concluded.

Friends and acquaintances issued their own warnings. My inexperience and lack of capital to fund the exhibition was a formula for financial disaster—or made the whole idea risky, at best. Yet, it was a risk I was willing to take. I breezed through their prophecies of doom and threw gloom to the wind. I'd figure things out as I steered the creative project from the dream stage straight to the reality stage.

PHASE ONE: *Find a venue*

The logistics of taking my wild idea through the phases from the dream stage to reality—the successful exhibition—began to take shape. I needed a presentation. I assembled a notebook of miscellaneous images of paintings by some of my Santa Fe artist friends: Carol Mothner, Dick Mason, Paul Sarkisian, Forrest Moses, and John Fincher. I had no proper transparencies, color photographs, or slides. Just a jumble of humble snapshots and a motley assortment of illustrations on out-of-date exhibition announcements from unknown, possibly defunct, galleries.

I purchased a plane ticket to Toronto and made a reservation at a fine old hotel. I still didn't know anyone in Toronto. However, I knew someone who knew someone. Ford Ruthling, a well-known Santa Fe painter and social friend, introduced me to his friend John Scoffield, a high-end Toronto interior designer.

Mr. Scoffield introduced me to Diana McMannus, a brilliant British woman who worked for an important business tycoon who was building an upscale shopping complex called Hazelton Lanes in a trendy part of the city.

In addition to being a billionaire, French-born Monsieur William Louis-Dreyfus turned out to be an engaging, attractive poet and art collector. In nervous silence during our two-hour lunch, I watched him page through my amateur notebook presentation. He smiled. I relaxed. My idea intrigued him. Would I like to mount the exhibition in an available, unfinished, five-thousand-square-foot space on the second floor of Hazelton Lanes?

Would I?

Phase One, mission accomplished! I had secured an excellent venue in which to present my not-yet-curated exhibition. I decided to call it *New Mexico in Toronto.*

William sent two dozen anthuriums to my hotel room.

PHASE TWO: *Find money*

My local banker loaned me $25,000. My unquestionably naïve entrepreneur-in-the-making earnestness must not have alarmed him. He even seemed to enjoy my enthusiastic presentation. I described my plan: the art, the artists, the venue. I summoned all my optimism and told him I was certain that this was "an idea whose time has come."

"I'm convinced I will succeed."

To my joy and relief, the banker responded, "Well, you convinced me."

Phase Two, mission accomplished!

PHASE THREE: *Find artists*

Once the loan was in place, I continued to seek out artists whose works I could include in the exhibition: Larry Bell, Allan Graham, Paul Pletka, Carl Johansen, Luis Jimenez, Georgia O'Keeffe, John Wenger, Ken Price.

At the start of this project, I had never heard of Ken Price. It was my friend Paul Sarkisian, the most accomplished artist I knew, who suggested I include him.

"Who is he?

"You don't know who Ken Price is?"

With undisguised surprise at my lack of basic contemporary art-world knowledge, Paul struggled to find a tolerant tone. Like an impatient adult speaking to a child who failed to understand a simple homework assignment, he instructed, "Ken is a very well-known artist who lives in Taos."

The shock and incredulity in Paul's voice at the embarrassing void in my art-worldly knowledge convinced me. Price belonged in my *New Mexico in Toronto* show. And so, I called Ken Price. I used my most confident voice when I introduced myself.

"Mr. Price, this is Linda Durham calling from Santa Fe. Paul Sarkisian suggested I contact you. I'm curating an exhibition in Toronto of paintings and sculpture by New Mexico-based artists. I would like to include your work in the show."

The next day, I visited Ken's Taos studio jammed with his art. He explained that he didn't have much work available since practically everything was reserved for *Happy's Curios*, his upcoming exhibition at the Los Angeles County Museum of Art.

Ken gestured toward a solitary piece in an alcove near his book- and paper-filled desk.

"If you want, I can let you have this."

We stood in front of a tall, narrow white sculpture pedestal, fitted with a Plexiglas box cover. Inside the box was an extremely small, silvery-lavender, peanut-shaped ribbed ceramic object, resting on a curved purple velvet stand—like a miniature chaise longue.

"Oh, yes, thank you. This will be wonderful." I would have accepted anything. I took out a homemade consignment agreement and began to record the particulars: artist, title, medium, dimensions. "And how much is this piece?"

"You can sell it for nine," Ken said.

"Great." I wrote nine hundred dollars on the form. We both signed it. I gave him the original and kept the carbon copy for myself.

What a very nice man. He didn't act famous at all, I thought, as I drove home.

Several days later, while having tea with a few "art people" at the home of Rosalind Constable, the former avant-garde arts reporter for *Time* magazine, I shared some details of the forthcoming Toronto exhibition.

"Ken Price consigned a fascinating piece to my show."

Rosalind launched into an effusive tribute. She fairly gushed with Price appreciation.

"I almost bought one of Ken's remarkable small tequila cups in New York not long ago," she said in her crisp British accent. "But it was nine thousand dollars, so I didn't get it."

My heart fluttered, then somersaulted.

Nine t-h-o-u-s-a-n-d dollars! Somehow, I remained poised. I dropped neither my teacup nor my jaw.

Late that afternoon, I called Mr. Price's Taos studio and launched into my affected "oh, careless me" voice.

"Hello, Ken, this is Linda Durham. I'm looking over my notes and...did I inadvertently leave a zero off the price of the sculpture on your copy of the consignment sheet?" Pause.

"Yes? I'll fix it."

"No problem." Surely Ken suspected.

PHASE FOUR: *Marketing and PR*

My business adventures and misadventures were underway. The advertisement I placed in a major national art magazine was truly atrocious. I know this only in retrospect. The graphic design for the invitation was also dreadful. The young, quasi-professional design firm that created the logo and ad (silly curlicue glyphs superimposed on an inappropriate painting) didn't know any better. Neither did I. Both the poster and the ad featured the landmark Canadian National Tower, simply called the "CN Tower"—emerging out of a surreal desert landscape painting by Dennis Culver. No wonder the layout staff at *ARTnews* placed the ad way in the back of the magazine—next to the classifieds.

That I had manifested an invitation and a color ad and a group of willing artists and a sophisticated venue for my project was enough to keep me active, enthusiastic, forward-moving, and oblivious to (or ignorant of) things like bad design and art-world faux pas.

Never underestimate the power of kismet. My vision of a successful, grand *vernissage* clouded. The day I posted two thousand lovingly hand-addressed *New Mexico in Toronto* invitations at the Santa Fe Post Office coincided with the first day of the Great Canadian Postal Strike. The little arrow-shaped cards inviting strangers to a show of artists no Canadian had ever heard of (not even icon Georgia O'Keeffe had achieved name recognition then), in an unfinished section of an under-construction shopping complex, remained undelivered during the exhibition's six-week run.

Now and then over the decades, I've wondered whatever happened to all those little abominably designed cards. I imagined them languishing in big canvas mail sacks somewhere in the wilds of Alberta, or buried beneath an avalanche of terminally undeliverable mail in Manitoba. Detritus. Landfill.

PHASE FIVE: *The 4.7 earthquake*

Determined and undaunted by minor adversities, I soldiered on. The artworks were safely transported across the country and over the border into Canada. Phew! Included in the international transport were Luis Jimenez's famous, life-size, fiberglass *End of the Trail* sculpture; Donald B. Wright's one-of-a-kind metal sculptures on his incredibly over-designed pedestals; John Fincher's suite of cacti paintings; Richard Thompson's cowboy caricatures; and a few small, delicate paintings by Carol Mothner.

We hung the show, installed the lights, and waited. And waited. We waited for the Torontonians to snap up the small (but wildly expensive by ignorant standards) Ken Price ceramic, or the Ford Ruthling painting of an eagle feather suspended over a stylized Native American pot, or the large Dick Mason gouache of Pilobolus acrobats, or the Larry Bell glass sculpture—shipped to Toronto, at my expense, from the Marian Goodman Gallery in New York, or Georgia O'Keeffe's *Red Pepper*—loaned to me by Warren Adelson, director of New York's Coe Kerr Galleries.

On opening night, I floated amid the trophy art in a pink and purple silk tie-dye gown that Anna Hansen (*aka* Anna Manana) had made for me. It was a lonely night. Other than a few close friends who traveled from Santa Fe to celebrate my inauguration, no one came to the vernissage.

In the days that followed, I sat in the gallery for hours and hours, alone. Occasionally a Hazelton Lanes shopper, who had gotten off the elevator on the wrong floor, checked out the art. The operative word was "occasionally."

One of those rare browsers told me she was quite certain she had been to my Santa Fe location. She was effusive in her compliments about the gallery that didn't exist. She remembered meeting me. I didn't amend her memory.

On another day, a well-dressed older couple strolled into *New Mexico in Toronto*. They shared their plans to visit Santa Fe in July.

"Where is your gallery? Is it near La Fonda Hotel?" the gentleman asked. Not exactly. I gave them my home address.

During the days and days of long and peopleless hours, I had plenty of time to think. Plenty of time to criticize myself. Plenty of time to immerse myself in the murky pond of disappointment in the five-thousand-square-foot space devoid of art patrons. To entertain and comfort myself, I invented names of nonexistent visitors and added their fictitious "signatures" to the otherwise empty guest book.

William sent anthuriums. William sent more anthuriums. Before the show closed, he purchased two large Allan Graham mixed-media paintings for his still-under-construction Four Seasons Hotel in Washington, D.C.

Each of those days, longing for the flock of collectors that failed to appear, my intimacy with the art in this improvised gallery grew. I fell in love with certain pieces. Shrugged off others. A few perplexed me, especially Ken Price's clay object. I struggled to understand it. Failed to understand it. It made me nervous. That little peanut intimidated me. I had not yet learned that to be intimidated by a work of art could be a good thing.

I cringed at the thought that I could have sold it for one-tenth of its actual retail value. A few years later, when I had become familiar with the market for Price's art, I bid on a set of small tequila cups at a fund-raising auction for Santa Fe's Center for Contemporary Art. When mine was the successful bid, I assumed that I was among the few auction patrons familiar with Price's work and its worth. After all, for the four tiny tequila cups, my bid was unconscionably—one might say obscenely—low. I paid at the check-out table and strolled over to pick up my great art score. The cups were gone! Someone had unobtrusively stolen them from the table of auction items. I couldn't get my money back. And the thief was never discovered. It was an ironic twist. I thought about Rosalind Constable and our shared passion for the "Price-y" tequila cups.

New Mexico in Toronto—my first solo adventure into the international art world—was far, far from a success. I returned to Santa Fe dejected, defeated, and depleted. Reality eclipsed my expectations for a stellar show, a launch that had fueled my early enthusiasm. I had fantasized that wealthy and cultured art collectors would flock to *New Mexico in Toronto*, marvel at the newness, the freshness, the vitality of the work. They would eagerly and happily write checks for John Fincher's cactus suite, Paul Pletka's large painting, O'Keeffe's *Red Pepper*, or even the mysterious Ken Price ceramic.

The Dick Mason figure drawing and the paintings that William Louis-Dreyfus purchased at a special (read "sharply reduced") collector's price represented the entire sales picture. And not a pretty picture.

When my imagined, magical windfall didn't materialize, my twenty-five-thousand-dollar bank loan produced an immediate twenty-thousand-dollar shortfall. As other bills came due, I faced a forty-five-thousand-dollar wall of debt.

On the plus side—because I always look for and usually find a plus side—I enjoyed six weeks in a penthouse duplex off Yonge Street. And I became acquainted with the many ethnic neighborhoods in culturally diverse Toronto. I met a few fascinating people who became long-time friends, and I returned to Santa Fe with some semi-possible follow-up prospects.

William sent more anthuriums to the gallery I did not yet have. Before the year was over, he purchased two more paintings and a group of ceramics by Gloria Graham for his D.C. Four Seasons hotel.

PHASE SIX: *The aftershocks*

With the artwork safely back from Canada, my husband and I decided to turn our historic adobe home into a private gallery. We moved the furniture out of the "grand sala" and walled up a big window to create more display space. We purchased track lighting and two chic white couches. Artists asked me to represent their work. I installed a group exhibition. Soon the walls were hung with paintings by Zachariah Rieke, Steve Catron, Sam Scott, Susan Rowland, Warren Davis, and many others.

I bought a beautiful white wool suit.

I threw a cocktail party for a group of collectors from a California museum.

I began to become "Linda Durham, Girl Art Dealer."

Our marriage ended soon after. We sold our house and divided the meager proceeds. My share was just enough for a down payment on an old brick schoolhouse on Canyon Road. I moved into the basement. Bart bought a small house a few blocks away. My children, Donna Lynn (Daisy) and Everett Andrew (Rocky), shuttled between. I hired my first gallery associate, Nancy Strell. We filled the rooms of the schoolhouse with art. Toronto was kindergarten. I graduated to *New Mexico in New Mexico*. I hung a hand-carved blue and white sign outside.

Linda Durham Gallery

…and I am waiting
for a rebirth of wonder…
and I am waiting
for the last long careless rapture
and I am perpetually waiting
for the fleeing lovers on the Grecian Urn
to catch each other up at last
and embrace
and I am awaiting
perpetually and forever
a renaissance of wonder.

–Lawrence Ferlinghetti, extract from "I Am Waiting"

Scotland and My Private Brigadoon

The gallery was still in its infancy when I received a call from two members of the Scottish Arts Council. They were traveling across the Southwest on holiday and wanted to meet me. "Could we discuss some of the similarities between the art communities of New Mexico and those of Scotland?" they asked. An artist working as a Santa Fe hotel concierge had told them about *New Mexico in Toronto* and my second major traveling exhibition, *New Mexico in the Bay Area*.

We met at my newly opened space in the old brick schoolhouse on Canyon Road to discuss the growing contemporary art scenes in Santa Fe and Edinburgh. Rob Breen and Gerald Laing suggested that I reprise the Toronto and Bay Area exhibitions at the 1979 Edinburgh Festival of the Arts.

New New Mexico took shape over the winter and spring, and the Scottish Arts Council approved and funded it. Serendipity, Providence, and Scotland! Art, travel, business, and friendship-making in one international project. It was the chance of a summer.

The exhibition at the Fruit Market Gallery during Edinburgh's lively theatre season proved a smash hit. Luis Jimenez, Susan Rowland, Richard Thompson, Georgia O'Keeffe, and the other Southwest American artists thrilled European visitors. We designed a tightly curated show, complete with a full-color catalog with a capstone essay by Taos author John Nichols. His words sang to exhibition goers:

> New Mexico [is a] surreal territory suspended between colorful yesterdays and frightening tomorrows. For some, it's an inspiration; for others, a castigation. Few states in America are more impoverished…or more magnificent.

And that is how I first got to Scotland—although my heart had been there since I was a stage-struck teenage apprentice at New Jersey's Camden County Music

Fair, where I saw *Brigadoon* fourteen times. An idyllic place unaffected by time and remote from reality, Brigadoon catered to my dramatic, romantic teenage self. It so captured me that I performed "The Heather on the Hill" at a high-school talent night. In Scotland, decades later, I felt my roots everywhere.

Exploring Edinburgh one afternoon, I wandered into an exhibition of daguerre-otypes at a small gallery off The High Street. I couldn't take my eyes off an image of a young man who looked exactly like me. Exactly. I asked if I could buy the photograph, but it wasn't for sale. The sensation swept over me: he must be an ancestor. The likeness was too great. Perhaps I was this lad in a former incarnation.

Everywhere, I felt the touch, the whisperings, the powerful mystery of St. Brigid, the Celtic Goddess. Roaming Scotland, I found great comfort know-ing that some of my invisible, long sloughed-away genes originated here in the heather-filled highlands. I reveled in the misty, brisk mornings. I thrilled at the stillness "in the gloaming" on Arthur's Seat. Scotland is forever in my soul.

On the heels of *New New Mexico's* success, Rob Breen advocated a second exhi-bition at the museum in Aberdeen. Some easy negotiations and the continuing generosity of the Scottish Arts Council catalyzed my return to Edinburgh in mid-November to see and publicize the show in "Granite City."

Rob and I motored from Edinburgh to Aberdeen along picturesque rural roads, through forests, moors, and magic. Scotland is the other "Land of Enchantment."

By late afternoon, we reached the museum. An arts reporter from a local television station interviewed us about the New Mexico installation. We lauded the ambitious transatlantic project and the history of the Scottish Arts Council. At the heart of the exhibition were two vibrant communities with important similarities and special differences. Each was distant from acclaimed art centers.

We came to Aberdeenshire to create a buzz about *New New Mexico* and entice residents to momentarily shake off the damp grayness of Granite City and expe-rience the warmth and ethereal light of the American West.

On the road again, this time, to the home and professional recording studio of a Canadian-American expat couple, friends of friends of Rob's who offered to put us up for the night. Our hosts, rock and roll music producers/impresa-rios, had purchased and restored a remarkable, centuries-old, fortified house.

A castle, actually. I don't mean that figuratively. Literally. It is known as "the Pink Castle."

We pulled up hungry, cold, and two hours late. A young houseman responded to our loud knocks at the hefty wood and iron door. He led us up a narrow, curving stone staircase guarded by mannequins in suits of armor. Historic coats of arms ornamented the granite walls. At the end of a baronial hall, a magnificent stone fireplace—the largest I had ever seen—caught our attention. Six leather chairs clustered around a heavy wooden table before the crackling fire.

The host, a burly man in a thick, gray Aran sweater, and his wife, a quiet brunette with a pleasant, steady expression, were warming their backs by the fire, watching the evening news on a large, then state-of-the-art television.

And there I was—in two places at once—walking toward the television across a gleaming floor that Robert the Bruce might have paced, and on the TV, extolling the virtues of *New New Mexico* in Aberdeen. Without speaking, the four of us watched, smiling. The synchronicity washed away all formality, and, despite the wife's shyness, we laughed heartily throughout dinner and wondered and marveled about the smallness of the world.

Just before midnight, the woman of the castle bid us goodnight and disappeared down a dark stone hallway. Minutes later, a celebrity from Glasgow arrived unexpectedly. His sonorous voice preceded him up the winding staircase. The imposing figure—perhaps six foot six—paused dramatically, his broad shoulders leading to a large face and an unruly mop of dark brown hair. He brandished a bottle of single malt Scotch whisky and a bottle of cognac as though they were dueling pistols as he paraded toward the table to his own accompaniment of triumphal trumpet sounds.

In a flash, the straight and sedate evening took a sharp turn toward the rowdy and bawdy. The brawny guest, a well-known Highland Games caber-toss champion, was a serious drinker and a professional storyteller, the funniest of funny men, the likes of Scotland's stand-up comedian Sir William "Billy" Connolly. We drank. He told stories. One after another. So thick was his Glaswegian brogue, the sexiest of all Scottish lilts, that I understood only the occasional phrase. It didn't matter. Everything he said caused us to double over in laughter.

Late, late into the night, the four of us drank and laughed more. We finished the Scotch. And when the brandy was gone, our host showed Rob and me to our quarters—up another flight of castle steps that led to a suite of sixteenth-century bed chambers, one room behind the other. For privacy, I chose the more distant bedroom.

It was beautiful. Cold but beautiful. I undressed quickly, slipped on my silky turquoise nightgown, and tip-toed silently through Rob's room to reach the icy bathroom. He had already climbed in bed. By my return, Rob had propped his head on several overstuffed white pillows and pulled the covers up to his chin. Motionless, he looked straight at me, or through me.

"This is so beautiful." My brandy-infused voice was excited and shaky. "Wow, I'm sleeping in a castle, I…"

Rob continued to stare at me as I rambled nervously.

"What a magnificent day…I loved the drive from Edinburgh…so exhilarating…and Aberdeen is fascinating, isn't it? I had no idea…and the TV interview went very well, I think…and the dinner was…and the castle is…and wasn't the conversation brilliant…and I'm still so excited…and tomorrow per…."

The energy in the room shifted. I could see my breath.

Rob threw aside the billowing covers and whispered, "Get in."

"Get in," he repeated, like a gentle command.

We are two people from different continents, fortified by spirits, tossed together in a fortified house where chainmail and long-handled axes hang on ancient walls. Nothing separates us, not even the linen sheets and fluffy down comforter. He is married. I am not quite divorced. He, the consummate professional. I, the novice art dealer. We, sharing moments out of context in…in a pink castle.

I am outside of my self, looking down from a carved, painted ceiling at a pale woman kissing, caressing, entangled, and intertwined with this man whose voice whispered, "Get in." Time and reality have disappeared. We are lost in passion. We hold tight to each other. He tells me stories, heartbreaking stories, of his boyhood in London during the blitzkrieg—more than fifty days and nights of horror—of his terror. We cry. We make love with abandon. This must be another life, another world, a faraway not-here, not-now place, a then-and-there place where life is pure, and there are no rules other than the rule of the Law of Yes. I hear the faint voices of the Brigadoon lovers singing "come to me, bend to me."

Just past dawn, we dressed in counterfeit formality. After a hearty breakfast, shared in earnest gratitude, with promises to return, Rob and I hugged our hosts goodbye. We traveled much of the road to reality in silence.

At the crest of a slight rise, however, I noticed a large rock cairn and asked Rob to stop. Bundled in an old fur coat, I walked toward it. Below, I saw a young girl in a blue and white pinafore, running with abandon across the gray-green field, her long red hair flowing in the wind. The instant I recognized my long-ago lassie self, she vanished. To what time did I return?

In Edinburgh, the night of love and touch dissolved into the illusionary. Perhaps it was enough to melt into the mystery of a Celtic spiritual union and release it into the universe. Two lovers, star-crossed, perhaps, who came together for a sacred moment outside of time, inside their hearts.

Pay Attention!

Midway through the 1980s, divorced and living in the pink-carpeted base-ment of the Canyon Road gallery with twelve hundred books, a sixty-gallon tropical fish aquarium, Toronto, the cat, and Tess, the comical standard poodle, I met and became friends with Allene LaPides, a smart, stylish, and very rich collector who responded enthusiastically to the art the gallery exhibited and the artists whose works we represented. When she purchased a large Richard Hogan painting, I was thrilled.

I trusted her impeccable taste to such a degree that I willingly adopted some of her suggestions for making the gallery chicer and expanding the collector base. Our friendship evolved, and soon we found ourselves discussing a partner-ship. I had the artists, the gallery name, and the charm (yes, I had the charm). She had the money, business acumen, and the East Coast connections.

As the possibility of working together developed, we decided that she would buy my entire business for a small and realistic sum. I would become the direc-tor of the state-of-the-art gallery she planned to open. Allene agreed that her new gallery would represent all the artists from Linda Durham Gallery.

The creative partnership would lift from my increasingly burdened shoulders the distasteful chore of chasing funds for advertising, rent, and staff salaries. The artists would benefit, plus, it would be a relief for me to receive a modest-but-secure salary with commissions. This win-win arrangement was an excellent way to expand the brand and assure the continuation of our participation in the major international art fairs. Best of all, Allene's buy-out meant that I could purchase a house of my own.

Her lawyers drew up a contract based upon our discussions. Added to my forty-thousand-dollar base salary would be commissions up to two hundred thousand dollars a year. I pored over the contract. Something seemed amiss.

"Allene," I said, my furrowed brows registered my concern, "this non-compete clause would bar me from working in the art business for five years if I resigned, or if you fired me. That's a deal-breaker."

"Oh," she replied with an elegant, Armani-jacketed brushing-off gesture, "the lawyers put that in there. We know what our agreement is. We don't have to sign that."

And we didn't. We jumped over the legal hurdles and raced into the partnership with a spoken handshake. I never doubted my contribution and commitment to Allene. I was a valuable asset. The arrangement pleased me. Totally. Financial responsibilities had never been my forte. It was a relief to relinquish them to Allene. I had the freedom to do the work I loved with the artists who I supported and whose work I represented. I felt strongly that, together, Allene and I would forge a powerful partnership.

Construction of an amazing space near the Santa Fe Plaza began. So, too, did the process of transitioning from my personal living quarters in the basement of 400 Canyon Road to something more upscale. I could afford to buy a house of my own. Dreams do come true.

I made an offer on a charming adobe on Camino Santander in Santa Fe's historic district. Allene's letter of support clinched the loan. Straight from closing, I drove to my exquisite little house, parked in the driveway, kissed the keys and walked to my very own front door. I must have stood there for a full minute before inserting the key in the brass-plated lock and tiptoeing inside. Then, I burst into tears of joy.

Our business arrangement began well. But, Robert Burns had it right: "the best-laid schemes o' mice an' [wo]men often go awry, an' lea'e us nought but grief and pain for promised joy." When it devolved, it was death by a thousand cuts. The joy bled out. The situation was rife with deception, stress, and cause for a lawsuit.

As planned, Allene took charge of everything financial. I fulfilled my role as on-site partner, dealing with art, artists, and collectors.

For the first two months, Allene paid my modest salary, plus commissions on my sales. On the third month, Allene handed me a check. "Congratulations," she said, "You've already made your commissions for the year."

"What? No, not nearly." Surprise and shock registered together.

"Yes. With this check, you've received your commissions on two hundred thousand dollars in sales."

"No, Allene, that's not right. The contract says, 'commissions *up* to two hundred thousand dollars,' not on two hundred thousand dollars of sales."

And Allene, who had been so complimentary of Linda Durham Gallery and so enthusiastic about forming this partnership, replied, "I never read the contract. And besides, it isn't signed."

She departed in a rush.

Collapsing against the closet door, I struggled to get my breath, find my voice. What just happened? Thoughts swirled, going nowhere. Had I been tricked? Swindled? Deceived by my new and mistakenly trusted friend? A case of Jekyll and Hyde? What happened to the person who expressed gratitude for helping her establish a positive presence in the Santa Fe contemporary art community? Did I misjudge her intentions; misinterpret the signs so completely? Was I blind? Fooled? A fool?

How could this have happened?

I. Lost. Everything. I lost my gallery, my precious house, my confidence, my Pollyanna nature. Worst, I lost my way.

I had no answers to dozens of questions. Did this devastating development result from a misunderstanding? Was I the victim of a deliberate deception? Was this vaporous partnership a clever, calculated piece of legal shenanigans plotted from the outset by her business-savvy husband, their lawyers, and someone I called friend?

I didn't and still don't know. Falling into an old habit, I wondered: what next? But wondering didn't keep me from losing my house. I could continue to wonder. Or, let it go. Chalk it up to experience. Consider it an advanced degree from the School of (extremely) Hard Knocks.

I went through the five stages of grief and loss, skipped around, revisited a few of the most comfortable stages, and finally graduated from abject despair to relative acceptance. The tears that accompanied my woe-is-me attitude dried, disappeared. Perhaps it was an over-simplification to say that I accepted responsibility for the decisions and actions that had wreaked such havoc. Clearly, it took time and effort for me to confess to myself that contracts have consequences—some good, some not so good. Seeing myself as the creator of my own challenging reality restored my optimism in my indomitable strength.

In that moment of clarity, I knew, without a shadow of doubt, that I was bound to recover what I had lost. Solidify my professional footing. Cultivate once again a stable "stable" of artists. Reinvigorate my optimism.

In nearly illegible scrawl, I counseled myself:

Hey, Durham, you are not even close to the end of your creative life in the art world. It is up to you to turn this unanticipated and heartbreaking business travesty into a chance to build a new path. Self-pity is unhelpful, unhealthy, and unattractive. It must not hold you captive indefinitely. This crash will pass. Crashes often punctuate journeys of conscience and consequence. Think of the Phoenix!

–Journal entry

Before long, I convinced myself that a setback was nothing more than a jumping-off place for opportunity. Onward was the only logical direction. What lingered was the perceived injustice. The enormous sense of betrayal and loss.

I felt compelled to fight. I filed a lawsuit.

Allene's legal team countersued.

Mornings, I awoke angry, broke, and broken. I worked and thought with fists clenched. The pain was agonizing. Someday, I must write *The Gullible Girl's Guide to Doing Business with Rich People*. For now, I write to myself.

> Not for the first time and probably not for the last time, I find myself floating in a limbo-esque place: I'm not dead—but part of me feels dead. I'm not doomed—but I feel doomed. Maybe I am doomed!
>
> —Journal entry

I careened back and forth among the stages of grief and loss, thinking I had achieved grace and gratitude only to fall into an abyss as the legal wrangling dragged on and on. All at once, the brutality of the litigious pummeling—that I had endured, milked, and perpetuated—shifted.

The Dalai Lama came to town.

"Come with me," my friend Henry Oat encouraged.

His Holiness the Dalai Lama was appearing at the Santa Fe High School gymnasium. In the car with Henry, I was full of enmity and antipathy and talked about nothing but the seemingly unendurable emotional and financial stress of the never-ending lawsuit. Vitriol spewed from my lips. Anger oozed from each pore. Henry was a patient listener.

"Let go of all that, just for the afternoon, and concentrate on the Dalai Lama's messages of peace and love," he whispered, taking my hand and squeezing it gently.

In silence, we joined the queue.

Devotees, enthusiasts, and the curious pack the bleachers and spread out in lotus position on the gym floor. Everyone has come to witness and celebrate the existence and presence of this holy man. Henry and I find seats with a view three-quarters of the way to the top of the bleachers to the left of the makeshift stage.

A tall woman approaches the podium and tests the microphone. She welcomes us and tells us that, after his talk, His Holiness will respond to written questions from the audience. She holds up a bundle of small white papers. "Jot them down and pass the little slips of paper forward," she explains. "Volunteers will collect them."

I write nothing, because I don't know how to put in words the question I most need answered. I just know that I need help. While others write their burning questions, I close my eyes and pray to find comfort in the Dalai Lama's voice and message. I tell myself that I will receive an answer to my ongoing predicament in His response to the very first question read—whatever it is.

The Dalai Lama finishes his formal talk and smiles broadly at the hushed and anticipatory audience. The tall woman stands with a microphone in hand and reads the first question drawn from the bowlful of folded papers:

"How do we forgive our enemies when we know they are trying to destroy us?"

Yes, that's my unwritten question. I close my eyes and feel blood pulsing in my eyelids. How, how, how do we forgive our enemies? I feel slightly dizzy. I don't hear the words of the Dalai Lama's response with my ears. I feel his benevolence and compassion wash over me. An almost tangible heaviness releases its hold on my mind and heart. I sense my resentment, rage, and guilt lift. The pain of betrayal and the debilitating sense of victimization coalesce and float up, up, up to the rafters. And away.

I forgive you, Allene. I forgive you, Linda. I breathe in freedom.

> As I walked out the door toward the gate that would lead to my freedom, I knew if I didn't leave my bitterness and hatred behind, I'd still be in prison.
>
> –Nelson Mandela

"Drop the suit," I instructed my attorney the next day. "Are you sure?" he asked. "I'm sure."

I recovered slowly. Magically, I found a way to keep my Canyon Road schoolhouse gallery. Most of the artists who had signed agreements with Allene found their way back to me. Disappointments and a range of setbacks and mistakes notwithstanding, the gallery and I survived that fateful challenge with "luck and pluck," as a friend put it.

One otherwise forgotten day, years later, I walked into a local dry cleaner's and waited my turn behind the small woman in front of me. She lifted her hanging garments from the rack, and as she swung around toward the door, we almost collided. Our eyes met. It was Allene. We hugged. We broke into tears. We made a lunch date. We never mentioned the lawsuit. I didn't say, "You tried to destroy me!" or "How could you?" I didn't need to hear her response—apology or defense. I pictured His Holiness, beaming to the crowd in the high school gym. I focused on all the exemplary things I knew about Allene: her love of animals, her generosity toward worthy organizations, her keen political instincts. We became better than fair-weather friends.

In time, Allene sold her beautiful downtown gallery to the foundation funding the Georgia O'Keeffe Museum. She renovated a property on Canyon Road not far from my re-salvaged gallery and moved her art business there. Not many years later, she sold that gallery to other rich people at a price—she confided—she couldn't afford to refuse. She remains an important mentor. I suspect that I will always remember her with fondness, respect, and just a bit of sadness. Among my wonderings, it occurs to me that the art business takes no prisoners—only temporary hostages. Think Stockholm Syndrome.

Disappointments and a range of setbacks and mistakes notwithstanding, the gallery and I persisted. There were lucky accidents and appearances of hoped-for, but unexpected, angels of opportunity. I had been blessed with both. It was my good fortune to have worked with artists of extraordinary vision and talent, such as Linda Fleming, Yozo Suzuki, Ciel Bergman, Erika Wanenmacher, Eugene Newmann, Harmony Hammond, Terry Allen, Robert Kelly, Sam Scott, Dana Newmann, John Connell, James Havard, Richard Hogan, Judy Tuwaletstiwa, Charles Thomas O'Neil, Barbara Zusman, Joan Myers, David Kimball Anderson, Frank McEntire, Joel Peter Witkin, Martin Cary Horowitz, Meow Wolf, and many others.

I have learned that if you must leave a place that you have lived in and loved and
where all your yesteryears are buried deep, leave it any way except a slow way,
leave it the fastest way you can. Never turn back and never believe that an hour
you remember is a better hour because it is dead. Passed years seem safe ones,
vanquished ones, while the future lives in a cloud, formidable from a distance.

–BERYL MARKHAM, *West with the Night*

The Piper Must Be Paid

By the end of 2010, when the Universe yelled, "Look out, ruin looms!" it was too late. The gallery was already doomed. My financial footing, creative edge, and confidence were lost. Art sales had diminished considerably (drastically). The false luxury of denial collided with the unwelcome wall of reality. Insolvency beat me to the finish line. Gone was my sense of myself as an unsinkable warrior goddess for goodness, truth, and beauty. The scope and scale of my dream must have been too grand for the uncertainty of a changing art world. The contemporary art-world club turned a corner without me. The Recession and Reality, two formidable opponents, out-played me. The gallery and its legacy of character, conviction, and passion for art did not survive.

When in disgrace with fortune and men's eyes
I all alone beweep my outcast state,
And trouble deaf heaven with my bootless cries,
And look upon myself, and curse my fate....
–Shakespeare, "Sonnet 29"

Credit-card debt and loneliness kept me awake nights. Days I spent bouncing desperate and impractical ideas against the hard surfaces of my intransigent mind. To little avail. Dead ends and detours met me at every turn. Potential solutions to my career-ending predicament dried up. Still, I fought against the obvious. Sell the business. Why not try?

A professional couple new to Santa Fe materialized and expressed interest in absorbing LDCA, purchasing my mailing list, gallery-owned inventory, consulting services, and (perhaps) representing the LDCA artists. That would work! I was giddily optimistic for several days, anticipating a positive response from the potential investors—in the form of a check. My optimism ran wild. I imagined the next exciting chapter in my self-salvation as I hobbled in from the lonely outfield. I awaited the investors' response. It came in a curt email:

> …with regard to our conversation regarding the possible purchase of your gallery inventory, etc., we have decided there is really nothing in it for us. It would just be getting you out of a difficult situation. So, we withdraw our offer. Good luck in finding a buyer.

Too stunned, scared, and ashamed to feel anger or disappointment, I sat at my desk and faced the computer screen for long minutes in motionless emptiness. I had pushed myself to the end of all known options. *You cannot save the gallery, Linda. Face it, this is your moment of resignation.* I pushed the delete button, condemning the nail-in-the-coffin message to the trash.

Fade to black.

Trembling, taking a shaky breath, I started down the staircase from my attic-like office to deliver the news to my staff. From that raven's-eye view, I stopped, peered over the banister into the main exhibition space, and watched a few afternoon visitors drift from painting to painting, pausing at each carefully conceived, rendered, chosen, and installed work.

For a long time, I sat on that step and listened to their whispering voices. No one could see me holding my pounding heart. Only angels saw the shroud of failure that engulfed me. Only angels heard my stifled sobs. My hard-fought dream, in all its "manic-festations" and permutations, was dying. Sitting on those wooden steps, dissociated from the past, present, and future, I declared under my breath: "The gallery is not for sale. The gallery will just close; it will cease to exist. Completely. The proverbial plug is pulled. The End. I am done with it."

I am done with it!

Those very words appeared scrawled in a shaky hand, in an old-fashioned script, on the back of an antique banjo clock that belonged to my great-great-grandmother Angelina Berry. The clock hung in the entry hall of my family's house. It didn't tell time. It had no use for time. It served an aesthetic purpose, not a practical one. It was just a beautiful old thing with a lovely face, a reverse-glass painting of a sailing ship on the compartment door at the bottom, and a golden-winged eagle perched on the top.

"I am done with it," Angelina Berry wrote to me across generations. Time moved. In no rush to catch up with it, I lingered in a timeless place.

Situations change. Time and Time's events occur in random, linear or non-linear, predictable or unpredictable fits and starts, overseeing an ever-changing constellation of possibilities.

> Imaginary time is a new dimension, at right angles to ordinary, real time.
>
> –Stephen Hawking

All earnest efforts to resuscitate my beloved gallery had failed. What would I do with the energy, obsession, and passion that had tumbled me along the rocky shallows of the dream that flowed through my heart and mind? I had no idea what might happen next. No ideas at all.

Eventually, rising from the step, I took a few deep breaths, clenched and unclenched my fists, continued down the stairs, and began to let go.

Passion for my work had never dimmed. It remained bright and alive in my heart—through thin and thinner. Yet, that sharp sting of failure confirmed that pride does "goeth before a fall." I segued from feeling something excruciating to feeling nothing.

> …I am aware of beginnings and endings,
> and life after the end, and something
> that I don't have to remember just now.
>
> –Anna Akhmatova

The days following my staircase descent existed in a blur. Within two months, my life-changing edict to close LDCA—to cease and desist—was accomplished. So many years cascaded into a few cycles of the moon.

I had come full circle, from knowing nothing much about most everything at the start of my blind climb toward unimaginable heights to knowing nothing all over again and beginning to search for another trailhead on the mountain of wisdom.

After making a few public announcements and granting a handful of interviews about the gallery's closing, I returned all the consigned art and swept away, threw away, or gave away disparate items from three decades of this casual archivist's accumulation of notes and letters, souvenirs and supplies. My friend Jax helped me truck some potentially useful or salvageable material to my house.

With my once-empty garage now full of tools, office supplies, gallery furniture, boxes of files, cardboard portfolios, and crates of owned or abandoned artwork and with no one to ask me what happened and no one to tell me what I should have done or what to do next, I sat on the cold cement floor and wept.

Once more unto the breach dear friends, once more....

—Shakespeare, *Henry V*

At the nadir of that pouty depression, I scrawled my feelings of hopelessness, anger, and loss on a yellow tablet with a black felt-tipped marker. Real and proverbial doors had shut. Softly. I didn't have to slam anything. The winds of change did that for me.

I feel empty. I want to disappear. I want to sell or give away everything I own and love, all the Burmese art, paintings, puppets, sculpture, photographs. I will sell all my books, including my well-loved set of the Oxford English Dictionary and all my art books—even the ones signed and inscribed. And I will leave the various notes, cards, articles, and ephemera that I saved and placed within the pages, for long-forgotten reasons, because I want to travel long and lightly, long and lightly. And alone. Resolved, I will sell everything: china; silver; jewelry; dolls; my Wonder Woman collection. Oh, I might hold on to the special Wonder Woman figure that Carol Sarkisian made. And I don't think I can bring myself to sell the small sculpture with the Datura flower under glass that Erika Wanenmacher gave me. And I'll keep one or two Eugene Newmann paintings and a few John Connell works on paper and the painting of the mass graves in Iraq that an artist gave me in Baghdad. I want to keep the Robert Kelly painting with the references to the Persian Gulf, a gift from Robert. And I couldn't part with the signed Wifredo Lam lithograph—not yet, not yet. Nor could I part with any of my wild Cuban drawings. I definitely am not ready to part with all the art I acquired in Myanmar, my soulful, self-described spiritual home. I'll hold on to the boxes and boxes of letters and photographs that document the decades of my wonder-filled life; my wonder-fueled life. Someday I'll sort through it all or give it to my children. Not now, though, not now. Now I'm preparing to disappear. I will honor my debts and take what money remains, and I will wander and explore and encounter and celebrate...until or...forever."

—Journal entry, March 2011

I carried out only part of that radical intention before abandoning it in favor of other ideas. Standing in my kitchen, I willed myself to re-appear on a new stage with a new or reconstituted attitude and newly corralled courage, to shuck the remnants of my old personas and to show up unmasked, unafraid, unapologetic, and with a more-resonant voice and a refreshed look. I pledged to shuck and show up!

But my encore could wait until tomorrow or another day. My inner *Gone with the Wind* was calling. Today, I would book a flight to Myanmar. Perhaps there in my spiritual home I could seek and find a new purpose to my life. Any issues that threatened to block or endanger my future could be shelved until my return—if a return was even in the cards. Quickly, quietly, with help from no one, using my over-extended, but not yet terminally declined, credit card, I purchased a cheap ticket to Bangkok and onward to Yangon. I vanished somewhere around the ides of March.

Now this is not the end. It is not even the beginning of the end. But it is, perhaps, the end of the beginning.

–Winston Churchill

*With two Myanmar friends, ready to participate
in the annual Kachin tribal dance, 2009*

Myanmar, the Golden Land

Fleeing the pains and disappointments of my failure to rescue and resuscitate the gallery, I sought refuge once again in the tranquility and ornate splendor of Myanmar's temples and stupas. The gestating possibilities of my un-experienced future rested in a remote corner of my mind, as I gave free rein to my wandering sense of wonder in "The Golden Land" that beckoned my return almost annually since the late 1990s.

During another visit years earlier, I was invited to a private lunch in the modest Yangon home of my great and wise friend Daw Pwa Yin. She had gathered family and a few friends to welcome a Venerable Monk and his fellow brothers who were transporting a single hair of the Buddha from one monastery to another.

The hair rests on a bed of shaved gold leaf in a beautiful blue glass goblet. It is about an inch and a half in length; black with a slight curl. It looks like a chest hair or a pubic hair. We peer into the goblet, my hosts, the monks and I. And we watch as the black hair moves. We are transfixed. It seems miraculous.

–Journal entry

After the meal, Pwa Yin—a most-refined woman who received a Fulbright scholarship to study at Temple University in the 1940s, and who spoke impeccable English—introduced me to the Venerable Monk. She told him of my journey to a remote area south of the town of Mawlaymine and of my visit to Win Sein Taw Ya, the largest reclining Buddha in the world. I was a little embarrassed when Pwa Yin shared with the assembled group that I had made a donation of a few hundred dollars to the head monk who oversees the ongoing construction of the amazing, 180-meter-long world wonder. In appreciation of my gift, which would fund the construction of a life-size seated Buddha beneath a Bodhisattva

Tree somewhere within the cavernous reclining figure, the Venerable Monk offered me a blessing.

My hosts instructed me.

"Kneel down in front of him." I kneel.

"Closer." I inch closer.

"Lower, lower." I lower myself.

"Lower your head." I follow their instructions. I am uncomfortable and self-conscious.

The VM presses a small Buddha figure against my forehead. I close my eyes. He mumbles a long and resonant prayer in Pali. On and on. I remain still. I hardly breathe. Tears well up. They waterfall over my cheeks. I don't know where they come from. And I can't stop them. I can feel the monks and the gathered guests watching me, knowingly. They can see me. I open my eyes and look around. Everyone is smiling. Beatifically.

I have received a transmission.

Before departing with the sacred hair of the Buddha, the Venerable Monk invited me to visit his monastery.

"It's an honor none of us have ever received," Pwa Yin confided. The remaining luncheon guests decided among themselves that my "brother-friend" Phone Kyaw and Ma Thanegi, a writer and scholar, would escort me to the monastery.

The next day, at the morning market near my apartment, we bought some fruit, a bunch of sun-yellow roses, and a basketful of dried bamboo shoots wrapped in leaves, tied with twine—a traditional offering, my friends explained. Phone Kyaw parked at a gate in front of a beautiful, crumbling, three-story teak building at the edge of the city.

Deep stillness enveloped me as we followed a dusty path across an overgrown garden to the main entrance of the monastery, which led to an interior courtyard. A solitary monk acknowledged us with a nod and gestured toward a narrow wooden staircase. At the top floor, we removed our shoes and entered a large room with a gleaming dark wood floor polished, no doubt, by countless hands and feet. And years. Fragrant incense filled my nostrils. Tall glass cases and ancient-looking, ornately carved chests displaying lacquer bowls, Buddha figures, and vases of dried and fresh flowers lined the far wall.

"Please be seated," instructed the young monk who had followed us upstairs. We positioned ourselves on the floor in front of the room's only chair. Moments later, the Venerable Monk appeared, sat in the solitary chair, and arranged himself and his robes. "Move closer," the young monk whispered. I presented my gifts. Once the Venerable Monk accepted them, the young monk removed them from the room. Phone Kyaw leaned slightly toward me and translated Venerable Monk's softly spoken words.

"The Venerable Monk knows you…" said Phone Kyaw. He paused as though preparing to share a great secret, "…from a former incarnation. You and he were monks together many hundreds of years ago. He welcomes you. He is happy to be with you again after so many centuries."

A Spanish monk who spoke a little English entered, placed a wooden bowl with fruit in front of the Venerable Monk, and sat on the floor beside me. The VM selected an orange from the bowl, peeled it, and offered me a section. As I reached for it, the Spanish monk stopped me.

"No, he feed you."

I accepted the orange wedge on my tongue. Communion. "You're to receive a second blessing," said the monk sitting next to me.

My tears begin even before the VM touches my forehead with the small Buddha. The prayer is long. I am as still as a boulder. Again, the sacred sounds transport me. I am far away. I see wavy lines. I hear watery sounds.

At the end of the prayer, the Venerable Monk presented me with gifts: the little black blessing Buddha; nine ancient, pebble-sized bone relics sifted from the cremated ashes of revered monks; and a small gold orb from the same period as my monastic past life. He instructed me to have the orb—which once belonged to an important ancient monk—made in a special way so that the little orb would touch my skin.

We said our goodbyes and prepared to leave. To my amazement, behind us the room had filled with people who had entered soundlessly and witnessed our ceremony.

Ma Thanegi, Phone Kyaw, and I returned to the car in silence. As we drove away, they wondered aloud to each other about the marvel of what had just transpired. I remained speechless.

Back home in New Mexico, my good friend Richard Hogan, a superb artist and jeweler whose work is minimal and meditative, mounted the gold orb to a simple gold band. The relic treasured by a fellow monk centuries ago rests day in and day out against the skin of my right ring finger.

Years after my sacred blessing at the monastery, when I returned to Myanmar, I asked Phone Kyaw about the extraordinary man who had given me such treasures. "Venerable Monk is gone," Phone Kyaw said. "No one knows where."

I like to imagine that the Venerable Monk and I will intersect yet again in a future incarnation.

Retreating to Myanmar for soul rebuilding had become a pattern. Two years before my gallery closed, during a Christmas holiday in Yangon and environs, my friends U Tin Win and Sanda invited me to experience a special New Year's tribal festival in Myitkyina, the small, riverside capital city of Kachin, the northernmost state of Myanmar. We would be guests at the home of Sanda's boarding school roommate. It sounded irresistible.

In Mandalay, I purchased a train ticket for the overnight trip to Myitkyina. Late in the afternoon, I located my single, forward-facing seat in the crowded passenger car. Opposite me, separated by a small table, was a young man whose fate would be to ride backwards for the eighteen-hour trip. As the train eased out of the station, my table mate was already asleep.

Boxes, bundles, and small trunks jammed the aisle. A colorful textile covered all but the calloused bare feet of an old man stretched out across a half-dozen boxes. Darkness came quickly, obscuring the rugged countryside as we chugged north. Instead of focusing outward, I studied the beautiful life in the second-class car.

Across the aisle, a young couple with two small children played games quietly. In another section of the compartment, two matronly women, wearing brightly patterned sarong-like *longyis* and bulky sweaters, shared a meal from a traditional multi-tiered, tin lunch box. Before long, we exchanged smiles, breaking an initial and typical reserve. The woman nearest me offered a thick wedge of pomelo, my favorite tropical fruit—like a big juicy and sweet grapefruit.

"*Chay su tim bah deh,*" I responded. Both women nodded warmly at the foreigner who could say thank you in their language.

Time moved in sync with the clack, clack of iron wheels on the tracks. Someone coughed. Someone snored. Someone whispered. Someone laughed. Every now and then, an ancient, orange-robed monk passed through the train car seeking donations.

"Hallew, where you fron?" he asked me in a big voice.

"United States." I looked into his gentle, dark eyes.

"Oh, veddy good. America." His wizened face crinkled with joy. He translated for the other passengers. Heads nodded and smiled at me. Hours ticked off. Perhaps I slept. Eventually, day broke.

The train pulled into Myitkyina just before noon on the first day of the week-long New Year's celebration. Three teenage girls, dressed stylishly in Western clothes, met me on the railway platform. They had been on the same train, but in the first-class sleeping compartments. From their various schools in other parts of the country and abroad, they were returning to attend the festivities. We piled into a shiny blue SUV.

Our hostess' sprawling estate included three major buildings: an impressive mansion, a separate sleeping house, and a cooking/eating house. U Tin Win and Sanda greeted me in the flower-filled circular driveway and introduced me to the regal hostess. Appearing in a shimmering *longyi,* a royal blue silk blouse, and a golden brocade shawl, the bejeweled matriarch sparkled with rubies and other precious gems. I later learned those gems were unearthed from her own mines. She embraced me. Smiles became our common language. Immediately, I was treated like family.

The whole small city was in celebration mode. Hundreds and hundreds of local and expat Kachin people had taken leave of their jobs, homes, and schools abroad and swarmed into Myitkyina for the annual "Manaw," the sacred festival composed of animal sacrifices, dancing, singing, and feasting. "I'm ready for the dancing, singing, and drinking," I told my friends, "but the animal sacrifices definitely give me pause."

That first night we attended an outdoor musical presentation. I sat in the front row between my elegant hostess and five sedate Myanmar generals with their expensively and exquisitely dressed wives (or mistresses). Someone placed small portable heaters by our feet and the feet of the generals' party. We watched act after excellent act. Each talented performer received multiple bouquets of flowers. The audience applauded with loud and sincere enthusiasm. In Myitkyina, I learned, everyone can sing and everyone loves singing.

The feast spread across several long tables in the large, covered pavilion. Fine paintings lined the temporary walls. The local rice wine kept flowing. I felt like a visiting princess. On successive evenings, elegant dinners honored the cuisine and culture of a Kachin expat's adoptive country: India, China, Thailand, or Korea. At each banquet my hostess dressed more exquisitely than the night before. Her motherly form dripped with rubies, emeralds, and jade. Every day, I dressed improperly in one of two plain travelers' shirts and either my serviceable *longyi* or khaki trousers. And every day, wherever we went, shopkeepers and café servers asked if I would be dancing at the Manaw. Of course, I will dance. I love to dance.

On that special day, my two sister friends and five Kachin women dressed me for the dance. They fastened a Kachin tribal *longyi* around my hips and slipped my arms into a heavy black-velvet jacket covered with real silver discs and small bangles. My wardrobe crew wound a multi-colored belt around my waist. They laughed and fussed as they wrapped, un-wrapped, and re-wrapped the ceremonial long scarf around my head. When they were satisfied, they applied my makeup. Still, it was clear—the mirror didn't lie—I was the palest person in the city.

The dance arena was almost the size of a football field. Kachin participants in multi-colored traditional costumes with distinctive headdresses denoting their clans surrounded the space that would soon erupt in dance. A cluster of drums—some six feet across—commanded the middle of the vast dance pavilion.

Our clan files in behind the single line of more than a thousand dancers, all following the tall leader with the elaborate feather headdress. The women in our clan hold fans. They demonstrate the steps and arm movements for me. They feel natural. We shuffle slowly around the wide pavilion in sync with the drumbeat, rhythmically, hypnotically. Pah, pah. Pah, pah. Thousands of dancers' feet pat the ground. The undulating line snakes and coils onto itself until everyone passes someone going in the opposite direction. Pah, pah. Pah, pah.

At every step I pass new costumes, new smiles. Pah, pah. Pah, pah. Outside the cycling of dancers, one or two travel photographers click off images, and a few for-eign-looking spectators—very few—seem mesmerized.

I am not a spectator. I am the only non-Kachin dancing. But, today, I am a Kachin. Pah, pah. Pah, pah. I feel in perfect rhythm with the women in my clan and the drums are inside of me. I am holding my fans and moving in just the right way, and I am following the friendly Kachin woman in front of me, in step, out of context, smiling. And there is no thought of war. There is no poverty. No evil. No boundaries. No strangers. No worry. No sadness. No loneliness. There is only the sound of the drums, the smiles, the love. And the wonder.

On the last day in Myitkyina, I traveled with a van full of new friends to the confluence of the Mali and N'Mai Rivers. Here, at this remote place in the Kachin State, the great Irrawaddy River begins and continues south through Bhamo, Mandalay, Bagan, and Yangon to the Andaman Sea.

Quiet thoughts and peaceful days of music, flowers, incense, and smiles helped me center myself. I picked up a shiny green leaf, stroked its waxy surface. I kissed it and dropped it in the water, sending it downstream with a wish attached. The little raft carried my perpetual prayer: "Please help me to stay in the light…." I watched it grow smaller and smaller, then disappear.

Something else was about to disappear, something anticipatory, veiled in sadness. With reluctance—because it's always difficult to leave my gentle friends and the Shwedagon Pagoda and the stupas and temples and incense—I headed back to my physical home, believing that the Myanmar renewal once again prepared me to confidently face the challenges of a changed art world, battered by the storm of the previous year's Great Recession.

The shrill winds of 2011 chilled me to the bone. My still-open wounds accompanied me as I traveled through Bangkok and disembarked in Yangon, exhausted and empty. I could have been just another aimless or nameless seeker. Who was I? I could pretend that I knew. But Linda Durham Contemporary Art and I were history. Who will I become? I stretched my spine and renewed the pledge I had made in my kitchen weeks before. I would succeed. I would return—defiant in the face of failure.

For ten days at sunrise and sunset, I prayed where "Thursday-born" people pray: in front of the stone standing Buddha at the magnificent Shwedagon Pagoda. The pilgrimage raised me from a place of hopelessness to one of hopefulness. As it had done each time I needed spiritual rebirth, the Golden Land offered strong medicine for my ailing psyche as it signaled the beginning of my next never-ending adventure and pulled and pushed me toward more parts of the unexplored and unknown.

But storms leave a swath of wreckage in their paths. The debris I left behind was now before me. What was I thinking? That a new job offer would be waiting for me? Not really. That the financial collapse of my gallery had been only a bad dream? No such luck. There were serious issues to confront, to contemplate, to correct. I knew there were answers to my questions and concerns. I began to convince myself that a new and desirable purpose would unfold. And because I believed that clarity would come, I succumbed to the kind of faith that H. L. Mencken defined as "an illogical belief in the occurrence of the improbable."

Now and then, during moments of seemingly unendurable financial stress, I comforted myself by fantasizing that a stranger—someone like Michael Anthony, who worked for billionaire J. Beresford Tipton in the old TV series *The Millionaire*—would knock on my door and remind me of a time long, long ago when I had been kind to an old derelict who was, in reality, a wealthy person who never forgot my kindness and had left me his entire fortune.

No, I wasn't seriously delusional. I was just resting in a place of temporary evasion—of taxes, debt, responsibility, reality. Sometimes it's helpful to indulge in a bit of the "what ifs" and "if onlys."

That spring, I said my Myanmar goodbyes resolved to search for a fresh direction for my life. Clearly, the signs and signals of the *something* that had hung over my departure were becoming increasingly apparent. Like the leaf I set adrift down the Irrawaddy River years before, something old and treasured was disappearing in my life and in the peaceful life in the Kachin State.

Fighting in the north between the ethnic minority elites and regional army commanders—over gold, amber, copper, rubies, jade, water, and drugs—accelerated, creating hardship for tens of thousands of people. Foreign investors exacerbated the troubles. The abundance of resources in that part of Myanmar had become a curse rather than an asset, bringing a virtual end to the way of life I had the very rare privilege to experience during that very rare and revitalizing retreat.

Retreat Furthers

Sitting on a stone bench in my neglected garden, meditating, I remembered a favorite hexagram from the *I Ching*. "Retreat Furthers." I repeated it over and over. "Retreat furthers…retreat furthers." These two powerful words, with their seemingly contradictory messages, shook, awakened, and reunited me with an important misplaced mantra. A key. A clue in my search for a way through the rip currents and roadblocks of the past year.

Hoping to find comfort and direction in the ancient wisdom of that venerable *Book of Changes*, I abandoned my meditation and retrieved a well-worn copy from my library, on a shelf of timeless inspirational works, somewhere between *Tibet's Great Yogi Milarepa* and *The Fruitful Darkness*, by Roshi Joan Halifax. I craved a message of optimism, a passage with the power to ferry me across troubled waters. Or a lantern to shine a glimmer of light on that dark and muddy landscape filled with the shaky footprints of my recent directionless meanderings.

Tun/Retreat. The power of the dark is ascending. The light retreats to security so that the dark cannot encroach upon it. This retreat is a matter not of man's will, but of natural law. Therefore, in this case, withdrawal is proper; it is the correct way to behave in order not to exhaust one's forces.

Retreat furthers. That's it!

Mountain under heaven: the image of RETREAT. Thus, the superior [wo]man keeps the inferior [wo]man at a distance, not angrily but with reserve.

I couldn't afford to exhaust my forces any more than I already had. It was settled. I listened to *The Book of Changes*. I needed to find strength by retreating, to move forward by stepping back. Clearly, I needed more than the wisdom of a hexagram—but the hexagram offered a clue. My immediate need was to seek guidance from an expert: Mother Nature. I needed the solitude of the desert.

Before I reached the village of Cerrillos, I pulled over, climbed between the strands of rusty barbed-wire fence, and trespassed. In the long-ago decades of my twenties and early-marital-bliss thirties, this deserted section of the arroyo, cholla, sage, and sandstone prairie belonged to Bart Durham, our children, and me.

I surveyed the landscape of my fractured life, with all its dead ends, U-turns, and lucky landings. *What in the world is leading me, following me?* My mind tumbled back to turning points that had propelled me forward. I walked.

In May 1966, Bart and I were in the midst of hand-building our home on the remote parcel of high desert on which I stood once again. A recent (and very tender-footed) transplant from the familiar canyons of Manhattan to the unfamiliar peaks and valleys of the American Wild West, I took to life in New Mexico slowly. Without my false eyelashes, I felt naked. There was no place to wear three-inch heels with my Fifth Avenue skinny, velveteen jeans.

Real cowgirls in the neighborhood wore denim jeans with ragged cuffs that covered the heels of their well-worn, barrel-racing boots, which, undoubtedly, coaxed many ranch horses to obey.

We were building our house in learn-by-guessing-and-doing early hippie fashion. Our construction technique was to make it up as we went along. We had no architectural drawings, not even sketches. We drew the floor plan in the dirt with a stick, then enclosed the space with boards and rocks. This was a year or two before the influx of rich, not-so-rich, upscale, no-scale, and off-the-scale escapees from conventional life swarmed into Northern New Mexico, a year or two before *The Whole Earth Catalog* and the "Summer of Love."

One particularly windy afternoon, I'd had enough of stacking two-by-fours and picking up six-penny nails with sawdust flying in my face. My own nails were split and broken. My fair, "mega" metropolis-shaded skin was parchment. My russet hair was dry and lifeless. I was exhausted, unhappy, and wistful for the glamorous life I left behind. My mind withdrew from the reality of my current geographical location.

I could be in Washington Square Park right now, watching kids and scruffy old men play chess. I could be having a manicure uptown. I could be drinking a rum and Coke with friends at The Ninth Circle in the West Village. I could be out of this relentless wind.

Seeking purpose and purchase in this strange land to which I had been delivered, I climbed a high ridge and onto a massive, sculptural sandstone formation that bisected our quarter section. The raw spring wind whipped my long hair into a tangle. I squinted to focus on the polka-dotted mountains in the near and far distances and surveyed the expansive landscape before me. The big sandy arroyo. Junipers with their gray-blue berries. Overgrazed buffalo grass. Teddy-bear chollas and prickly pear cactus. I watched feathery high clouds form and change their wispy shapes and vanish. Yet, I yearned for the sights, smells, and sounds of life in the skyscraper city that had defined and confined me. I felt totally alone.

I faced the sun and shouted through the wind…all the way to God.

"God, please help me. I'm so confused. Did I make a good choice by marrying Bart and accompanying him to his chosen land and helping him manifest his dream? His land, his dream, not mine. Is there a reason for me to be here in this windy emptiness? If so, please tell me, please send me a sign."

At that moment, two ravens flew over my shoulders from the east. They hung in the updraft in front of me. Their iridescent, blue-black feathers glistened in the sun and rustled in the incessant wind.

"Caw," they called. "Caw, caw."

It was a moment of awe. I considered the powerful appearance of the two ravens an immediate and true message from God. The magical encounter settled in my cells. I embraced the call to honor those messengers whose commanding presence showed me the link between a call to God and a response through nature. From then until now, ravens have symbolized my connection to the mysterious world in which I had come to dwell. Overflowing with the wonder of that encounter and a new feeling that this high desert, its inhabitants, and I could truly belong to each other, I returned to my husband and our half-built house.

Since then, I have greeted every raven as a messenger and mentor. At each encounter, I pay attention to where I am, what I'm doing, thinking, and feeling. Always, I say, "thank you." Aloud.

I'll get tattoos on my shoulders of two ravens in flight, I pledged to myself and the Universe that day. In my mid-fifties, I fulfilled that pledge. The image of me on the cover of the *Santa Fe Reporter* reveals my first raven tattoo.

Ravens taught me to pay attention. The desert taught me to see. Art and artists taught me to see more…and better…and to appreciate, savor, and protect.

–Journal entry

As is sometimes the case, transformation waxes and wanes. It can take a while to stick. One moment you think you've become a different person, only to find that in the next, you've lapsed into your old self. Turning points, burning points can happen instantaneously. "Proud Mary" keeps on turning, as Creedence Clearwater Revival sang to us since 1969 and sings to me still.

In those first years of ranch living, blinders shielded my metropolitan eyes from the beauty of my new homeland, and my mind balked at embracing its subtle secrets. My perspective changed one morning in the late 1960s when the consummate artist Paul Sarkisian and I hiked together in the desert.

Everything seemed fresh, new, and exciting, scanning the desert environment with Paul as he pointed out one visually wondrous thing after another. So much captured his super-observer eye: a spindly winter plant pirouetted with the wind, tracing concentric circles in the sand. We studied the intricate geometric patterns of the shiny, cracked clay at the edge of the arroyo. We stopped and touched and stooped and climbed for hours. My inexperienced and otherwise-inclined eyes opened to the subtleties of nature's endless treasures and surprises that I had overlooked during all my solitary walks. And I received the everlasting gift of "slow seeing."

That day, Paul took my spirit in hand and gently guided it with his desert-lover's soul, heart, and mind. A new sensation arose. I cherished much more than the rocks, or plants, or dirt. With blinders off, I recognized and reveled in the beauty and wonder of it all. For too long, I misinterpreted nature's chaos. With a new perspective, I sought and found its patterns and order mirrored in the Universe. The mystery and unity of "as above, so below" captured me and opened me to receive messages and insights from that "somewhere," which is beyond naming.

I continued to discover and explore opportunities to move forward by stepping back. It takes more than the wisdom of a Chinese hexagram and more than nature's guidance for permanent change of the self to occur. It takes time. And the gift of opportunity.

I am myself and what is around me, and if I do not save it, it shall not save me.

–José Ortega y Gasset, *Meditations on Quixote*

Life's Purpose

Peace—that was the topic of the 1989 stopover friendship conference in Leningrad/St. Petersburg, Russia. By invitation, I had joined Santa Fe Mayor Sam Pick, a small delegation of New Mexico dignitaries, and experts on international relations on our way to meet officials of our new Sister City, Bukhara, Uzbekistan.

During the conference's introductory, get-to-know-the-other icebreaker session, I found myself randomly paired with Nicholas Devyatkin, an intense young man with hazel eyes and a piercing gaze. We sat face to face on old wooden folding chairs at the edge of a dreary Soviet-era room. We smiled, shook hands, and exchanged greetings in English and Russian.

Before I had a chance to recite my carefully memorized Russian sentence: *Kak vy dumayete, budet li mir na nashem veku*? ("Do you think we will we experience peace in our time?"), Nicholas blurted out his question: "What is your life's purpose?"

My eyes widened, then closed. I was uncharacteristically speechless. My life's purpose? I hadn't contemplated the topic, not consciously. Did I have a special purpose? If so, what was it? My entire repertoire of charming or acceptable responses to philosophical inquiries eluded me. Glibness failed me. There I was, in Russia's most hauntingly poetic city—the birthplace of Alexander Pushkin, Anna Pavlova, Vladimir Nabokov, and Igor Stravinsky—and I was struggling to respond to this Russian scholar's existential question about human existence.

I must have I managed to say something interesting or stimulating, because our conversation continued so warmly and deeply that when we received instructions from the conference leader to move to new partners, Nicholas and I stood up, looked around, shuffled our feet, and sat down again in our same seats. We grinned like junior high school classmates who had successfully defied their teacher's instructions. Nicholas and I continued to deepen our rare and mutually welcomed opportunity to have a special one-on-one talk, in face-to-face time, with a seeking, open "Other" from another Motherland.

> Our conversation was brilliant, daring, colorful, insightful, thought-provoking, intimate, playful, honest, and when we parted, Nicholas said (and I would agree) that he had never had such a conversation in his life. We spoke of art and peace and kayaking and propaganda and life aims and travel and fantasy and children. He and I began our communication at a place where most communications only hope to reach after a long time....I am learning about reaching across distances quickly and finding truth and that which is enlightening. Nicholas and I did this. It was extraordinary.
>
> —Leningrad Journal

Since that afternoon in the old government building across from the Neva River, sitting where Anna Akhmatova and Fyodor Dostoevsky might have sat, the answer to the question Nicholas posed still eludes me.

The mystery of human existence lies not just in staying alive, but in finding something to live for.
                                                            —Fyodor Dostoevsky

Still Naked After All These Years

Hans Christian Anderson's fable "The Emperor's New Clothes" has particular resonance for me. Often, when acknowledged art experts (with power, position, or wealth) champion their favorite artist or work of art, the "madding crowd" tends to nod and concur. Whether or not the viewer or collector truly likes or understands the painting, or sculpture, or artist's manifesto may take a back seat to being trendy about one's tastes.

Many high-end collectors secretly dread (even fear) making "wrong" choices. At all costs, we avoid being put in a position of feeling disrobed and exposed. We fear looking ignorant or unsophisticated in the lofty circles inhabited or controlled by the money and media-created art-world elite. I know this firsthand.

One autumn day in the mid-1970s, I was standing in front of an abstract painting in a small, well-respected Santa Fe gallery. The handsome and suave gallery director approached me. We exchanged a few cordial words. Then, unaware that I was about to commit a common, but grave, contemporary art-world faux pas, I gestured toward the painting and asked, "What's that supposed to mean?"

Mr. Suave sighed audibly, paused, took an indulgent breath and said something like, "When people ask me that, I usually tell them, 'If you can't see it, I can't take the time to explain it to you.' However, I'm willing to make an exception and give you a quick lesson on looking at non-objective art."

I don't remember what he said, but I'll never forget the lesson. My pedestrian question labeled me an unsophisticated outsider—naïve about art. I felt ignorant and exposed.

N-n-n-naked!

Shortly after that unsolicited tutorial, while standing in front of another abstract painting in another art venue, a well-known Chicago art collector sidled up to me. He stood behind me, a bit too close. His breath ruffled my hair.

"What do you think of this painting?" he asked in a disturbingly low, almost confidential tone. My mind spun. Froze. I remained silent for too long. I thought there must be a correct answer, and I didn't know what it was. Should I like it? Was it a masterpiece? A second- or third-rate work? I had no idea. I remember neither my response nor the painting, only the discomfort of being unsure and self-conscious of my opinions and knowledge, feeling naked and exposed once more.

It took time, experience, and a bit of courage for me to be able to look at a painting and see more than size and color and subject matter and technical skill—or the absence of technical skill—and to see paint and brushstroke and composition and depth and quality—or the absence of quality—and to be brave enough or certain enough to have an opinion or no opinion.

Eventually, I developed a personal and mysterious skill of "feeling" a painting or sculpture. I felt comfortable (not smug) with my points of view. Developing connoisseurship and educated opinions doesn't happen in a "sight-byte." Perhaps developing confidence in one's ability to find and assess quality and authenticity in works of art is an act of bravery. Whatever the case, I ceased to be automatically affected by the opinions of others. It was liberating. Not that I was always—or even usually—right in the eyes and pronouncements of others, just right for me. That confidence was widely convincing during all those years.

Early in my gallery years, I had a conversation with a plumber who had spent the afternoon fixing a misbehaving faucet in the gallery's kitchen. As I wrote out his check, he leaned against the office doorjamb and gazed around at the show in the main exhibition room.

"So, that painting over there," he said, gesturing with his head in the direction of a large Richard Hogan canvas, "looks like electric worms to me."

"Hmm, yes," I responded, "I see what you mean."

"You mean I'm right?" He registered surprise. "It's supposed to be electric worms?"

"Well, I don't think the artist was painting electric worms, but I can see what you mean. The bright colors and the wavy, snaky lines are quite electric."

"And that one on the far wall…" He pointed to a large, dark brown and gray canvas by Zachariah Rieke. "It's kind of like looking at outer space."

"Oh, uh-huh, very much so."

"I'm right again?"

"I can see how it might evoke that notion. It's quite ethereal."

I handed him the check. He thanked me, smiled, and shook his head in a satisfied manner as he sauntered out the door.

The next morning, a Saturday, the plumber returned with a friend. The two men spent more than an hour going from painting to painting, assigning each descriptions, meanings, and interpretations. Their laughter and whispers warmed me and made me smile. Before they left, the plumber popped his head into my office.

"Hey, thanks again. My friend really liked the painting in the other room, the one that looks sort of like a picket fence. He's a carpenter. The tag says 'Robert Kelly.'"

The priceless exchanges with those workmen have stayed with me. I know that permission to be right and to have one's interpretation of a work validated and received in a respectful, judgment-free manner creates a welcoming introduction to the world of art. Particularly for abstract art.

I add four postscripts to this story. First, neither the electrician nor the carpenter ever returned to purchase a painting. Second, I didn't buy that abstract painting at the Santa Fe gallery where Mr. Suave gave me an early lesson in art-world *what's what*. I could have, but I didn't. Third, years later, however, when that gallery closed and the director moved to New York, I invited the painter of that abstract work to join my gallery. He did. Eugene Newmann became one of my favorite artists. We worked together for more than twenty-five mutually successful years. We remain great friends. Several of his paintings and drawings hang in my home, part of my forever private collection. I owe thanks to the gallerist whose approach to answering naïve questions—leaving the questioner naked and shamed—I reconciled and adapted differently. Fourth, showing up with enthusiasm, with or without a clue, is an honest, rewarding, and liberating path to pursue through the art-world thicket. And in many other societal thickets.

I am glad I am a woman who once danced naked in the Mediterranean Sea at midnight.

–Mercedes McCambridge

Around the Fucking World

On an autumn afternoon in 1963, sitting alone at The Hip Bagel, a small café near my Greenwich Village apartment, sipping coffee, smoking Tareytons, and trolling for experiences, I watched two ruggedly handsome men enter the restaurant and pull up chairs at the table next to mine.

They were fully engaged in an animated, rapid-fire conversation. I listened to the energy in their voices (admiring their broad shoulders) as they talked about coal leases (whatever they were) on the Kaiparowits Plateau (wherever that was). These two men fascinated me. They were so unlike the stuffy, gawking men in their buttoned-down suits and buttoned-up truths who frequented the New York Playboy Club, where I worked as a Bunny—a glorified cocktail waitress.

One of the good-looking Marlboro men noticed the box of Playboy matches, which I had placed strategically and conspicuously at the far edge of my table. "Could I borrow it?" he asked.

I responded in an Irish brogue, something I slipped into from time to time to amuse myself, my Playboy Club customers, and intriguing strangers. A casual conversation continued. I told them that my father was with the diplomatic corps, that I had traveled with him throughout Europe. Now, he was in New York for meetings at the United Nations. A version of this act always played well at the tables of the nervous Playboy Keyholders. Toward dusk, the Marlboro men walked me to my apartment. The matches borrower asked me to dinner for the next night.

He took me to a Greek restaurant in Midtown. We drank ouzo and retsina and dined on moussaka and spanakopita. All evening, I regaled this tall wrangler with stories of my life in Ireland and of travels with my father, the diplomat. I described the imaginary village of my childhood and recounted my mother's tragic death when I was only three. "Sometimes, late at night, I think I can hear her singing," I told him, wistfully.

He asked me out again. Again, he seemed delighted by the tales of my make-believe girlhood in Ulster. My energy for the Irish deception quickly became tiresome to me if not to my eager cowboy admirer. The theatrics ceased to amuse me. Plus, what I knew about things Irish was running out. How long could I continue to quote lines from Yeats or Joyce in my imitation of a Siobhán McKenna accent?

On our third date, this sincere and gentle man suggested we go for a ride on the Staten Island Ferry. The evening was perfect: full moon, gentle breeze, laughter with a handsome companion. We stood on the deck of the old ferry, looking into the starry night. I leaned against the railing. He pressed his body against my back—a strong, protective closeness. I was beginning to feel real affection for this tall and thoughtful man. I wanted to extricate myself from my short-sighted deception. But how? Haltingly, I summoned up the courage to tell him the truth.

I began wistfully, brogue-ishly. "Ya know, there's somethin' I gotta be tellin' ya."

"What is it?" His breath caressed my ear.

"Oh, an' it's a shameful, shameful thing...." I directed those first true words into the inky harbor.

"What is it?"

"Oh, and to be sure you're not gonna wanta be seein' me anymore, once I tell ya." For the third time, he coaxed me.

"What is it? Tell me."

"Well, ya know...(pause)...I'm not *really* Irish...(long pause)...I'm from Philadelphia."

In silence, we watched the ferry approach the lower Manhattan dock. My heart raced. I ran out of words. A minute passed. When he told me that he didn't care if I was Irish or Polish or Martian, I cried. He liked *me*! He cared about *me*! Me—the embarrassingly ordinary, untraveled, inexperienced, credential-less me.

My shell cracked. For the first time, in a long time, I had a meaningful indication that I was okay; an indication from someone for whom I was developing respect bordering on awe; an indication that defied all my mother's threats, admonitions, and curses; an indication that who I *really* was was better than any two-dimensional theatrical character my insecure, fantasy-filled mind could ever invent. I felt safe, was safe, just being myself.

And that was how I met my husband Hobart Noble Durham, Jr., called "Bart" by all who knew him. That night, I packed up the masks of lies and deceit that had hidden me from myself. It was life-changing. At twenty-three, I left my most-burdensome baggage behind and followed Bart and my heart to New Mexico, the "Land of Enchantment," where we raised a house and two children and where *my* self grew over the next fifty years out of the dry, high-desert dust.

The other rugged, handsome man with Bart on the afternoon of that memorable first encounter at The Hip Bagel was his best friend, John Allen. Shortly thereafter, John left on an extended world trip—first stop, North Africa. I declined his "Meet me in Morocco" invitation. I didn't want to leave my Playboy life, and I didn't want to leave Bart.

John wrote to me from Tangiers:

...If only we could always (or even often, or even once or twice) be "worthy" of life that is open to the full surge of forces, shadows, lights, conflicts, creations, evanescences, in as well as out, but this is what I feel in you and ever more strongly—that this is your direction and that you have the strength, sensitivity, and intelligence to survive and to flow.

The day after John returned to New York from his year-long adventure abroad, the three of us rendezvoused outside our favorite café near the corner of Bleecker and MacDougal streets. Bart and I were eager to hear about John's global adventures. We spotted him from a block away. He sauntered in our direction, sure-footedly, shoulders back, head up, smiling. He wore a safari jacket and a jaunty canvas hat. As soon as he saw us, he waved and bounded across the street. The two "brothers" embraced roughly, in a best-buddy way. Then John grabbed Bart's shoulders, looked him square in the eye and proclaimed: "I've been around the fucking world!"

...around the fucking world...

It was on that special corner in 1964 that John Allen's words awakened in me a long-dormant longing in my otherwise occupied come-and-go cells. Those cells shouted to me, "If John can do it, you can do it. You can go around the fucking world." That imperative lodged in the crease of my unfolding life plan. It catapulted my dreams of travel forward and gave my unstructured life a compass.

"Around the fucking world" became a private mantra, a slow-growing intention on my chart of accomplishments-to-come. I visualized the earth: me circumnavigating it. New York to France, Italy, Morocco, Madagascar, India, Vietnam, China, Japan, Hawaii, California, and back to New York.

I have an existential map. It has "You are here" written all over it.

–Steven Wright

Rendezvous with Death

Decades ago, on a November afternoon, I was working the lunch shift in The Playroom of the New York Playboy Club, where, in my role as "Bunny Jill," I served roast prime rib platters, vodka martinis, sidecars, bullshots, and Cutty Sark on the rocks to an assortment of executives from midtown corporate banks and other financial and investment-centered companies.

I had taken the drink order at a table of three wide-eyed Iowa and Kansas bankers who were the guests of Stirling Adams, vice president at CIT Financial Corporation. Mr. Adams was my favorite steady customer (Playboy Club key number NY15336). Almost every day, he brought important out-of-town clients to the club.

Having sashayed my Bunny tail back to the service bar, I was setting up a tray of drinks when Andrew, the Greek busboy, stepped off the service elevator and announced, in a matter-of-fact tone, "They just shot the President."

"Andrew, that's not funny." Andrew was inclined to say bizarre things that were rarely funny.

"No," he insisted, "somebody shot President Kennedy."

Bobbie, the bartender, switched on the little radio behind the bar, and, in a matter of seconds, we heard the news: The President had been shot in Dallas. I set the tray down and hurried out to the Playroom floor to tell the men in my station what had just been reported.

No one finished his drink. No one ate his prime rib. Everyone abandoned the Playroom to return to their offices. The Bunnies rushed upstairs to the Bunny Room, changed into street clothes, and filed out of the already closed Club. Soon we knew. The country knew. The world knew.

Walter Cronkite reported: "From Dallas, Texas, the flash apparently official, President Kennedy died at 1 p.m. Central Standard Time—2 o'clock Eastern Standard Time—some thirty-eight minutes ago."

As I walked down Fifth Avenue to my apartment near Washington Square, people in the streets wept unselfconsciously. Strangers wrapped their arms around each other and sobbed. Stores shuttered. Shopkeepers shrouded their holiday-decorated windows in black cloth. The city instantly plunged into the first throes of mourning. New Yorkers were shocked and numb.

I called my parents. "Oh, don't be so dramatic," my mother mocked. "And remember to call your Grandmother Graves. It's her birthday." If only my father had answered the phone.

Unfamiliar and uncomfortable thoughts and emotions churned in me all day and for many days that followed. As an uninformed or ill-informed twenty-one-year-old citizen of the United States of America (*one nation under God*), I had taken for granted that the country of my birth was a safe and powerful place. That's what we were taught in school.

Born in the "City of Brotherly Love," a few miles from the Liberty Bell, Independence Hall, and the Betsy Ross House, I was now living within view of the Statue of Liberty. My youthful and unquestioned understanding of America—symbolized by righteousness, goodness, safety, and strength—could not assimilate such evil. Everything in my world turned upside-down. The Commander in Chief of the United States had been targeted, shot, and killed.

Before the assassination, I lived in my small Manhattan bubble with no interest in politics, war, famine, drought, or other world issues. I had never been anywhere but Philadelphia and New York. I didn't listen to the news. I wasn't old enough to vote. I was a young girl with a faux-glamorous job, fantasies, and false eyelashes.

Kennedy's murder shocked my consciousness. Suddenly, two gunshots penetrated my tenuous connection to a universe outside my narrow yesterdays and vague tomorrows. They jolted me into a growing understanding that there was so much more to wonder and worry about than shopping, men, marijuana, sex, and girlish musings about faraway Paris. I began to pay attention to the world beyond my tight circle of friends and my studio apartment in Greenwich Village, beyond my few years of running away, dropping out, dreaming, and yearning. I sensed, or began to, that I was a part of something enormous.

My mind replayed the events of that momentous week: Jacqueline Kennedy pushing through the day in a blood-stained pink Chanel suit; Lyndon B. Johnson being sworn in aboard Air Force One; Little John-John snapping a final salute to the man he called Dad; Caroline kneeling at her father's flag-draped coffin in the Rotunda; Jack Ruby pulling the trigger on Lee Harvey Oswald in the basement of the Dallas Police Department. In the blink of an eye, in a shot from a textbook repository window (or somewhere), the relentless march of history took a sharp and unanticipated turn. I was determined—destined, perhaps—to be a part of that march toward justice, truth, or salvation.

Eight months after Kennedy's assassination, during the tumultuous political season of 1964 and the Democratic National Convention in Atlantic City, I watched a television program honoring Mrs. Kennedy. Fredrick March and Florence Eldridge read selections from President Kennedy's favorite poetry and prose. March's reading of Alan Seeger's "I Have a Rendezvous with Death" moved me to tears, an emotion I didn't know I could feel.

> I have a rendezvous with Death
> At some disputed barricade...
> ...And I to my pledged word am true,
> I shall not fail that rendezvous.

Perhaps for the first time, I wondered about my rendezvous with death. But more, I wondered about now. To what "pledged word" should I be true? Where should I go? What should I do as I march toward that ultimate rendezvous?

Death Be Not Cowed or Cowardly

Caveat lector: I am not proud of everything in my past. Still, certain personal stories of death, near-death, or the death of shadows deserve inclusion in this work. Otherwise, how am I to shine light on those life lessons that have lain hidden in the darkness of shame and denial?

I had a near-death experience. At least that's what I called it in an effort to give a name and meaning to an incident that still confounds me. I'm not sure what it was, except surreal. *La petite mort, peut-être.*

It happened one night long ago in a hotel room in my town. My tryst with a secret lover, a big-city art dealer, dragged out plotless like a Hollywood B-movie shot over three years. We had wandered into our illicit affair through a shared connection—marital ennui—a path circling on itself, leading nowhere. Two selfish, self-absorbed people with spouses and children, who didn't hold marriage vows to be sacrosanct. What we did hold sacrosanct was the lofty art of business and the business of the lofty art world. The ramifications of our libido-driven rendezvous were of little concern.

Sex was exciting, liberating, and daring. He was attracted to my old Playboy Bunny nouveau-geisha flirtatiousness and my saucy repartee. I was attracted to his attraction to me. The more erotic the sex, the more uninhibited we became. We played an increasingly daring game. And, professional roulette.

That night, we slipped into our familiar routine. Sex progressed. For the first time, time was irrelevant. Strangely, I made no attempt to control how he saw me—the angles and lines of my legs, the fullness of my breasts, the curve of my torso. A strange wave of energy rose within me and outside of me, and suddenly I lost the sensation of being in my body. The sense of him, the room, and family waiting at home drifted away. I no longer saw, heard, tasted, or felt my partner. I found myself in deep and distant darkness, balanced on a small, shiny, white, free-form, platform-like vehicle about four feet long and two feet wide. It seemed to be zooming into deep space with me on it. I felt sturdy, secure, and alert, sailing into an extra-terrestrial beyond. Lucidly, I wondered how I was able to see the blazing whiteness of this mysterious vehicle in the pitch blackness? How was I able to keep my balance?

My transporter stopped in a familiar deep, pitch-dark place in the middle—or toward the end—of a distant nothingness. I stood tall and straight, my feet anchored safely to the white platform, arms outstretched. At that moment, it became clear. I must make an immediate and ultimate choice. Life or Death. This way or that. I sensed that I was facing twelve o'clock, and if I sent my strange chariot in the direction of two o'clock, it would take me "into the light." I didn't know if "into the light" meant death, or heaven, or God, or the final abyss. If I turned to travel in the direction of nine o'clock, I wondered if I'd return to the place from which I came.

In a flash, the decision was made, or not made. It just happened. I was back in bed with my bewildered lover. I heard myself crying, sobbing. His voice grew less faint and distant.

"Are you okay?"

I couldn't answer, couldn't speak. I had an overwhelming urge to get out of that room, out of the hotel. I had to flee.

"What's wrong?" he asked.

Crying, unable to reply, I got out of bed and dressed quickly. I grabbed my handbag and reached for the doorknob before turning to look at him. Still in bed, with the sheet pulled up to cover his chest, leaning on one elbow, he reached for his designer horn-rimmed glasses. I fled.

I didn't go home. Instead, I crossed the Alameda and walked along the dirt path by the side of the little Santa Fe River—a glorified creek. I sat on a wooden bench under a park light and took a small journal from my handbag.

I wrote, "I will never be the same."

That was the end of the affair. In a snap of my fingers, I went from intimacy to indifference, from desire to desertion, from self-absorption to heaven knows where.

How was I not the same, I wondered? Did I realize that I had made a dreadful mistake by indulging in a superficial affair? Or had I finally and suddenly moved away from the shallowness of a tryst that no longer aligned with a new path that was mine to walk on my own? No doubt that shallowness would resurface some-where else—like the child's game of Whack-a-Mole.

The next day, I shared the saga of the whole affair and the "near-death" experience with a trusted friend and psychic who worked with crystals, Tarot cards, past lives, and distance healing, among other new-age and age-old beliefs.

"I think you might have become a walk-in," she said.

"What's a 'walk-in'?" I asked.

"It's a higher-consciousness being from another dimension who replaces a lower-consciousness being during a near-death, or psychedelic drug experience."

"Really? Why?" I was instantly attracted to the idea that I might have become a higher-consciousness being. Perhaps I had been a higher-consciousness being all along but had simply failed to push the right button, or switch to the right channel. I sat up straight and leaned toward her.

"It's an attempt by superior beings not currently in human form to bring higher energy to the planet before it's too late."

"Too late?" Did she mean too late for the planet, or just too late for me?

I held onto the proposition of walk-ins and onto the puffed-up notion that perhaps I already was or had become a higher-consciousness being sent, challenged, or destined, to seek and find and celebrate higher consciousness in my world. Sometimes, an irrational part of me chooses to unearth and dust off an opportunity to indulge in short flights of fancy self-flattery.

It is not more surprising to be born twice than once; everything in nature is resurrection.

–Voltaire

Yearning.
Spurning the dull, the mundane, the safe, and predictable…
Burning unrequited desires…
Setting inextinguishable fires.
Churning, chomping at the bit,
Biting the hand, the bullet, the forbidden fruit….

Amid my notes and journals, I found that emotional (for lack of a better adjective) poem scrawled on the back of an old envelope. I don't know when I wrote it, but my handwriting indicates that I was in a hurry or in a mood where yearning dwells. Naturally, I wondered what I yearned for and when this yearning began. Perhaps it was for Paris. Oh, yes. I yearned for Paris.

Summer vacation, 1948

Destination: Paris (At Last!)

Decades before manifesting a trip around the world, I managed to manifest a trip to the city that had inhabited my dreams from my earliest childhood and all through high school and college: Paris. I wanted to see the Eiffel Tower and Notre Dame. I wanted to wear a beret and stroll along the Rue de la Paix, speaking French and smoking cigarettes at street cafés in the Quartier Latin.

There was a large map of the world on a wall in "Phlegmside," the off-campus house in Ithaca, New York, where my boyfriend and three other drama students lived. With color-coded map pins, each roommate had indicated the faraway—or not-so-faraway—countries he had visited. Three had been to Europe; two had visited Mexico; all four had been to Canada; one had been to Bermuda. I envied them their travel experiences. To me, those red, yellow, blue, and green map pins authenticated worldly sophistication: I've been here and here; I saw this and that; I climbed that; I dined there.

Me? I didn't even have a passport.

One of the housemates had a souvenir image of the Eiffel Tower on a shelf in the living room. He bought it in Paris; lucky Bryn had been to Paris. My yearning to know Paris was borderline painful. How could I get to Paris? When will the postponement, the waiting, and the excuses end, and when will I experience myself in The City of Light?

I was seventeen. Practically every day, I dreamed of fleeing my stuck-on-the-shelf life and flying to Paris, to London, to Amsterdam, to "somewhere I have never traveled, gladly beyond…," as the E. E. Cummings poem taunted me.

That wretched "Phlegmside" map of the unexplored world I yearned to know teased and tormented me. I indulged in an imaginary, one-sided competition with it. I plotted. Maybe I'd get purple pushpins and stick them on Siberia, Northern Rhodesia, and Tasmania. Could my fascination with the map be a harbinger of my certain destiny, a path that would lead (inevitably) to the wherever I would discover and (ultimately) the whatever I would become in this world?

Faraway places with strange-sounding names…calling, calling me…

On the beach at Cape May, New Jersey, during the inquisitively fertile six-year-old time of my life, I set an intention.

I'm wearing baggy red and white striped shorts and one of my Dad's big white t-shirts, so I don't get a blistering sunburn. If I get too many more freckles, my mother says, they will merge, and I'll look like I belong to a different family.

My Dad and I are standing ankle-deep in the ocean. I know we're looking east because he taught me that.

"That's France over there, right, Dad?"

"Right." He tugs on one of my wet pigtails.

"But we can't see it, can we Dad?"

"No, it's farther than the eye can see."

"How far can the eye see?"

"It depends. Here, we can see to the horizon."

"How far is that?"

"Mmm. Maybe ten miles or so."

"How far is France?"

"Oh, France is about two thousand miles away."

"Wow, two thousand miles!"

The foamy water rushes up, curls around my feet, and then pulls the sand out from under my toes. I stand there for a long time, just looking far away.

"Someday I'm going to Paris, France!" I say.

Dad smiles.

I had forsaken Manhattan for love and adventure in New Mexico. My early declaration to go to Paris took a while to put in play. That fantasy reignited twenty-one years later during a conversation with an old woman who lived alone in a crumbling adobe casita in Cerrillos, not far from our ranch.

One afternoon, as we sat drinking tea, she shared one of her life's disappointments with me: she had never been to Paris. For most of her life, she dreamed of going to La Ville Lumière. Sadly, she had never created the opportunity for herself. She postponed her dream again and again because of time and money issues and other obligations or choices. As we chatted and nibbled *biscochitos*, I realized that my worn-out reasons and excuses for failing to make a trip to Paris a priority were the same as hers: too little time and money, and too many family obligations. I studied the sad, old woman with gnarled knuckles who needed to hold on to the furniture and walls when she walked.

It was too late for her to go to Paris, but it was not too late for me.

Then and there, I made a promise to myself: I'm going to Paris this year, not next year, not some year, this year—any and all excuses or obligations, notwithstanding. That evening, I confronted the woman in my mirror: "Don't let what happened to that lovely, old woman happen to you, girl. Go to Paris. Find a way to get to Paris before the year is over. Before it's too late."

The seaside declaration by my six-year-old self began to materialize. The pulsing imperative merged with an opportunity, long-planted, but slow to germinate. A creative and workable idea finally sprouted through the dry, unfertilized soil of possibility. *Je vais à Paris!*

I financed that first trans-Atlantic adventure by selling an unusual object from my accumulation of unusual objects: an ancient mummified baby crocodile in a small, molded papier-mâché sarcophagus. This strange artifact was a gift from my favorite Playboy Club customer who relished listening to my excitement about Egypt and Egyptology. Mr. Adams had received the little mummy as a joke birthday present from someone in his wealthy, waspy social circle. I was thrilled to receive it. The day after he gave it to me, I called The Metropolitan Museum of Art and made an appointment to show the fascinating *objet* to an expert.

The chief curator of Egyptology examined the curious treasure and surmised that the sarcophagus was most likely a nineteenth-century piece, craftily faked more than a hundred and fifty years before coming into my possession. However, after studying the cloth and the style of the wrapping, the curator concluded that the object inside was most likely an authentic, mummified baby crocodile, probably from a late Egyptian dynasty. He posited that the little object could contain either the actual remains of a baby crocodile or just a bunch of wrapped sticks signifying the little reptile.

Years later, in pursuit of money to purchase my ticket to France, I sold my Egyptian treasure to Dr. Rudy Kieve, a psychiatrist in Santa Fe, who, in turn, gave it to the artist Fritz Scholder, who sold it (or traded it) to a Texas-born, wheeler-dealer art-gallery owner and my future employer, Forrest Fenn.

Shortly after I began working for him, and more than three decades before Forrest Fenn made international news by purportedly burying a million-dollar treasure in the Rocky Mountains, I stumbled upon "my baby crocodile" in a fancy display case in the back showroom of his gallery. The little sign next to it read: "Deaccessioned from the British Museum." Knowing that it actually came from an executive at a midtown bank in New York City, who had given it to a Playboy Bunny who was fascinated by anything Egyptian,

I proudly shared this accurate information with Forrest. He was not pleased. His displeasure intensified when I brought him a clipping of a short article I had written for the "Life in These United States" section of *Reader's Digest* (circa 1967). It described the time I asked an obstetrician friend, at the suggestion of the curator at the Met, to X-ray the little mummy and prove or disprove if someone, millennia ago, painstakingly embalmed a baby crocodile to honor one of the deities.

> I sat in the doctor's waiting room with a group of women in various stages of pregnancy. Presently, the doctor entered the room. "Linda," he called. I stood expectantly. "Congratulations, you have a baby crocodile!"

The baby crocodile paid for my round-trip ticket from New York to Luxembourg on Icelandic Airlines. My intention was to sell fine Native American jewelry to Europeans to pay for the additional expenses of the trip.

It was 1971. I was about to become an international traveler, a woman of the world. At last, my long-held dream was underway. This dream made no sense to anyone in my family. To them, it seemed reckless and selfish. Many times, I tried to persuade Bart to accompany me to France, or Italy, or Spain (with or without the children). Over and again, he told me that he had absolutely no interest in going to Europe. "I'd just as soon read about it in *National Geographic*."

I used his disappointing rejections to free my conscience to go it alone.

I left our toddler son at the ranch with his father and flew our three-year-old daughter to New Jersey to stay with my parents. Booking a super cheap Icelandic Airlines flight to Europe, I flew away to manifest my fantasy destiny.

From Luxembourg, I boarded a train to Paris, along with six young American backpackers who had been on my Icelandic flight. Like me, they were first-time European adventurers. Paul, a recent law-school graduate, planned a month's escape while waiting to hear if he'd passed the California bar exam—or not. On adrenaline, drugs, or both, we were all on a high that first night of our first trip to Europe.

A few hours before midnight, we arrived in The City of Light. None of us had hotel reservations. Most of the train gang decided to stay at a youth hostel near the Gare du Nord. *Mais, non!* A youth hostel on my first night in Paris? That would be an insult to all my long-running fantasies. My unplanned plan was to find a charming small hotel—something sexy and romantic. My Bohemian self leaned toward the Left Bank. From a pay phone near the train station, I called the underlined hotels in my small *Guide de Paris.*

"*Complet.*" "*Complet.*" "*Complet.*" No available rooms.

Paul waited with me while I made more calls, eventually securing the last available room at a slightly too-pricey hotel near the Arc de Triomphe. The Rive Gauche would have to wait. Paul offered to escort me to the hotel. He waited outside while I registered and quickly dropped my bag in the sweet, small room with a single bed, one tall window, and a tiny private bath. Minutes later, he and I were strolling arm in arm along the Champs-Élysées, talking and marveling at the fabled city that had captivated our dreams and our imaginations for years.

The adrenalin rush eventually subsided, and a gust of tiredness overtook me. It was late, and I yearned for my first night's sleep in Paris. Paul still had no accommodations. He asked if he could leave his backpack in my room while he searched for a place to stay. Of course, I said. We tip-toed through the deserted hotel lobby. Once in my room, I agreed, with very little persuasion, to let him sleep on the floor. *Pourquoi pas?* It had been an extremely long day, we were both exhausted, and Paul was a very polite soon-to-be lawyer. He could find a proper place to stay in the morning.

Oh, Dear Paris,

You know how my young and overly dramatic self has romanticized you. You know how I have continued to fantasize about French love and beauty and Paris fashion and sex. Imagine, Dear Paris, my ecstatic realization upon finding myself—at last, at last—in the embrace of your grace, your magic, your je ne sais quoi. Countless chic-seeking mademoiselles, hungry for love, have been enveloped by your avenues of desire. We lose ourselves in the long-imagined, hallowed destination of our dreams and we sense— with the full power of our hormonal innocence—that the nearness of the promise of romance awaits us. In story, song, and dreams, oh, cher Paree, you have enchanted us. You have beckoned us. Now, we aspire to turn our long-held fantasies into reality. J'arrive! Nous arrivons!

The crisp white linen sheets feel cool against my skin. I dim the lamp, and the floral-papered wall recedes. Paul is standing on a faux-Persian area rug in the middle of the lovely small room, his back to me. He arranges his sleeping bag. My eyes follow the contour of his spine from the top of his neck down, down to the waistband of his pale blue boxers. Considerations disappear. The magic of Paris asserts itself.

Heavy drapes frame the narrow window. I see the glow of Paris. I feel the weight of him. I feel the weight and weightlessness of time. Frame by frame, the enchanting night captures us in late or early hours of unexpected timelessness.

Time is like that—somersaulting, nonlinear. One minute this man I met hours earlier is standing in the train station. The next retrievable minute, he is in my arms, in this narrow bed, and we toss all logic, all considerations, all possible repercussions to the wind of this first perfect and sensual Parisian night. Our bodies and our French fantasies yield to the intimacy that the Other offers, tentatively at first, and then to an erotic crescendo.

Paul and I had found an opening in the fabric of our encumbered lives for a week of love-making, hand-holding, boulevard-strolling, museum-wandering, café-lingering connection. At the end of the week, Paul traveled on to Munich, and I moved to a modest hotel in the Quartier Latin and recast myself as a woman of great mystery, a poet, maybe, alone in Paris.

Full of sexual satisfaction and empty of remorse, I sat in cafés and dark jazz clubs, smoking foul-tasting Gauloises. I lingered in museums, and I fell in love with Rodin's *Burghers of Calais* and the Degas' ballerina pastels. It took some effort to direct my attention away from fantasy and romance and back to the task of introducing Paris shopkeepers to the exquisite vintage Zuni and Navajo jewelry that I had brought to Europe with the intention of dazzling Europeans.

I wandered the streets, browsed in shops, showed shopkeepers the fine assortment of silver bracelets and necklaces, strands of coral, silver, shell, and the ornate Navajo squash blossom necklace. One very serious jeweler examined the heavy silver and turquoise piece. I detected the hint of a smile on his face and assumed he must be enchanted by it. But, no. He handed the ceremonial treasure back to me, rather dismissively, and turned his attention to a well-dressed matron who had just entered the shop. The collection aroused curiosity, but not buyers.

On my last evening in Paris, I came close to selling a small silver and turquoise bird pin to a man in a bar. Clearly, the piece delighted him, and my quoted price seemed fair. As he reached for his wallet, he asked me, "What is ze name of ze bird?"

Smiling at the good fortune of a sale, I replied, "It's a roadrunner."

Distaste registered on his face. He shoved his wallet back into his pocket.

"Oh, non, non, non!" he exclaimed, waving me away. "No cartoon bird. No beep, beep, beep."

I couldn't save the sale. Even when I told him that the official name was chaparral cock.

"Non, non. No beep, beep, beep."

After a week in London, a few days in Amsterdam, and a weekend in New York, I reclaimed my daughter from my parents and flew back to New Mexico with all the jewelry—minus my cowboy hat with the silver hatband. That, I sold to a man on the corner of Madison Avenue and 60th Street. It crushed me to acknowledge that I was an absolute entrepreneurial failure. However, I quickly discounted my initial disappointment and recognized that I had become an international traveler with a working/walking knowledge of the shops in the Quartier Latin and on the Rue de Rivoli and the Rue de la Paix. The *pièce de résistance* was a glorious Parisian affair.

Pushpins dotted my visionary map: France, England, the Netherlands. My journal overflowed with self-endorsement. I climbed the Eiffel Tower. Marveled at the Rosetta Stone in the British Museum. Smoked hashish in a small Amsterdam hotel. Gazed upon Rembrandt's *The Night Watch*. Succeeded in creating a magnificent, memorable, mini-grand tour with the stamps in my new passport to prove it. And I betrayed my marriage vows, betrayed something in myself. The affair was a secret I kept from my husband. The repercussions of the secret I kept from myself.

I connect these decades-old episodes with a beautiful passage about cowardice and the absence of courage I've read aloud to myself countless times.

> Long before morning, I knew that what I was seeking to discover was a thing I'd always known. That all courage was a form of constancy. That it was always himself that the coward abandoned first. After this all other betrayals came easily.
>
> –Cormac McCarthy, *All the Pretty Horses*

Lie Lady Lie

SCENE ONE: Manhattan

"Taxi!"

It's just after dawn, and the cabbie picks me up on the corner of 9th Avenue and 23rd Street. I'm on my way back to New Mexico after a busy week in the city. I settle back in the cab for the half-hour drive to LaGuardia Airport. Bob Dylan's "Lay Lady Lay" comes on the radio, and I ask the driver to turn up the volume.

"You like Dylan?" he asks, with a sense of surprise and approval in his voice. To him, I may look too old or too *establishment* in my Calvin Klein suit and knock-off Louis Vuitton bag to appreciate a skinny, mazy-haired, American folk-rock idol.

"Like him? I reply off-handedly. "I used to live with him."

"You did? You lived with Dylan!" The excitement in his voice fills the cab's interior.

All the way to LaGuardia, I answer this young man's fan questions about my (made-up) years with Dylan.

"We lived in the Village" "Yes, he was moody." "No, he never wrote a song about me—at least not anything I could recognize." "Yes, we're still in touch, occasionally." "Of course, I love many of his songs."

No, I never lived with Dylan. But I know someone who did. And I know plenty of people who hung out with him regularly. Plus, I'm the right age, and I came out of the same music circles and places.

I didn't see these out-of-context fabrications as lying. To me, assuming the part of a former lover of Dylan's was nothing more than a harmless, pre-rush-hour conversation in a random cab with a gullible, curly-haired, Dylan-worshiping music lover who was charmed by having a former lover of Dylan's in his taxi. No, I did not feel guilty about my made-up story. No person was harmed in the course of this charade.

I didn't want the driver to think that one of Dylan's exes was a cheapskate so, when we reached the airport, I gave him an enormous tip, along with my gallery business card.

SCENE TWO: My Gallery in Santa Fe

I was in my office when I overheard an exchange between a gallery assistant and a young man.

"Is Linda Durham here?"

"May I tell her who's asking?"

"Oh, she wouldn't know my name. It's just that she was a passenger in my taxi in New York last year, and I..."

I rose to greet him. He recognized me immediately and began to relate our taxicab conversation. I gently stopped him, acting as if I didn't want those within earshot to be privy to my Dylan history.

He nodded his understanding, binding our secret as co-conspirators. He explained that he and a friend were on a cross-country adventure and that the tip I gave him was the largest he had ever received. It was the impetus to start a travel fund. I neither remembered—if I even knew—how much I gave him— nor did I know what constituted a proper "guilt tip." Whatever the amount, it impressed him.

On exhibit, in front of the gallery, there was a six-foot-tall bronze hand grenade sculpture gilded in twenty-three-carat gold leaf by Martin Cary Horowitz. The controversial sculpture intrigued the cabbie, and he asked if I would pose with him in front of it. Of course. Full of excitement at having introduced his friend to one of Bob Dylan's former lovers and eager to continue their cross-country adventure, the two young men closed a chapter in their journey.

SCENE THREE: My Office, Months Later

Journalist and friend Kathryn Davis had been assigned to write an article about me for a regional publication. Before our scheduled afternoon interview at the gallery, she had done her research.

"I didn't know you used to live with Bob Dylan!" were the first words out of her mouth.

"What? No, I never lived with Bob Dylan. Who told you that?"

"Well, I googled you and found this page by a taxi driver who blogged about driving you to the airport. He wrote that you shared some stories of your life with Dylan. He posted a recent picture of himself with you in front of Marty's grenade."

It was time to come clean. I told Kathryn the story of the early morning taxi ride in Manhattan.

"Oh, Linda, how could you do such a crazy thing! Suppose Bob Dylan sees that blog and claims you never lived together—that he doesn't even know you!"

"I'll tell him that he must have forgotten."

Hanging Out with Ishmael

By the Christmas Season, following the demise of the gallery and months after my regenerative trip to Myanmar, I thought I had entered the acceptance stage of grief. No fairy god friend was going to appear and magically eliminate the growing financial issues that were fast plummeting me into unwanted territory—bankruptcy, foreclosure, and homelessness.

All summer long, through the fall and into December, I toyed with a recurring idea of selling everything in one giant, creatively staged estate sale, taking that net bundle of cash and disappearing into a new and unexplored existential wilderness. Instead, I sold a few treasured paintings and photographs from my personal collection and continued to stay a month or two ahead of complete financial disaster.

But my least-favorite season snowed on my progress. Wrapped in the middle of some sad and lonely feelings, with money low and temperatures even lower, I decided to get out of town, to get away from holiday commercials and hollow festivities, and to find some much-needed comfort and warmth in isolation and anonymity. From the refuge of my car, I reasoned, I could drive away from the depressing, infernally omnipresent Christmas gaiety that is inescapable in town.

By the day after Hallowe'en, and all through my Scorpio birthday, Thanksgiving, Chanukah, Kwanzaa, and the Winter Solstice, Santa Feans are surrounded (inundated, bombarded) by displays and advertisements for holiday everything, most of which mean nothing to me. Frequently, Christmastime fills me not with love and joy, but with great disappointment, sadness, anger, confusion, tragedy, and a sense of being betrayed. In other words: unhappiness. I dislike corporate Christmas cards signed by twenty people I don't know and with whom I'll probably never engage. I don't like tinsel. I don't like poinsettias. Bah, humbug. I feel it approaching—the shopping mania, obligatory gift-giving, commercialism, family dynamics, parties, Santa Clauses, the songs. Not the carols; I love the carols. It's the chipmunk jingles I want to avoid.

So, I mapped out a scenic, snow-free route to the elusive sunshine that my bones and mind urgently sought. On the 22nd of December, with my dog, Ruby, my hiking boots, a journal, and Herman Melville's unabridged *Moby Dick* on nineteen CDs, I got in the car and headed south, determined to find the warmth and comfort that I could not find in my drafty house or in my isolated life. A week or two of unstructured adventure seemed a perfect way to fill the emptiness I almost always felt at Christmas.

"We're heading for the Mexican border," I announced to Ruby. "We'll find a little cabin in nature, and we'll hike in the warm, dry desert of Sonora or far southern Arizona."

I inserted disc one of Melville's great tale into the CD player. Call me Ishmael's eager listener.

> …having little or no money in my purse, and nothing particular to interest me on shore, I thought I would sail about a little and see the watery part of the world. It is a way I have of driving off the spleen and regulating the circulation.

As I put Santa Fe County behind me, the first snowflakes floated onto my windshield. They continued to fall gently through Albuquerque, Socorro, and Elephant Butte city. Because I was in no particular hurry and because my destination was vague at best, I decided to take the scenic route through Hillsboro, Kingston, and the Black Mountain Range, a perfect road for my mood and Melville.

By the time we reached Silver City, the snow was falling fast and accumulating significantly. "Tonight, Ruby," I said to my backseat passenger, "you and I will go no farther. Let's find a place to spend the night."

We took a snow walk along Main Street, checking out the town, and approached an interesting-looking woman dressed in wildly colorful clothes who was loading groceries into her truck.

"Excuse me, do you know of a dog-friendly motel or guest house nearby?"

"Yes. Bear Mountain Inn is dog-friendly. I can call them for you to see if they have room." We stood in the snowfall while she got out her cell phone and called the inn.

Yes. They had a room and, yes, my dog was welcome. It was pricey, but it was snowing harder and harder, and with each passing minute, I grew hungrier and more tired. As the friendly woman, who called herself a "gyno-lanthropist"— one who donates money to women in need—drew an overly detailed map to the inn, Ruby's black coat turned snow white.

We found our way down the long, slightly rutted, snow-covered lane that led to the beautiful WPA-era lodge. It appeared through a ghostly navy-blue night and curtain of white. Lights blazed. The proprietress and two large dogs waited for Ruby and me at the edge of the circular drive. A fire crackled in the great room. A lodge-cooked dinner and a glass of wine capped off eight adventurous hours. After a long and tiring day, filled with miles of weather, a bag of trail mix, and Melville's "dreamy quietude," Ruby and I arrived at the current best place in our world.

The night's deep snowfall closed roads in and out. We lingered over an elegant breakfast. By noon, the Highway Patrol radio report announced some roads were open. Ruby and I bid farewell to the inn's inhabitants and unburied the Outback. Through ice and snow, we headed into the unknown with Ishmael and Queequeg in our ears, filled with expectations. In my case, sunshine. In the case of Melville's characters, fortune, adventure, or revenge.

> But we had not gone perhaps above a hundred yards, when chancing to turn a corner, and looking back as I did so, who should be seen but Elijah following us, though at a distance.

Sunshine eluded us. The road over the mountains was closed, and the State Police turned us back. We retraced our tracks until we reached the alternate highway headed southeast. The route lengthened our journey to warmth, which I craved more and more deeply, but I was in no hurry on this day before the day before Christmas, and I permitted myself to rejoice that no one expected me anywhere, at any time.

We negotiated the ice and snow-compromised roads all the way to Deming and Interstate 10, the major east-west highway. Parked cars and giant semis jammed Deming's main road. Vehicles lined the grimy, slushy streets from one end of town to the other in both directions. I-10 was closed. Motels were full. Shadows were long. Ice and snow covered everything. While Ismael commented on the whiteness of the whale, I surveyed the whiteness of the land.

> But not yet have we solved the incantation of this whiteness, and learned why it appeals with such power to the soul: and more strange and portentous why, as we have seen, it is at once the most meaning symbol of spiritual things, nay, the very veil of the Christmas deity; and yet should be as it is, the intensifying agent in things the most appalling to mankind.

Two nights before Christmas, is there room at the inn for one disappointed, stranded woman and her dog? There is. Ruby and I headed back to Bear Mountain Lodge to spend a second night by the roaring gas fireplace in the cozy cabin reserved for dogs and their owners.

Morning brought more discouraging news for my dream of a sunny sojourn to the border or beyond: frigid temperatures; unseasonably cold weather in Arizona; roads throughout the southern corridor snow-packed, closed, or only going north. I couldn't afford a third night at the inn. Besides, it was fully booked with happy holiday travelers. Reluctantly, I made the difficult decision to head back to Santa Fe. Slowly. I definitely did not want to find myself in the middle of Christmas Eve revelers on Canyon Road.

With no place to go and no one to meet, we were in no hurry to hit the road. My only plan was to drive for a while and stop before dark wherever we could find a manger or motel. I followed Ishmael as he journeyed, mused, and observed.

Before this equatorial coin, Ahab, not unobserved by others, was now pausing. 'There's something ever egotistical in mountain-tops and towers all other grand and lofty things; look here,—three peaks as proud as Lucifer. The firm tower, that is Ahab; the volcano, that is Ahab; the courageous, the undaunted, and victorious fowl, that, too, is Ahab; all are Ahab; and this round gold is but the image of the rounder globe, which, like a magician's glass, to each and every man in turn but mirrors back his own mysterious self. Great pains, small gains for those who ask the world to solve them; it cannot solve itself. Methinks now this coined sun wears a ruddy face…. From storm to storm! So be it, then! Born in throes, 'tis fit that man should live in pains and die in pangs! So be it, then. Here's stout stuff for woe to work on. So be it, then.'

Hour after hour, listening to the flawless reader's voice, I realized that, although Melville's novel is certainly about whales, whaling, and the search for Captain Ahab's nemesis, it's also about isolation, obsession, loneliness, and revenge. So be it.

Lost in a deep and silent monologue about destiny, the search for life's purpose, and the comfort that surely must lie ahead, as I drove in the bitter, unreasonable late afternoon of December 24th, I found I longed for no one.

Not seldom in this life, when, on the right side, fortune's favourites sail close by us, we, though all adroop before, catch somewhat of the rushing breeze, and joyfully our bagging sails fill out.

Once we hit Interstate 25 northbound, it was smooth sailing at last. Beyond the metal borders of my warm car, the icy air was practically visible, casting a steely veil across a giant billboard as it came into view. ELEPHANT BUTTE INN AND SPA—5 MILES AHEAD.

"Let's spend Christmas Eve at Elephant Butte, Ruby, if they have a room, and if they accept well-behaved black Labs."

Just as the sun began to set, we pulled into the unplowed parking lot of the less-than-glamorous motel in downtown Elephant Butte, which is not so much a city as a few abandoned RV courts, some secured storage businesses, and an empty boat marina overlooking a partially frozen manmade lake.

We plodded through the crusty snow to the lobby office. The place looked and felt deserted.

"Hello, hello!" Eventually, a smiling, plump woman wearing red ribbons and jingle bells in her elaborate upswept hairdo—à la 1940s Hollywood movie extra—greeted me. She smelled like cinnamon and candle wax and was on her way to a Christmas Eve party in Socorro. For a slight additional charge, Ruby was welcome, and we became the establishment's only guests.

Our room was charmless but warm, and the television worked. The movie *Jaws* had just begun. The beautiful teenager in the sun-splashed ocean was making her first startled expression as the screen filled. I postponed my thoughts on whales, madness, and the cold in favor of thoughts of sharks, panic, and sunny summer days.

Sometime before ten o'clock, I ventured into the hotel tavern. Two or three groups of local Christmas Evers slouched around a few knotty-pine tables, drinking and chatting festively. Juniper boughs and sprigs of holly festooned the bar. I ordered a steak dinner and a bottle of Burgundy to be delivered to my room. At midnight, the steak devoured and most of the wine drunk, I took Ruby for a walk.

Bundled up against the sub-freezing temperatures, I felt a strange, frozen isolation at my core. The absence of any longing for another struck me. I didn't miss my children or my granddaughter. I didn't miss old lovers or friends. I didn't miss my parents or siblings. I no longer missed my past. I did miss warmth—not the kind I sought by escaping frigid temperatures and driving off into the sunset. No. I missed my imaginary, faded-to-almost-invisible sense of family warmth—a warmth that was almost never part of my Christmas experiences. I drank the last of the wine and wrote in my travel journal.

It's Christmas Eve...heading toward morning. Ruby and I took a cold walk on the snow and frozen mud here in deserted Elephant Butte City. The stars appeared particularly small tonight, unconcerned. Strange, there is nowhere I am supposed to be. I am just here. I stood by a fence with my dog, where we could have viewed the lake if not for the dark, and I sang "O Holy Night" at the top of my icy lungs.
                                                              –Journal entry

Full of Captain Ahab, Moby Dick, and Ishmael's clarity and closure, I returned to Santa Fe and the aftermath of holiday madness with a reignited intention to perfect a plan and to pursue (at last) the lifelong fantasy I kept in hibernation for decades. My adventure with Ishmael inspired me, filled me with a resolve to prepare myself to leave again. I began to plan my trip around the world. Like Ishmael, I vowed to "survive the wreck."

Go East, Old Woman!

Early on an overcast morning in 2012, months after the close of Linda Durham Contemporary Art and the Myitkyina retreat and days after my winter road trip with Herman Melville's *Moby Dick*, I began to map out a plan to manifest my dream of going all the way around the world. Having assembled an atlas, a blank notebook, some pens, a few inspirational books, and my calendar, I sat at my kitchen table with a big bowl of cold red grapes and a mug of chai latte. With no appointments on my calendar and no tasks at hand, I vowed to stay "on message" until the beginning of a viable plan developed, or at least until the grapes were gone and the notebook pages filled. To get started, I referred to my personal, tried-and-true Road-to-Success Process.

Step One
Identify the goal: To manifest and execute a plan to go around the world—this year!

Step Two
Declare the goal: "I am going around the world—this year." (This must be said in a forceful and positive manner.)

Step Three
Proceed: Begin the first draft of a comprehensive to-do list.

Things To Do in Preparation for My Going Around the World Project:
1. Find money
2. Clarify the goals of the trip
3. Investigate places
4. Set a date for departure
5. Buy an airline ticket
6. Arrange to be gone
7. Find a house sitter and pet sitter
8. Etc.

I tackled those preparations, jockeying the intricacies back and forth, multi-tasking. The biggest hurdle, of course, was money. In my forward-thinking, visionary, damn-the-torpedoes-full-speed-ahead optimistic mind, I was already on my way.

> In my secret heart, I am beginning to embrace the notion that I am a pilgrim, that I have always been a lonely, dedicated seeker of something unnamed and not quite known…something "out there somewhere." I used to think the term "pilgrim" applied only to people of a serious and devout religious persuasion, people seeking enlightenment or connection with God in places like Mecca and Santiago de Compostela. Now I realize that I, too, am seeking something—something deep or elusive or maybe even "otherworldly." And, yes, it might be enlightenment or connection with God. I don't know yet. I know this: Somewhere in this big world, there is something I have been looking for, for a long time, something I almost understand, something I yearn to understand, something that is already an unexplored part of my essence. Perhaps it's also looking for me.
>
> —Journal entry, 2012

My sorrow over the end of LDCA and the accompanying low-level depression stemming from various post-gallery-life unknowns motivated me to pack my real and emotional bags and abandon the temporary emptiness of my circumstances. I was seized by a powerful urge to throw what caution I still possessed to the proverbial wind and its disciples and to experience whatever risks and revelations might be encountered in the uncharted territory that lies outside the commitments, boundaries, and realities of my suddenly shrunken life.

Risks and torpedoes be damned.

Excitement, freedom, and resolve pulsed through me. I was about to go from Here to Here. Eternity could wait. I shouted my intention to the air and to the Universe. I told my dog and cats. "I am going around the fucking world."

By beginning to search for something new, I could plot my escape from something old. Would I recognize what I was looking for when I stumbled upon it? Would I know what I had been running from when I outran it—or when it stopped pursuing me—or blocking me? I vowed to seek out, embrace, and relish the dreamed experiences that had whispered to me from the fallow fields of my tomorrows.

With no job, no savings, no identifiable prospects for gainful employment, I had only the vague and comforting notion that I would succeed in climbing over this temporary, self-generated, personal wreckage and land on a new path. Understandably, friends and family viewed a trip around the world in my current financial state as misguided and potentially dangerous. *Tant pis.* I could do it. I could create a pathway through this bothersome conundrum. An unknown but not unknowable solution loomed.

My soul yearned to surrender to beauty. I drove to the ski basin above Santa Fe to hike my favorite mountain trail, trusting that Mother Nature would guide me to that quiet place where thorny problems are solved and creative solutions are generated. Walking slowly and deliberatively in search of answers, I would open myself to the calmness and wonder of the forest. Summon clarity. Question the quaking aspens. Hug a ponderosa or two. Pay attention.

The previous year, I had gotten quite lost in that very forest, hiking much farther than I intended. It was a glorious July day—no appointments, no pressing obligations. I had driven into the mountains to commune with the natural world. While sauntering along a favorite trail, filling my senses with the varied gifts of wilderness—soft earth, sounds of birds, warm sun filtering through tall pine branches—and conversing with my inner voice instead of paying attention to my direction, I became disoriented. Lost in thought. Lost in the forest. Where was I? I turned and retraced my steps. Nothing looked familiar. Yes, I was lost.

How has this happened? I don't recall drifting from the main trail, but this is not that trail. It was confusing, but not alarming. It was a beautiful day, and I was in no hurry. I would just follow my woods-savvy instinct (Ha! What woods-savvy instinct?) until I reconnected with the familiar trail. *Maybe it's this way... this seems to go in the right direction...no, maybe not...maybe left instead of right.*

I chastised myself for failing to pay attention, not only to the forest but also to the basic tenets of hiking alone: tell someone where you're going; take water, a jacket, and a cell phone. Finding myself lost in the forest, I had the opportunity to test some of my survival skills. (Ha! What survival skills?)

As the afternoon sun waned, it became clear that I was going in the wrong direction, on the wrong path, which no longer looked like a path at all. I was forging a new and possibly futile trail over logs, brush, and rocks, attempting to use my innate sense of direction (Ha! What innate sense of direction?) to point me toward the parking lot and the road. My prescription sunglasses had served me well earlier in the day, but once the sun began to fall below the rugged horizon, dark glasses were no longer helpful. And without corrective lenses, I would be rendered semi-blind in the night.

Confident that I could survive whatever ordeal was ahead of me, I did not panic. I considered my situation and calculated ways to deal with the impending cold, pitch blackness, and other unspecified dangers of the forest. *I'll dig a big hole with my car keys. I'll curl up in the hole, cover myself with pine boughs, and shiver my way to first light. Maybe a curious bobcat will sleep nearby and watch over me. No one will miss me for a day or so. I'm not expected anywhere. Surely, I'll find my way to my car by morning.*

At dusk, I found a fence and began to follow it downhill. In the distance, I heard gunshots. This was disconcerting. Possible gun scenarios shot through my imagination. *Maybe hunters would save me. Maybe drunken men would alarm me. Maybe an errant bullet would injure the bobcat who would hole up with me in my emergency shelter. We would hide. She would keep me warm, and I would slowly and gently remove the bullet from her shoulder....*

Before I had to resort to digging my own grave-like shelter, I heard traffic in the distance. I stumbled toward the sound, descended down a brambly slope, and crossed a creek. I was just yards from the road but quite far from my car. Two young women—properly dressed for the mountains in boots, hats, and carrying backpacks—were returning to their truck. They drove me to my waiting Outback.

But that was then. This time was different. I hiked a short way up the trail, sat on a downed tree that had fallen across the path, and closed my eyes. With each breath of pine-scented air, peace filled my lungs. In a heartfelt voice, I spoke aloud.

Dear God, or Angels, or Spirit, or Whatever, if you can hear me, will you please help me to develop a workable plan to achieve my identified goal of going all the way around the world? I seek direction and clarity of intention. Help me find an idea that will bring my long-desired dream to fruition. Right now, I have the time and energy to do it. I'm lacking only the money and a concrete plan. With complete sincerity, I seek your wisdom.

This time, I retraced my steps and drove home, listening to my breath and the surrounding sounds of the town. A plan unfolded.

I drafted a letter to twenty of my favorite former collectors. I described my intention to celebrate my 70th birthday by going around the world in seventy days, planting "seeds of peace."

During the circumnavigation, I would record my adventures and observations in a special journal and, upon my return, develop those impressions into a book—a journey of my footprints and my breath from here...all the way to here...around my beautiful Mobius Strip World.

I asked these kind people of means if they would be willing to send me a check for one thousand dollars in exchange for a drawing or painting from my personal art collection worth two or three times that much.

Fifteen collectors responded with checks. I gave a public reading at the Everyday Center for Spiritual Living, a Science of Mind center. Generous members of the audience donated money and wrote wishes and prayers for peace on the backs of small, round, handmade papers embedded with wildflower seeds. An abstract image of the earth was stamped on the front of each disk. I pledged to plant these seeded prayers around the world.

I purchased a bargain Round-the-World (RTW) airline ticket and outlined my itinerary: South Africa, the Kingdom of Lesotho, Madagascar, Thailand, Myanmar (again), and Hawaii.

I don't like the term "bucket list." It has an unattractive tone that says, "I'm getting old, and I might die sooner rather than later, so I better get some accomplishments accomplished." This imperative is not that. Bucket list/schmucket list.

For almost half a century, my friend John Allen's powerful "I've been around the fucking world!" lived in my cells. Years ago, I altered his cry and made it my own: "Someday, I will go around the world!" That someday had arrived. Ready, get set, go! *I am going around the world!*

> If a man set out from home on a journey, and kept right on going, he would come back to his own front door.
>
> –Jan de Langhe, *The Travels of Sir John Mandeville*, 1356–5

Mission in the Accomplishing Stage

"Oh, my bags are packed, I'm ready to go…."

Dateline: 24 December 2012, Albuquerque Sunport. My black, many-pocketed satchel already left my possession. Like me, it's waiting to board a flight to Atlanta and then, beyond Atlanta, onward to Johannesburg, South Africa. For a few minutes, last night, while packing my suitcase and choosing my traveling clothes, I thought it would be a good idea to have a picture of me at the beginning of this Pilgrimage, for Posterity, I guess—not that I think Posterity would care. Perhaps I thought it would be good to have a visual indication of my mental and physical state on the morning of the big departure—an image for my older self to study. The once-and-future archivist in me might wonder: How did I look on the day I left on that around-the-world journey? What did I wear? Did I choose comfort over style? Is there evidence of some sort of image I intended to portray as I embarked on this circumnavigation of the planet? Considering that I'll be flying for a long time, I nixed the khaki-colored Eileen Fisher suit. I didn't think it would sleep well all the way to Johannesburg—although it might be useful in Bangkok. And I didn't choose the turquoise jeans with the almost matching Indian tunic—too summery. It's freezing here in my starting city. In the end, I didn't get a photo. So, imagine this: a bit of make-up, touch of lip gloss, a good haircut, black linen pants, coral linen and jersey shirt, black jersey sweater jacket, buttery yellow Hush Puppies (from a foot-blistering adventure in Cairo two years ago), black socks, and a yellowish, filmy, animal-print scarf. Under it all—black silk long underwear. I'll keep a "mental selfie" of that departing look.

—Round the World Travel Journal

Planting "Seeds of Peace" in Soweto, winter 2013

South Africa – Together Apart, Apartheid Together

I had been to Egypt, Kenya, and Tanzania, but I had never been to South Africa, "The Cradle of Civilization." What I knew I gathered from some of that country's most brilliant contemporary writers: Nadine Gordimer, J. M. Coetzee, Alan Paton, and others. Still, my knowledge was vague, incomplete, even unsettling. Apartheid. That was unsettling. The word brought an ache to my social justice advocate's heart. Translated from the Afrikaans' meaning for "apartness," the apartheid system is nearly as old as I.

For half a century, journalists and evening news anchors painted a painful picture of Africans' bloody struggle to achieve racial equality, overcome the ideology of white supremacy, and overturn segregationist legislation. We who paid attention to world events witnessed the reprehensible white domination through the filters of television, radio, and newspapers. What little I knew or understood about the violence and the resistance movement of anti-apartheid crusaders—such as Steve Biko, Nelson Mandela, and Bishop Tutu—was shocking at first, then painful. Perhaps it has become hopeful, nearly two decades after the end of apartheid. My interest led me to Johannesburg with pilgrimages to Soweto and the Apartheid Museum. My plan was not to plan, but rather to experience, with grace and curiosity, whatever and whomever I encountered.

I will slow down. I will adjust to being gone. And I will plant Seeds of Peace and make friends of strangers.

Who said, "Seek, and ye shall find"?
   a) A pilgrim
   b) St. Matthew, chapter 7, verse 7
   c) A character from *The Brothers Grimm Book of Fairy Tales*
   d) Your parent
   e) Your 5th-grade teacher
   f) All or most of the above

Answer: b or f

Somewhere over the Atlantic Ocean... As I sit in my budget seat, at the very back of the budget section of the plane, in front of the toilet, in the seat that doesn't recline, somewhere between Atlanta and Johannesburg, I chuckle. I have succeeded in creating this adventure out of "coal, air, and water." I have dreamed a vision into a reality. Amazing. Why am I going? I don't actually know. To escape something? To embrace something? To find a missing part of myself? To prove something to someone or to myself? To become someone else or something else? It's too soon to know. And now, to recline–oh, wait. I can't recline. No matter.

–Journal entry, still December 24, 2012

On Christmas, the warm, sunny Johannesburg afternoon welcomed me. The email message from the Sleepy Gecko Guesthouse, where I had reserved a room for my first two nights in South Africa, was comforting and correct: "Mike will meet you at baggage claim. He will have your name on a sign. You will recognize him. He is very tall."

Yes, I recognized him immediately. This soft-spoken giant from the Czech Republic was close to seven feet tall. After retrieving my bag from the carousel, we made our way through the surprisingly sparse and quiet holiday crowd to Mike's dilapidated car.

As we drove to the Sleepy Gecko, it became readily apparent that the wealth of the city was unevenly distributed. The contrast between rich and poor was disconcerting. My initial views of the city supported what I had read while preparing for the trip: modern roadways, lush greenery, considerable economic growth and activity—and slums. Johannesburg's crime rate is among the highest in the world. Highway signs, brochures, and internet travel sites warn visitors to avoid certain areas of the city. To ensure safety, tourists are advised not to show any signs of wealth, and not to carry a good handbag, but to keep personal items in a plastic bag while sightseeing.

We passed through lovely upscale neighborhoods with impressive houses encaged in concertina wire, enclosed by walls topped with shards of jagged glass or barbed wire. Defensive, ugly signs warned: IMMEDIATE ARMED RESPONSE. It doesn't take a political scientist or a lengthy investigation to conclude that fear or suspicion of "the other" continues to create tension in this sprawling city of three million.

Early quiet morning in Jo'burg: It's damp, having rained. No one else is staying at the Sleepy Gecko. I have a feeling that Christmas in Johannesburg is like August in Paris. The owners of this bed and breakfast are on holiday in Swaziland. Only

"Christian," the blasé young manager, is here—but he's not here. The doors to the reception building are locked. Two cats have joined me in my room as I sit at the writing desk, writing absentmindedly (in lieu of musing motionlessly) and waiting for breakfast and adventure—or as the artist Agnes Martin said to me many times, "waiting for inspiration." I have two special pilgrimages to make while I'm in this city: to Soweto and the Apartheid Museum. At both places, I plan to "plant" the seeds of peace disks that I brought from New Mexico.

—Journal entry, first Sleepy Gecko sunrise

Skyscraper Mike and I spent an afternoon at Soweto—an acronym for South West Township. We befriended two young boys who live near a vacant lot around the corner from Bishop Tutu's house and the Mandela Family Restaurant. At first, the boys watched from a distance, no doubt wondering what this strange blond woman and an equally strange tall white man were searching for. Curiosity brought them close.

"What are you doing?" the smaller of the two boys asked.

"I'm looking for a place to plant prayers for peace." I showed them the small, round, wildflower seed-encrusted papers with the abstract image of the world on one side and various hand-written messages of love and peace on the other side. I explained my intention, and they eagerly jumped in to assist in the planting. We dug holes in the hard, parched earth using a couple of sticks and a sharp rock. I gave the boys a pen and two blank world seed papers. The younger wrote his name and a message on it. The other boy couldn't write. Instead, he made a few squiggly marks on one of the disks. I did the same. We planted five prayers. They found an old can and filled it with water from a mud puddle in the road. We watered the places where the prayers were buried. I encouraged the boys to water the spot every day.

What a sweet miracle it would be if real-life flowers grew out of that tough ground. In the interest of encouraging miracles, I imagined determined green shoots pushing their way through the earth, reaching sunward. With the help of rains that would surely come, and from the effort of the two young boys who would return daily with rusty cans of mud-puddle water, sweet little leaves and buds would appear, their tender roots fortified by the protective sky-blue seed paper and encouraged by our prayers, wishes, or the secrets of those who prepared them. Then, there would be wildflowers. Daisies? Poppies? Dandelions?

Would the existing weeds in that lot make room for prayer-infused wildflowers? If those efforts of love and caring produced a plant, and if that plant grew into a sunny yellow flower, perhaps someone would pick it, give it to a loved one. What could happen to wildflower power if luck, intention, and optimism aligned to support it?

A brief feeling of despair washed over me as Mike and I drove away from the boys and the fragile, intentional prayers on paper planted in the rough—maybe unforgiving—earth. Back at the Sleepy Gecko, I wondered about those of us who began life as anonymous seeds, sown in neglected, challenging, and emotionally dry environments. Planted by preoccupied passersby, we, nonetheless, managed to find purchase in the soil of our inauspicious beginnings, and we continued to plow through the brambly paths of experience, aided by strangers, puddles, and the sun. Determined to survive. And here we are.

> Consider my rootlessness,
> The seeds of my un-sprouted flowers:
> How they wait
> Impatiently,
> Underground,
> Where existential joy
> Meets existential sadness
> And tears quench everything.

To be free is not merely to cast off one's chains, but to live in a way that respects and enhances the freedom of others.
—Nelson Mandela, June 1999, quote on a wall next to a reflecting pool at the Apartheid Museum

At the museum's ticket window, I received a card directing me to the non-white entrance. Visitors randomly selected for this experience could momentarily imagine the separation, humiliation, and injustice of the radical discrimination practices that permeated South African society. For decades, national laws dictated which buses one could ride, which doors one could or could not enter depending solely upon the color of one's skin.

The excruciating examples of unbearable human cruelty and suffering exhibited throughout the museum stunned me. In display after display, visual proof of man's inhumanity to man crushed me. Several times I sat on a museum bench for long minutes to still my heart and find my breath before moving on. How unconscionable! What's wrong with humanity! One rarely hears of woman's inhumanity to man or hu-Man-ity. Still, we have surely been complicit by our silence, fear, or sense of powerlessness. Or by threats to our lives and those of our children. Or by the burden of age-old traditions. Me? I was complicit by ignorance.

With shame—and through embarrassing obliviousness—I confess that long ago I inadvertently and unintentionally supported apartheid. In the '80s, on the advice of a rich and influential Texas businessman and client who purchased a Picasso drawing that was consigned to my gallery by a rich New York collector, I purchased a gold Krugerrand. "Gold is the safest place to put your money," the confident Texan puffed. *Safer than a Picasso drawing?*

Spiritually, a gold Krugerrand was not a safe investment. Not for me. But back then, the racial and economic turbulence of South Africa was far away from my poorly informed and narcissistically occupied mind. The day (the minute, the instant) I learned what my ignorance had purchased, I got rid of the ugly coin.

There are also some examples of bravery in South Africa's lengthy and difficult struggle for equality. I read about Jim Richard Abe Bailey, who was born in London and moved to South Africa in 1951. He did more than rail against apartheid; he started *African Drum*, the nation's first Black lifestyle magazine that dared to challenge the segregated system by bringing African men and women into mainstream urban culture. He and my maternal grandfather, Thomas Bailey, have the same surname. They're both from England. I wondered if I might be distantly related to this "hero." I'd like that.

Late in the day, I stopped at a neighborhood shopping center to buy stamps for my Wonder Postcard project and found a nearby café where I planned to write in my journal. Instead, for over an hour I conversed with the two well-dressed white South African women at the next table. Weather and tourism small talk turned political, and the walls between this American stranger and these Johannesburg women tumbled. They freely expressed their deep disappointment with the emergent societal level labeled "the new Black elite."

"It's like we're now, somehow, beneath them," said one woman, brushing biscuit crumbs onto the tea shop floor. The next election and its political consequences raised their apprehension about the future. "However, as far as I know," said one to the nod of the other, "South Africa is still the best country in the world."

My thoughts flashed to something I read at the Apartheid Museum. "South Africa's struggle for liberation has been a journey of pain and strife." That journey traced its footsteps from the dark days of bondage to a place of healing founded in democracy. May it hold.

Everywhere it is so. The peace of God escapes us.

–Alan Paton, *Cry, the Beloved Country*

I wonder if I will meet someone special on this journey. The possibility lingers in the wishful thinking part of my mind. Is there a person "out there" with whom I might bond for more than a day or a week or a month? Can I overcome the feelings of doubt about my desirability or compatibility quotient? Do I, a seventy-year-old "going-to-seed" woman, believe that I could or would encounter someone with whom a mutually desired intimate relationship could spring or sprout? And endure? For the evening sport of it, while I am sitting alone at this pleasant outdoor restaurant in an upscale (incredibly white) neighborhood, drinking a very lovely chardonnay, surrounded by a variety of relatively low-key, local-looking diners, I'll indulge myself by describing that unmet person, that man who may or may not exist, who may or may not be waiting for someone exactly like me. OK. He's within a few years of my age. He's divorced or a widower. A traveler. He's in good health, financially comfortable, curious, an intellectual, a raconteur, kind, with a sense of humor. He's politically savvy and fascinated by me, comfortable around me, wise, and interested in a relationship. I'll let you know if I meet him. I'll let you know if I succeed in resisting the impulse to fuck it up.

—Journal entry

The Kingdom of the Sky

Lesotho (pronounced Le Sue Too) is a landlocked country surrounded by South Africa. It's known as "The Kingdom of the Sky." Its name alone beckons. Before I began to plan the South African segment of my journey, I knew nothing about Lesotho, not even that it's also known for pony-trekking, hiking, climbing, and for a magical prehistoric culture, or that it has a dark distinction: its abject poverty. Tragically, the kingdom suffers the second-highest per capita prevalence of HIV/AIDS in the world. One in four people live with HIV, and, to date, more than 200,000 children have been orphaned. On a map, the Basotho homeland looks like a small free-form shape near the southern tip of Africa. Determined to learn about its people—who they are, how they live, what they need, and who rules them—I put Lesotho on my itinerary.

Giant Mike and I spent over an hour in the seediest parts of downtown Johannesburg looking for the location of the depot for the bus to Lesotho. No one we asked seemed to know. Eventually, we encountered an enterprising hustler who had been hanging outside the main bus terminal and noticed our confusion. For a handful of rands, he agreed to lead us to the minivan depot.

"Follow me," he said and raced off through the congested parking lot and haphazard market mayhem. He rushed down blocks of busy, garbage-strewn streets while Mike and I struggled to keep him in sight. Weasel-like, he darted between double- and triple-parked cars on a major commercial street. Every hundred yards or so, he glanced around to see that we were still following him. Near the destination, he stopped, caught our eye, and pointed at an opening between two boarded-up storefronts, then rushed away.

We walked down the crowded alley full of trucks and minivans. Dozens of people milled about, moving crates, and talking in small groups. I approached three official-looking men who were leaning against a van smoking and joking.

"Hello, can you tell me how to get a bus ticket to Lesotho?"

A portly man wearing a plaid shirt and an almost matching cap responded, "I can help you."

We chatted at length. He told me about time tables, prices (180 rands), and border requirements. I asked if it would be possible to be picked up at my guest house. Yes, possible. I offered to pay for my ticket in advance, but all the men agreed that I should pay in the morning. Much conversation, curiosity, and laughter ensued. We discussed the pick-up time, confirmed the address, and Mike gave directions to the Sleepy Gecko Guesthouse. We thanked them and left.

It's the middle of the night. A Sleepy Gecko cat is on the bed. I keep waking up. I am overly excited about the start of the Lesotho adventure. I had a disconcerting dream: I was planning to go to a big social fundraising event back home. I didn't know what to wear. Fancy friends were wearing fancy attire. I put a proper outfit together: black pencil skirt, lace top, and velvet jacket. I hung it on a rack with other people's outfits. When the event was beginning, I couldn't find my clothes, and so I didn't attend. I just waited outside. When it was over, I checked again for my outfit...and there it was, right where I had been looking for it. I analyze the dream myself since Freud and Jung are not available. The dream is a message from one part of me to another: go naked, if you must, or you'll miss the point, the opportunity....There may be other interpretations (I'm smiling).

–Journal entry

Early in the morning, I buckled my money belt/pouch inside my pants and put my travel papers and extra cash in my wallet, which I stashed at the very bottom of my small, green backpack. I tossed my underwear on top of it. To be prepared for all sorts of weather and other unknowns, I packed black jeans, leopard print pajamas, and the African sarong I bought on a beach in Tanzania years ago. It would double as a towel if need be. I put on my white jeans, a sleeveless t-shirt, a long-sleeve shirt, pink socks, and my trusty Tevas. I was ready for the minivan trip to the mysterious kingdom on my itinerary.

Lesotho calls. *Hello! I'll be right there.*

The seven o'clock van pickup at the "Geck" failed. Of course, it failed; those guys were just jiving me. Get your savvy and grown-up pants on, Durham! Fortunately, Mike got my call and drove me to the minivan station, where I became part of a circus of baggage-laden people. Most women wore fancy dresses; most men wore dirty clothes. I wore self-consciousness, dressed in my nearly clean white jeans. There is much pushing—not mean pushing—just the kind of absentminded pushing that occurs when one is not aware of the world beyond one's immediate circle of bundles and conversation. I jostled in a long, non-linear cluster queue that snaked in, out, and around parked or moving vans and trailers, loading people up and nearly running others down. For more than two hours, van after van loaded up and drove off to destinations other than Lesotho. We stood and waited.

A woman in a pink and lavender flowered dress tapped my shoulder, pointed at a spot behind me, and kept me from stepping backward into a pile of recently deposited feces. She and a young man in faux military clothes became my informal guides on the seven-hour journey from dirty, congested downtown Johannesburg through the open, clean, pastoral South African countryside all the way to Maseru, the capital of the Kingdom of Lesotho.

The kind young man in the pseudo army outfit shepherded me through the customs/border crossing, a rabbit warren of gates and lines and waits and papers to complete. Once through the ordeal, he introduced me to a taxi driver who spoke a little English and could help me find a place to stay. His name was David. He had a beautiful smile. I smiled back at him as I slipped into his old car.

What is the point behind my strong desire and strange quest to get to Lesotho? I know so little about the Kingdom, and I am perplexed about the origin of my urge to go there—to come here. It's not the pony rides for which the country is quite well-known—at least to those who have heard of the country in the first place. It's not the mountainous landscape; not the King; not Prince Harry's Foundation, the orphanage he purports to support, in a princely gesture, for the care of children with AIDS, or children whose parents have succumbed to the insidious disease. Before this trip, I wrote to the Foundation (twice!) to arrange a visit. No response. No response. I think I will discover something very important in this Kingdom in the Sky, something about the difference between deep and shallow compassion....

—Lesotho journal entry

My pre-selected quest on my first Sunday in Lesotho was to visit an orphanage. When Sentebale, the charity founded in 2006 by Prince Harry, did not respond to my request to visit, I asked David, the taxi driver, if he knew of a children's charity or orphanage near Maseru that I could visit. Yes. He knew of an orphanage somewhere on the outskirts of the city.

For half an hour, we drove west through a rural area. Houses and small businesses lined the two-lane highway. We made numerous wrong turns onto rough dirt roads and asked directions four or five times. Eventually, we found the far-off-the-beaten-path orphanage compound. As we approached, I saw yards and yards of children's clothes drying in the sun. I could hear children singing. A statuesque woman dressed in a lacy Sunday-best outfit walked toward us, smiling warmly. She and David exchanged a few sentences in their native Basotho. Seventy children live here under this woman's care, he translated. "Everyone calls her 'Mama.' HIV/AIDS-stricken parents abandon their children here when they are no longer able to care for them."

"Mama, how do you pay for the children's food, clothes, and other needs?" I asked and David translated.

"I go to the capital and beg on the street," she said.

"What about the king? Does the king help?"

David and Mama looked at one another. We stood in a spell of silence.

"No, the king does not help." David interpreted, looking at the ground. Again, no one spoke.

In the distance, I heard the children's voices. Although I was concerned about finances, I was not so concerned that I would walk away from this place without making a donation. I had been given some unexpected, last-minute financial support for the trip from my friends Eugene and Dana Newmann. In honor of Dana, whose life revolves around early childhood education, art, and kindness, I gave Mama the Newmanns' kind contribution—a crisp hundred-dollar bill.

Mama folded it in three, covered it with her hands, and prayed over it. David and I prayed with her. She invited us into the rec-room-like church, or church-like recreation room, overflowing with singing children.

"Jesus is Lord," proclaimed the big banner at the front of the space, hanging above a low platform. I sat on one side of the room and listened to the children's repetitive songs, sweet-voiced hallelujahs, and prayers in the soft Basotho language. It sounded like they were speaking in tongues. Mama summoned David and me to join her on the stage. I stood close to her as she introduced us. Everyone applauded. Mama motioned for me to step forward. As I did, I looked out at a room of young, scrubbed, smiling faces—all looking back at me expectantly. I didn't know what to do or say until a long-ago Sunday School song came to me. I took another small step forward, paused, found courage, and my voice.

"Jesus loves the little children, all the children of the world, brown and yellow, black and white, they are precious in his sight…Jesus loves the little children of the world."

A tiny girl with wonderful braids, wearing a crisp white dress, ran up to me, hugged me, and buried her face in my shirt. She examined my face, kissed my hand, and softly caressed my freckled arm. I felt loved. And richer than the King of Lesotho.

Following a few days in Maseru, my new friend David drove me to Mmelesi Lodge, a paradise of flowered walks and charming thatched-roof "rondavels." My small, round, free-standing cabin with its own tiny bathroom was furnished with a small table, chair, comfortable bed, and a nightstand with a drawer full of condoms. I arranged to stay through the new year.

At six-thirty in the morning on my second day in this restful place, I decided to climb Thaba-Bosiu, a UNESCO World Heritage Site, where the first King Moshoe-shoe and his people defended the land from their enemies, the warring Zulus.

At the trailhead—a half-mile from the lodge—I paid the small fee to a pleasant volunteer at the empty visitor center and began the climb. Alone. It was quite a rocky uphill hike—long, steep, and winding. It began to get hot, and I thought about turning back, but I didn't. Instead, I whispered the powerful Maasai climbing refrain: *pole, pole*—slowly, slowly. And upward.

Unlike the dreaded Zulu enemies of 1827, who were turned back by magical powers, as the legend goes, I made it to the top. My eyes took in the panoramic views of the vast unspoiled landscape—cliffs and hills, an arroyo, rolling meadows, and blue sky—not unlike the landscapes of my New Mexico. I captured great shots on my trusty iPhone, including a picture of my elongated shadow outlining my Lesotho safari-style trekker hat.

I descended even more slowly than I had ascended, reminding myself that the climb was simply about making it to the top, while my descent was about not falling and breaking anything.

It's evening, pre-dusk. I am sitting at a picnic table in the garden of the lodge, drinking a local beer and feeling pleasantly invisible or ignored, a true stranger in a strange land. Mmelesi Lodge. That's where I am on this earthly journey of mine. I trust my world. I trust the people I encounter. I trust the passengers on the buses. I trust the drivers, the road, the destination, the discoveries, the synergy, the rightness, the miracle of it all. I do not yet grasp my real direction or intentions on this RTW trip. That has to be okay for now. What did I or do I expect? Is this a pilgrimage yet? How do I turn this rambling into something meaningful? Where are the thoughts beneath these chatty scribblings?

–Journal entry, New Year's Eve 2012

On New Year's Eve, smoky light drifted over the cottages, gardens, and giant soccer field at Mmelesi Lodge, where a raucous and rousing music festival was in progress. Posters pinned throughout the lodge advertised the event as an eighteen-hour extravaganza with traditional and tribal music by well-known groups from as far away as Swaziland and Botswana.

Attractive, confident, and upbeat Lesothoans arrived in casual dress. They parked their big, shiny cars and clambered down into the pit-like football field. No one looked at me; no one said hello. For most of the night, I sat at the edge of the action, alone, contentedly invisible, the only white person for miles in any direction. Late in the evening, five older ladies from Maseru invited me to join them in comfortable chairs at the edge of the ridge, overlooking the musical action. They wore haute, tribal-style clothes with lots and lots of jewelry. We smiled, laughed, danced, and ate delicious barbecue and mashed potatoes. It felt so good to be included.

In the pre-wee hours, I strolled back to my cozy round cabin, stretched out on the bed, and listened to the muffled rhythmic beat for the first minutes of a promising new year. I was at peace.

A few hours later, on the first morning of 2013, I was having breakfast in the surprisingly deserted dining room of the lodge, writing, thinking, and planning great things for the new year. Sounds of drumming and ululations came from the reception room. For a few minutes, I stood and watched from the entryway as the entire staff sang and danced themselves into the new year. One of the kitchen ladies grabbed my hand and pulled me into the room, where I joined a circle of joyful, uninhibited dancers and singers. The rhythmic beat of the traditional Lesotho music was infectious. I tried to ululate. It would take practice. Everyone hugged me, kissed me. Everyone hugged and kissed everyone else. It was so unrestrained, so natural, so beautiful. Despite all social, racial, generational, linguistic, and cultural distances, I felt connected to this place. In that now, we were all just dancers, singers, and ululaters, celebrating life, welcoming in our shared new year. The operative word that morning was "fullness."

In this small African kingdom, the friendly staff had embraced this sister from another mother. I drink in an unexpected and deeply appreciated sense of belonging—here, with these gracious people. Perhaps this is what I have been searching for: a sense of belonging to the world, to the "faraway nearby." I just thought of a favorite African proverb: "If you are ugly, you must either learn to dance or to make love." Or to do both, I hasten to add. New Year's Day, 2013.

—Journal entry

Back in Maseru, I began to plan the next step of my journey—I didn't want to leave Lesotho. I wanted to visit the orphanage again, go back to the Lodge and dance and drink up the spirit of the Basotho people. I still wanted to pony trek, find Prince Harry's compound, be part of this little-known kingdom. It saddened me to think how unlikely it was that I would ever come this way again. My world excursion, as I developed it, did not permit me to linger. The few iPhone shots would have to serve as precious threads connecting and reconnecting me to soulful Lesotho: the picture of my shadow on top of the sacred mountain; the inclusive women in the countryside; the smiling young man in a black t-shirt with its brightly colored slogan announcing I LOVE MY LIFE. The very words I have said aloud every morning for years.

Saying "I love my life" helps make it true.

In Johannesburg, at the deserted bed and breakfast, I had just enough time to add some new impressions and experiences to my journal, ponder and record my new-year thoughts, have a last meal at the neighborhood Italian restaurant, and get a good Sleepy Gecko night's sleep.

Giant Mike hugged me goodbye at the airport, and I hurried off to catch my flight to Madagascar.

L'Avenue des Baobabs, Madagascar, 2013

To See the Baobabs

This is a great moment, when you see, however distant, the goal of your wandering. The thing which has been living in your imagination suddenly becomes a part of the tangible world.

–FREYA STARK

I'm en route to Antananarivo, the capital of Madagascar. I'm on a smallish plane with an interesting assortment of travelers: some Madagascar Nationals returning from holiday; a few Peace Corps volunteers; two or three families that look like they're from India, or a place where everyone has shiny black hair and dark-copper skin and speaks loudly in a tongue I cannot identify. No obvious Americans. My intention is to travel to a remote part of the island where the giant baobab trees are found. A magazine picture of a beautiful young woman wrapped in a colorful sari, standing on a dirt road among the majestic *Adansonia grandidieri* baobabs, has drawn me to this island nation. The light in the photograph is perfect. It gives a magnificent glow to the tall and distinctive "upside-down" trees that grow in certain parts of Madagascar—and nowhere else in the world. I plan to stand where the sari-wrapped woman stood. I want to touch those trees, kiss them, hug them. I'm almost there.

–Journal entry, January 2013

Linda, what are you doing?

It was a rhetorical question. I knew what I was doing, unlikely as it would have been years earlier. Crammed in an overcrowded minivan, stopped at a checkpoint in the pitch dark on a mountain road somewhere in Madagascar, I was on my way to Morondava, a coastal town not far from my intended destination, L'Avenue des Baobabs.

My journey to the trees started auspiciously. I had waited for hours at the crowded, chaotic *taxi-brousse* terminal at the edge of Antananarivo, the sprawling capital of the vast and intriguing island of Madagascar. I became part of the aggregate of passengers, onlookers, drivers, packers, and hawkers of sunglasses, pillows, toys, maps, and food. I watched a young boy throw small stones against a broken board while his mother dozed on a big crate. As we waited to board the dilapidated van to Morondava, I leaned against a shady wall while a dozen men and boys loaded, unloaded, and reloaded miscellaneous baggage atop the rusted, stripped-down minibus. The rooftop carrier cargo had the same volume as the van's interior. Only my determination to see the famous trees and to succeed in this pilgrimage kept me from catching a taxi back to the relative safety of La Ribaudière, the small French-run hotel in Antananarivo, where I had spent the past few days. To reach my dream destination, I was more than willing and totally able to endure a grueling but bearable overnight trip. But, just in case, I took the advice of the Parisian expat hotel owner and purchased an extra seat for a bit more comfort.

Tick, tock, tick, tock. The man who sold me the ticket for the noon departure to Morondava assured me that the van would leave at one thirty...or by three thirty...or four o'clock, perhaps. Shortly after five o'clock, at a signal from one of the three designated drivers, everyone scrambled aboard the already over-loaded vehicle.

I took my assigned seat next to a window, two rows behind the driver. My little backpack served as an armrest on the extra seat to my right. The engine started. Passengers clapped. With careful and skilled maneuvering around animals, cargo, people, and vehicles—all parked or moving willy-nilly—and with helpful yells and instructions from members of the ground crew, the driver eased out of the congested so-called terminal and onto the crowded, garbage-strewn side street. Slowly, the *taxi-brousse* passed little children playing, food fires smoking, friends congregating. We turned onto the highway and settled in for the overnight ride.

My pilgrimage to the best place on Earth to see the remarkable Grandidier's baobabs was underway; my destination was just a day away. My pack contained everything I needed for the five- or six-day adventure: camera, journal, a few clothes, malaria pills, insect repellent, and a good book. For the long haul, I carried a liter of water and two fruit pastries from a fancy patisserie in down-town "Tana."

Thank you, Universe, for everything.

Contemporary Malagasy music, almost loud enough to cover the congestive cough of the engine, filled the van. Some passengers sang or hummed. As we sped along the winding highway in concert with the music, I felt content. The driver had a reassuring command of the vehicle and a firm feel of the road, but no patience with slow traffic, and he deftly passed truck after van after cart. I caught glimpses of small villages as we made our way along increasingly curvy mountain roads. Horns honked. Music blared. I felt in tune with the other travelers and with the rhythms of the road as we swerved and lurched.

Just before sunset, we stopped at a wide place in the road. The driver honked three times, and a young woman in a flowered sarong ran down a hill lugging a backpack. She handed it through the shotgun window to the younger of two relief drivers. He threw kisses up the hill at a small girl holding a baby. Onward to Morondava!

At dusk, we encountered the first of many armed checkpoints. What were the guards checking? Were they looking for guns? Drugs? Lemurs? It all seemed very friendly, nonchalant.

The music continued. It united us. Then it began to rain. Around ten o'clock, we stopped for fuel and food at a dark, muddy truck stop. The friendly French-speaking Malagasy woman who occupied the seat in front of me took my hand.

"*Mangeons*," she said. Let's eat. She, her little girl, and I found seats in the big, dark cafeteria with rows of tables and benches filled with truckers and passengers—all Malagasy, except for me. At my companion's suggestion, I ordered the cutlet from the serious server in a green Mickey Mouse sweatshirt. She placed two bowls of rice in front of us, along with two bowls of a clear soup. I took a sip of the soup. Bitter and undrinkable. The greasy, fatty, gray cutlet arrived. I ate rice. My bill came to three hundred ariarys, not much money at all.

A toilet? There was no toilet. Luckily, I realized that before inquiring. I followed Madame and her child outside. We walked to the darker side of the building—a wet expanse of a vacant parking lot—pulled down our pants and peed. Mid-stream, in the drizzling darkness, not far from me, my eyes connected with those of a very old woman who crouched similarly, slowly stood, adjusted her trousers, and smiled at me. I smiled back.

The second relief driver took over the wheel for the next stretch. The rain accelerated into a downpour as our overloaded minibus zigged and zagged, narrowly averting (in my mind) accident after accident. Passengers snored or whispered behind me.

By well after midnight, the deluge exceeded the wipers' capacity to clear the cracked windshield, and the van felt like it was hydroplaning. I sent a mental message to the driver to slow down. He did. The young man on the other side of my backpack was leaning forward, wide awake, clenching two cell phones. Together we peered over the dozing mothers and their sleeping children, past the three drivers, beyond the rain-sheeted windshield to the glossy-slick road, alert to our problematic circumstances. My fate awaited me. I took a few bites of my apple croissant. *What the bleep!*

The van slowed to a crawl. Parked trucks and vans lined both sides of the road.

Passengers woke up and mumbled. Uniformed guards with rifles milled around in the wet, waning-moon night. Our *taxi-brousse* inched to the side of the road toward the front of a long queue. The driver and older co-driver got out. I opened my window and listened to the relaxed, muffled Malagasy voices. Nothing seemed alarming or out of the ordinary—but what was ordinary? I didn't speak Malagasy. No one spoke English. No one spoke French. I was in the dark in many ways. The third driver, still in the van, turned off the engine. Passengers whispered. In pitch black, we waited and waited. The only light came from my glow-in-the-dark bracelet with the phrase "Brand New Day." Yes, I looked forward to it.

Forty minutes later, the guards waved us on and into the wet night. At last, I dozed, my head on my backpack. But not for long. Passengers were disturbed again. This time, by a loud crash and a bump. The van swerved and stopped abruptly. Did we hit an animal? A person? A fallen tree? A boulder? The three drivers piled out to inspect the damage, if any. Babble…babble…babble.

"*Que s'est-il passé?*" I asked the friendly woman with the little girl.

"*Nous allons maintenant.*"

Whatever we hit was history—and to me, a permanent mystery. The van pulled back onto the road.

Dawn approached, damp and foggy. I entertained and comforted myself by imagining that I was standing among the amazing baobab trees.

There were already people on the road, herding cattle and goats, hauling water in big yellow containers. We took a few mud-rutted side trips to a few small villages that were not on my cursory map. Cargo was off- and on-loaded, money exchanged. The young man with two cell phones departed. New passengers got on. People shifted and shuffled for seats in the crowded van. No one crowded me. People seemed to know that I had purchased two seats and that I was, therefore, entitled to two seats.

Suddenly, I was embarrassed. Who was I to require two seats? A graceful young woman clutching a coughing infant climbed into the van. I moved my pack to my lap and made room for them. The sick baby coughed weakly and continuously. In grandmotherly fashion, I reached out and gently touched his thin leg. His pretty young mother gave me a sad smile.

"*Mon fils est très, très mal. Il a une fièvre.*" When she put him to her breast, he did not suck.

We reached Morondava just before noon. The driver maneuvered bumpily through a labyrinth of rutted, rain-gutted alleys until we reached the *taxi-brousse* terminal. At last.

Hoisting my backpack onto my shoulder, I made an awkward exit from the van, stepping into ankle-deep mud. It didn't matter. I had arrived and survived the amazing journey from Antananarivo to Morondava in the company of people who were the heart and soul of this island.

On the far side of the muddy expanse, three tall men stood next to a small jeep. One held a sign: WELCOME MADAME LINDA DURHAM. The helpful woman with the little girl hugged me goodbye. We turned to speak to the pretty woman with the sick baby. She had already made her way through the mud toward the street. We didn't get to say *bonne chance*.

I sloshed my way to the vehicle with a baobab tree painted on the door.

Early morning…sitting on the porch of my little cabin at Kimony Lodge, miles and miles of seriously rutted roads from the town of Morondava, a cornucopia of distractions and ideas tumbling from somewhere in my head: A grasshopper invites himself inside my sarong; amazing bird sounds caress my ears; the heat is practically tangible—I close it in my fist; longhorns are grazing on seagrass; smiling, silent young hotel staffers stare at me from the terrace by the dining room. I wonder what they think of this solitary woman with birds tattooed on her shoulders. They watch me writing—on my porch, at the edge of the pool, at meals, and between meals. I am deep into an ongoing conversation with myself; it has no special form. I have no rush to be profound nor to identify a particular agenda. I'm just nonchalantly noting what my senses sense: the smell of insect repellent and sunscreen on my skin, the taste of brackish pool water, the sound of goats chewing vegetation, the sight of a beached blue boat, the touch of a breeze after stillness. Here, inside, I am still and still moving. Still. Just after dawn on my second day at the remote resort, while strolling around the grounds, I discovered a small private zoo. I spent time watching a gang of lemurs climb and frolic about in their big, tree-filled environment. I looked at the caged birds. They weren't singing. I thought of Maya Angelou's book *I Know Why the Caged Bird Sings*. And, I wondered.

—Madagascar journal entry

> I know why the caged bird sings, ah me,
> When his wing is bruised and his bosom sore, –
> When he beats his bars and he would be free;
> It is not a carol of joy or glee,
> But a prayer that he sends from his heart's deep core,
> But a plea, that upward to Heaven he flings –
> I know why the caged bird sings.
> –Paul Laurence Dunbar, "Symphony"

Two days after my arrival in Morondava, as I was finishing my lunch, the hotel manager introduced me to Manatera, the driver who would take me to

L'Avenue des Baobabs. I liked him instantly. He had a beautiful smile and an infectious laugh.

We set off to visit the trees, Manatera and I, in a shiny four-wheel-drive vehicle. First, we made a few stops in town to purchase extra batteries for my camera and to get some additional ariarys—in case I wanted to sponsor a tree or something. As we drove, Manatera and I shared stories about our families and our lives. We listened to talk radio in the Malagasy language. I mimicked the sounds as closely as possible to the amusement of my gentle guide. We were two friendly strangers: a middle-aged (I flatter myself) woman from America and a smiling Morondavian man of indeterminate age—two people cohabiting this Earth, not pretending, not hiding—just experiencing connection, friendship, and respect. Manatera was another brother from another mother in another Motherland.

And then we arrived at the destination of my wild intention: The Avenue… the Trees.

The strange-looking Grandidier baobab has been called a "freak among trees": tall poles, fatter at the bottom and narrowing as they go up and up—to almost one hundred feet—with a jumble of leaves at the very top. Six of the nine species of baobab trees grow only in Madagascar. It's not known how old the oldest trees are. Some guess 900 years. But since these trees do not have growth circles, it's difficult to tell. Methuselah might know!

I'm giddy with happiness at finally arriving at this faraway place that has called to me so strongly. With the help of the Earth's rotation and a few planes and a car and a bus and a truck and my feet, I have—at last, at last—arrived at a magnificent "here and now." I touch the trees. I buy a few baobab fruits. Manatera and I crack one open, and I taste the fruit of the Grandidier's baobab for the first and last time in my life. "No, thank you," I say to the offer of a second piece. My palate screams, "This is disgusting!" The local people love the taste, but I barely manage to eat one fuzzy seed pod for a private pilgrim's communion. Take. Eat this seed pod in remembrance…yes…in remembrance….

> To be great is to go on
> To go on is to go far
> To go far is to return.
> –Lao Tzu

On my return trip from Morondava, on another overloaded van, I could see the magnificent countryside that the dark, rainy drive from Antananarivo had obscured. Fresh air and a gentle breeze wafted in from the open window by my seat. I was feeling drowsy and comfortable when, suddenly, something hit me in the face. A big bug. Quickly, we all closed our windows. In a matter of a second or two, the bright day turned dark. We were driving through a plague, a murmuration of locusts, or some type of giant grasshopper.

It was biblical! Two people crouched by the roadside and covered their heads. A moment later, they were invisible. The event was remarkable. Other passengers took this once-in-a-Linda-time spectacle in stride. Oh, Madagascar, how you and Maman Nature awed this stranger wandering in a strange and wondrous land.

That evening, the van from Morondava dropped me off (rather unceremoniously) in front of a small, dimly lit hotel, where the manager of Kimony Lodge had reserved a room for me. The van driver barely stopped long enough for me to grab my pack. It was already dark, and he must have been in a hurry. Four tall young men, almost invisible against the night, escorted me to the hotel lobby. The receptionist broke the bad news: the highly recommended restaurant was closed for renovation. Worse, there were no other restaurants open in the town. I had gone all day with almost no food. I was tired, confused, and in the dark—in more ways than one. I had counted on a relaxing meal.

The four young men and I stood in the gloomy reception area of the gloomy hotel. In silent confusion, they studied my thoughtless, unattractive, food-deprived outbreak (breakdown?) in haughty, falsely privileged English. I couldn't speak fast enough or convincingly enough or pissed off enough in French. *Merde.* I knew I was expressing my frustration inappropriately, yet, I had looked forward to (and needed) a lovely dinner with a glass of good wine. *Tant pis.*

It had been a long time since such brattiness emerged from my better traveler's nature. After a few huffy minutes, I returned to my more-reasonable self. Still, the only opportunity for sustenance of any kind on this late, lonesome night was to accept the singular suggestion of everyone in the lobby: order pizza and a Coke Zero from the only open food establishment in town. That was my choice for dinner: pizza and a Coke Zero, or just plain zero! I choose the former.

The obliging young men arrived with my no-other-choice dinner. The soda was hot—not warm, hot. The pizza was cold and rubbery, as if it had been made in Europe the previous year, shipped by sea, delivered to this town by horse cart, and then kept in a closet until a hungry stranger ordered it.

My appetite was gone. I was unhappy and grouchy. I hated my room. It was shabby and dingy. I hated the weird turquoise polyester sheets and the vile-colored mosquito netting. I fell asleep, clasping my ugly American attitude to my breast. I was too hungry, stressed, and out of sorts to acknowledge the unacceptable way in which I handled myself with the people in the reception area in the no-name hotel, in an unnamed town, somewhere between the baobabs and my chic-by-comparison French hotel in Antananarivo.

Morning arrived. Still hanging on to my critical eye, I opened the putrid puce and orange curtains that concealed dark wooden shutters, which, when unbolted and opened, revealed a small balcony facing a huge garden filled with flowers and birdsong and greenery and a charming bridge across a shimmering pond. It was like finding myself at the beginning of a Disney movie.

I stood on the little balcony and smiled at the scene. I felt the gift of a fresh perspective on the age-old adage, "It's always darkest before the dawn." I apologized to myself for my tired-princess snobbery.

Filled with light, my room became pleasant. I looked for a sign, or a word of inspiration, to get me back on an optimistic track. That sign appeared in the sink, in the small bathroom with the odd shower that did, in fact, finally yield hot water. That word was "Anchor," the name of the bathroom fixture company. Anchor: a way of connecting to the "reality of experience." I recounted a fragment from James Joyce:

> Welcome, O world, I go to encounter for the millionth time the reality of experience and to forge in the smithy of my soul the uncreated conscience of my race.

Months later, I studied my photographs of exotic Madagascar with a new vision. I knew, then, that the most memorable aspect of the journey to L'Avenue des Baobabs was not the rare upside-down trees—awesome as they were. No, it was the eighteen-hour van adventure. It was the helpful woman with the little girl who invited me to sit and eat with her at the strange way station in the middle of a rainy, dark nowhere. It was peeing in the rain and the mud with the same urgency as that of the weathered, old woman who crouched beside me. It was the pretty young mother with the sick baby who stirred my empathy and cosmic connection. It was Manatera, soul brother from another mother, country, and culture—but from the same heart of God. It was the Connection. The Love. It was the word "anchor" in the sink in the nameless hotel, in the forgotten town on my way back and forward.

> I have no right to call myself one who knows. I was one who seeks, and I still am, but I no longer seek in the stars or in books; I'm beginning to hear the teachings of my blood pulsing within me. My story isn't pleasant; it's not sweet and harmonious like the invented stories; it tastes of folly and bewilderment, of madness and dream, like the life of all people who no longer want to lie to themselves.
>
> –Hermann Hesse, *Demian*

Mount Kilimanjaro

No one has explained what the leopard was seeking at that altitude.
—ERNEST HEMINGWAY, "The Snows of Kilimanjaro"

My inspiration to climb that majestic African icon was not triggered while rereading Ernest Hemingway's short story "The Snows of Kilimanjaro," which is not about climbing the volcano, but rather about contemplating suicide. No, the truth is that I experienced a touch of traveler's envy when my good friend and world adventurer Steve Berger told me he was making plans to climb that highest peak in Africa. Summit Kilimanjaro? His goal quickly and firmly planted a new intention—or call it an impulse—in my head. If Steve could do it, I could do it.

Hmm. How might I proceed to achieve this lofty goal? I bought a few books and articles on climbing. I assured myself that since other ordinary, fit people reached the summit of Mount Kilimanjaro, it followed that I—an ordinary, fit person—could do it, too. For no particular reason beyond that, I began to set in motion the steps to the achievement of that wild goal. At the start of this quest, mountain climbing was neither a hobby nor a sport I pursued. My hobby or sport had always been wild goal-setting and achieving. My expedition application and deposit to Mountain Travel Sobek were on their way. In the words of Jean-Paul Sartre, "Commitment is an act, not a word."

To get in shape, I spent the summer of 1999 working out and summiting peaks in New Mexico, including 12,622-foot Mount Baldy.

In September, I flew to Nairobi and found my way to the Norfolk Hotel, an updated Colonial landmark. It almost exceeded my Hollywood movie idea of a perfect African inn: revolving mahogany ceiling fans; guests in khaki and tan safari shirts and pants. I envisaged Teddy Roosevelt, bush pilot Beryl Markham, William Holden, and Karen Blixen—"I had a farm in Africa..." I dreamed of melding into the grand, century-old tradition of those intrepid, romantic explorers.

That first evening, I met Clive, our leader, a genial, bush-jacketed, British expat, straight out of Central Casting. Six additional summiting hopefuls shared this climbing adventure: a Maryland dentist and her businessman mate; a sixty-nine-year-old Florida couple; a marathon runner from California; and a fitness trainer from Texas. I felt ready, able, and more than willing to climb the highest peak on the continent.

After gazing at cloud-encircled "Kili" for a week, while camping in Amboseli and Tsavo game parks and hiking and feasting with the Maasai, our group, including porters and guides, was delivered to the trailhead of the Rongai Route.

From that six-thousand-foot base, Clive and Justin, a Tanzanian mountain expert who was making his one-hundredth climb to the summit, led us to our first camp at nine thousand feet. By the time we reached camp, tired and hungry, the porters had already set up our tents, carved out a semi-discrete toilet area, and prepared our evening meal: bean and corn salad, potatoes, peas, and bread with chocolate peanut butter. I slept like a hibernating bear.

The following day, we climbed to more than twelve thousand feet, the same elevation as my summer climbs in Santa Fe and as high on the planet as I had ever been. The expedition's third-day trek took us from the Mawenzi Camp to the Outward Bound hut at more than fifteen thousand feet. Exhausted and cold to the core, we arrived at a weathered wooden bunkhouse at dusk.

"Eat the vegetable soup," the guides urged. No one was hungry. I organized my pack for the midnight start to the summit. Excitement kept sleep away. My biggest concern about this final push was neither the altitude nor the fear of falling or failing. It was the cold. I was as prepared as possible for the sub-freezing temperatures. I donned all the suggested layers: underwear, thermal base layer, two pairs of socks, trusty climbing boots, fleece jacket liner, gray and black North Face jacket, weatherproof mackintosh, waterproof over-pants, liner gloves, over mitts, woolly hat, and balaclava. I tossed my daypack on my back, tightened the shoulder straps, and adjusted my headlamp. I was ready to climb.

Justin is first in line. I am right behind him. There is no moon. It's very, very cold and very dark. We climb slowly, slowly—or, in Swahili *pole, pole!* One foot in front of the other. Deliberate, effortful. Almost immediately, the batteries in my headlamp freeze. I am blind; there is no time for my eyes to adapt to the blackness.

"Justin, I can't see!" There is a hint of panic in my voice. Justin holds his flashlight down by his side so I can see his boots and lower leg. I match his gait and speed. *Pole, pole!* We continue to climb.

My mind is working very slowly…my thoughts are vague…or maybe I'm not thinking… just stepping…stepping…stepping. The cold…the cold. In these slow mind moments, it occurs to me that my toes might freeze. Maybe they are already frozen. I feel no real alarm. Frozen toes are not an unreasonable price to pay for this experience. One can maneuver quite adequately with a few missing toes. Oxygen deprivation plays dangerous tricks on my virgin, high-altitude mountain-climber self. I inhale, slowly. Step, step, exhale…step, step…inhale. "Please, God, don't let me lose any toes."

Hours pass. A faint glow seems to lighten the faraway blackness. I am not thinking clearly. The realization comes slowly that those hints of light must mean dawn. And dawn means…I have been climbing…about six hours. My math skills are frozen solid. My toes still tingle, but not as much as hours ago. The cold feels less cold. I continue to stumble up the steep path. There is now one thought: conquer the summit or die in the attempt. I am incredibly sleepy.

I feel extremely drowsy. *Am I saying this aloud?*

"Central Casting Clive" steps in front of me. He puts his face very close to mine and yells, in a big commanding voice, "Breathe! Breathe! Breathe deeply!" I breathe deeply. "Again." he commands. After a few hyperventilating moments, my energy returns.

Justin turns to me.

"May I carry your pack for you so that you might walk more freely?"

"Yes, please!"

Pole, pole.

We reach Gilman's Point at the rim of the crater. It's early morning. Finally, the sun greets us. We pause to take a picture. Now I know. I really will reach the summit.

Pole, pole.

Suddenly—and, really, it seems like suddenly—Clive, Justin, Rex, the personal trainer, and I are standing at the top of the continent. *Uhuru! I am triumphant!*

> For an hour and a half, we trekked onward around the crater rim. As we approached the summit, I became gloriously happy. Yes, I had climbed to 19,341 feet—on my own two fifty-six-and-five-sixths'-year-old feet. I was too tired to get my camera out of my pack, but it didn't matter. The moment was indelible.
>
> —Journal entry

We stayed on top for a very brief time before beginning the arduous descent at our own pace. I made my way alone for most of the afternoon. I "escalatored" down the long scree slope along the Marangu Route, called "The Coca Cola Route," at about fourteen thousand feet toward camp. I noticed two fit climbers in bright pink ski outfits accompanying Jim, the long-distance runner, down the mountain. This comforted me, because I was concerned about him and the slowness of his descent.

As I entered the camp, a small group of tomorrow's summiters welcomed me with expressions of awe. I felt puffed up, elated, proud to be a "shero."

"Linda Durham, Girl Wonder. I did it! I did it!" I whispered to myself as a porter directed me to my little tent. I crawled inside, utterly exhausted. He brought me a small bowl of hot water—precious hot water. I looked in my tiny hand mirror to wash my face. A ninety-nine-year-old woman looked back at me—dehydrated, deeply wrinkled, and dirty. I searched for words to console myself. *That woman just climbed Kilimanjaro! She is…I am awesome. Powerful.*

Humming, I began to remove my clothes. "Climb every mountain…." Oh, no! I stopped singing. I made a humiliating and shocking discovery. There, in the privacy of my tiny tent, nested in my silky, peach-colored panties, was…a frozen turd. *Oh, my God! How did that happen?* I regained some composure. Yes, I remembered an innocent little "poof," what I assumed was a bit of air escaping my body as my right leg stretched to find purchase on that flat place with the sign that read "Gilman's Point." It was just a tiny poof. Now that tiny poof had become frozen proof of the altered physical and mental state that had taken me to the top of the dark continent and then had brought me down to reality. I was mortified. No one must ever know.

It turns out that the pink-clad mountaineers that I saw accompanying Jim were invisible angels. Jim never saw them. He said he made his descent alone. This is bewildering.

—Journal entry

The next day, when we were off the mountaintop, breathing easily and hiking on gently descending but very muddy terrain, Justin and I talked about God and nature and family. He told me that he (and especially his wife) hoped one day to have a milk cow of their own.

"How much is a milk cow?" I asked. I can't remember if he said one hundred or two hundred dollars. I do know that I split that amount with Jim, the summit partner who descended "Kili" with the pink angels. He and I gave that money to the amazing man who had gotten us to the top of the highest peak on the continent—and back down again.

Lodged most deeply in my heart and mind about the Kenya and Tanzania trip is neither the ego-gratifying moment standing atop Kilimanjaro, nor the physical achievement of summiting. And it's certainly not the peach-panties experience. No, it's the connection with my guide, Justin Sianga. Justin, full of grace and kindness. Justin, the soul skilled at encouraging me beyond my perceived limits. His assistance was the difference between success and…I don't want to think about it. Without him, I might not have made it to the top of Africa. I will always remember and be grateful that he carried my pack for that final distance so I could "walk more freely."

Later, Justin wrote to tell me that he and his wife had purchased the milk cow—plus there was enough money left over to buy a foam-rubber mattress. I am forever grateful for his kindnesses. I like knowing that he and his family have a milk cow and a foam rubber mattress. And love.

I have a confession. The secret, less-than-lofty goal in my quest to conquer the summit of that famous mountain was to have the ability to boast of my accomplishment to friends and acquaintances near and far. Now, that humbling, privately embarrassing, totally unanticipated surprise in my silk panties presented my inner narcissist with an unexpected lesson. Maybe I'm not the awesome character I have always pretended to be. Maybe I'm just a not-too-conscious, moderately adventurous woman-of-a-certain-age who made her way down a powerful mountain, all day long, with an icy, ego-shattering turd in her panties.

Years later, in an effort to comfort a close friend who was mortified when she wet her pants in a first-class seat on an American Airlines flight from Dallas to Albuquerque, while sitting next to a tall, intriguing gentleman, I confided my own story of an unintentional *toilette faux pas*. A minor mountaineering misdemeanor!

Guided by Providence on many of my wild journeys to places that have challenged the usual comforts of my life and extended my search for the outer reaches and risks in the world, I have encountered angel guides, like Justin, guides who have blessed me with opportunities to experience some of the heights, breadths, and wonders of this world.

Asante sana. Thank you.

My Inner Portugal

Saudade is the only Portuguese word I know. An old New England sailor "gave" me the word long ago. I can sense the meaning, but not quite define it. I know it's connected to feelings of longing and yearning—like something or someone is missing and missed. The word evokes a physical sensation in me. I close my eyes and wonder who or what is missing….

—Journal entry

From time to time, when life overwhelmed me, I transported myself through meditation to my secret life in Portugal. With eyes closed, I would breathe deeply and take refuge in my imaginary, exquisitely furnished stone cottage on a cliff overlooking the sweeping expanse of the Atlantic. Twice a week, in these fantasies, I strolled the gentle mile to the idyllic village, where I bought crusty bread from the balding baker and crisp, sunny fruits and vegetables from the smiling market vendors and shopkeepers.

One autumn day, somewhere in the mid-1990s, during a busy year in which I hadn't ventured abroad, I checked my demanding gallery calendar and realized that there were very few windows for travel before the new year and before I would have to break the pledge I made to myself long ago: Every year I will go somewhere exciting and mysterious and foreign, and I will never say that I don't have enough time or money.

My inner monitor reminded my peripatetic self that there might always be obstacles and excuses for postponing my personal journeys: time, money, responsibilities. I vowed not to let surmountable barriers stop me from propelling myself over those inevitable hurdles and into the world that called to me. Of course, I intended to honor my business commitments almost as much as I intended to honor my youthful promises to live a full life. Clearly, I had to make choices and plans very soon.

The day of that time-sensitive realization, I booked a flight to Portugal. Three days later, I packed a few clothes, a journal, and some psilocybin "magic mushrooms" in my carry-on bag, and flew to Lisbon. I had no itinerary. I knew no one in Portugal.

Years ago, a jazz-loving friend introduced me to *fado*, the soulful, emotive music of the Portuguese. Serendipitously, about the same time, an astrocartographer revealed—after careful, lengthy, and ephemeral calculations—that Portugal was one of my power places. Her words rang true for me. Music, providence, and imagination beckoned me to Portugal. A search for my secret stone cottage overlooking the Atlantic gave the trip a spirited purpose. Might I have imagined something that already existed or dreamed a fantasy into existence?

In song and story, we have been told that dreams are wishes your heart makes, "when you're fast asleep...." Lyrics from that Cinderella movie of my childhood accompany me in many of my fanciful dreams. Except, on this autumn night, I am not fast asleep. I am in an oceanic trance, somewhere over the Atlantic. I am in a blissful state of wakeful sleeping, a place where I go to spend private time, peaceful, restorative time. I am revisiting my familiar fantasy Portuguese house—with the claw foot bathtub and the beautiful linens and the great library and the pots of red geraniums on the window sill in the simple yet perfect kitchen. How can something that seems so real, not be real? Or might it be real?

—From the beginning of my Portuguese journal

The taxi driver at the Lisbon Airport loaded my bag and headed to the hotel that I had circled in the *Lonely Planet* guide. When he pulled up in front of the grand entrance, I could see that it was all wrong: too big, too corporate. It didn't fit the Lisbon of my imagination. The cabbie spoke virtually no English, matching my level of Portuguese—yet, he sensed my disappointment. With a few friendly gestures and soothing words, he convinced me that he knew a better place.

The small, welcoming hotel in the middle of a modest residential neighborhood suited me. My simple room overlooked ordinary buildings where all sorts of extraordinary humans strode, or rode along, oblivious to this observing traveler.

So, Lisboa, my new friend, now what? A plan took shape to explore the country by foot, bus, and car and seek out *fado* venues. I would search for what I had always searched for: insight, home, adventure, true love...as well as my secret cottage.

I noticed a Lisbon license plate: LD 03.15. *Hmm. Could that be code for Linda Durham? Ides of March? Beware. It could be an omen.*

By my third day in Lisbon, I had attended *fado* performances in a few nearby nightclubs, but they didn't offer me the mystical experience of my imagination. They were too overproduced, too geared for tourists seeking a single night of entertainment before heading back to the cruise ship.

I felt a pull or a push to move on, to go somewhere else. But where? I studied the maps in my guidebook, rented a car and set out in hither and thither fashion to search for my meditation-manifested cottage, or for something unforgettable, something different, something else.

I explored the middle of the country—its pine forests and picturesque towns. I stayed at small inns, absorbed the beauty of the countryside, met friendly people, drank green wine, and dined on grilled sardines.

That "something else" happened toward the end of my second week in Portugal. I wandered into Obidos, not far inland from the coast. The medieval walled town with narrow streets had a magnificent government-run hotel, the Pousada Castelo Obidos. Sadly, there was no room at the inn for this road-weary pilgrim. I must have looked lost and lonely, because the sympathetic desk clerk directed me to a small boutique inn nearby. I walked my dejection down a narrow street to the recommended establishment. The inn consisted of three or four exquisite rooms and an attached cantina. Marvelous! I was off the road. I had a luxurious room. And the genial owner informed me that, steps away, there would be *fado* that night.

It was a perfect time to ingest the few psilocybin mushrooms that, from the start of my journey, remained inside a tightly folded plastic bag, secured with rubber bands, in a small velvet pouch, deep inside my zippered leather makeup case, at the bottom of my small valise. *Bon appétit!*

Soft light brushed the dark patinaed walls of the taverna. Couples and clusters of friends talked, and laughed, and drank as they waited for the *fado* to begin. The innkeeper gestured for me to sit at the owner's table with a perfect view of the stage a couple of feet below. He introduced me to my tablemates: two musicians performing that evening; a bespectacled, gray-haired architect from Lisboa; and his svelte lady companion. Her ebony hair—pulled back from her regal face—glistened under the lights. Beneath the collar of her tailored ivory linen shirt, a smooth gold choker encircled her long neck. The mushrooms were beginning to work their magic on me as I imagined myself, sometime in the near future, truly becoming a part of this sophisticated continental class. She and the architect fascinated me; I admired their understated, continental elegance. *Would I achieve such style when I reached her advanced, but indeterminate age?*

Other friends and strangers joined us. Our lively conversation drifted effortlessly between Portuguese and English. Perhaps the combination of music and mushrooms heightened my ability to understand and communicate. We listened to the voices and guitars with our mouths agape. Our rousing applause ignited the musicians, who, in turn, responded with ever-increasing passionate interpretations. Heartbreakingly sorrowful songs of betrayal and lost love wrapped their sounds and sentiments around me. I recognized them, internalizing the meaning of my one Portuguese word: *Saudade.* I cried.

Hours dissolved in the drinks. An elderly English couple and a group of noisy young Belgian students departed. Those remaining kept the energy alive—infused with the individual cultural experiences we brought to the night. Sometime after one a.m., with most of the *fado* lovers gone, the owner invited the architect, the beautiful woman, a few musicians, and me to move the party to his place.

We regrouped around the large table in the main room of his modern home. He poured more drinks, and the musicians performed by turns. A young woman with a voice like an angel, fully nine months pregnant, enchanted us. My imagination zeroed in on the child in her womb. How blessed was that tiny life to await birth nestled in such acoustically perfect surroundings.

Waves of sadness, beauty, loss, longing, and ecstasy ebbed and flowed through me. A nascent part of me rested in those musical notes and in the haunting spaces between them. I felt complete, in a calm and contemplative womb of my own, in concert with the baby soon to celebrate its birth day. All through that night of music, while we talked and drank and listened, beauty engulfed me. The umbilical of passion, truth, love, music, companionship, and laughter connected me to this jubilant place (with a little help from the mushrooms) as a welcomed stranger who belonged. A pilgrim in a medieval tale. Cautionary? Not at all.

For weeks, I had searched for my imagined cottage. I drove up and down deserted dirt roads with magnificent views of the Atlantic. I explored small villages and idyllic dead ends. I didn't find my magical house. But I found, entered, and explored another chamber in the heart of my earthly dwelling place.

Remembering

Wearing the blue satin and tulle ballerina tutu with silvery sequins that my Grandmother Bailey made for me, I twirl around and around in the living room. My father stands in the doorway.

"What a good dancer you are," he says, applauding. "Someday, there will be color television. Then, when you dance on TV, everyone will see my wonderful daughter with her beautiful red hair...."

I whirl round and round, spinning what-I-will-be dreams. I want to be on color television. I want to be a ballerina. I want to wear fancy costumes. I want to recite poems. I want people to clap for me. I want to please my father. I want to be special.

There is a soliloquy in *The Fantasticks*, the long-running, off-Broadway musical that has lived inside me since I first saw the play in 1963. The ingénue muses about her life and her future. "*I am special...*I am special. Please, God, please, don't let me be normal." Or *ordinary*, I added.

Like that ingénue, as a child, I wanted to be "special." OK, I confess: I still want to be special. To whom, though, and for what reason? I'm not sure.

My mother used to shake her head and point a finger at me when I shared my ambitious and theatrical plans with her.

"Don't get too big for your britches," she would say. Despite her rebukes, I did my best to remain full of grand desires. And dreams.

When I was eight or nine, my family moved from "The City of Brotherly Love" to a forlorn, brown-shingled house in Haddon Heights, New Jersey. I lived there for six years with my much older brother and my much younger sister. We were like three "only child" siblings. Every day my friends and I played outside in back yards, on sidewalks, in the adjacent woods, and in vacant houses nearby. We had 1950's style kid gangs. We rang doorbells and ran away. We made pesky telephone calls. *Ring, ring.* "Hello, is your house on Station Avenue? It is? Well, you better move it—there's a bus coming!" We spoke Pig Latin and Op language. *Opi copan stopill spopeak opop lopanguopage!*

We climbed trees, dressed up, had tea parties, made paper dolls, read Nancy Drew Mysteries, and spent our allowances on movies and candy.

One August, I wrote a play and performed it in my backyard for the kids and parents on our block. It was about a little girl who wanted to be someone other than who she was. She wanted to be a ballerina, or a princess, or a Gypsy. To be glamourous. Famous. At the end of the play (at my mother's dramaturgical suggestion), the little girl discovered that she was content to be herself.

That was a summer lie. I was not content to be my ordinary self. Not then. Certainly not now.

It was during those formative years that I learned how to disavow, criticize, pretend. How to justify, obfuscate, envy, pout, and lament. How to create problems and solve them. How to entertain and hide in plain sight. I learned that I loved insects, puzzles, books, birds, and secrets.

I learned how to wonder. I wondered about the size and contents of the world. I wondered why I was born into such an ordinary family.

Blond, curly headed Becky Fox, my best friend in the fifth grade, moved to town from Bloomington, Indiana. She talked about Bloomington in glowing terms, making it sound like the most exotic place in the world. A paradise. I wanted to go to Bloomington, Indiana. I wanted to go everywhere. I wanted to see what everywhere was like. Someday, some way, I would get away and discover how to become something bigger, something beyond my restrictive early circumstances. I attached my wandering dreams to an inner and abiding intention. And I attached the intention to a growing collection of dreams.

> I haven't been everywhere, but it's on my list.
> –Susan Sontag

Six decades ago, I stopped wanting to be a ballerina for reasons too obvious to enumerate. A princess? That, too, seemed an unrealistic reach.

However, the free-thinking child filled with wonder and a wanderer's spirit clung in her survivalist way to the romanticized notion of a nomadic people who traveled alongside her caravan of dreams. Still many years off was my lesson of "gypsy" as a pejorative label for a marginalized Romani culture, which in the sixteenth century was named after the mysterious realm from which they were thought to emerge: Egypt. But the truth that a milennia and a half ago they dispersed out of northwestern India, painting their cultural color all the way to westernmost Europe, was not yet unveiled. I, a child, saw what I needed to see.

Who were Gypsies to the little girl whose father invited her to wander endlessly around a Mobius strip?

   a)   People who dressed in delightfully bright traditional clothes
   b)   Free-spirited, adventurous souls unboxed by cardinal rules
   c)   Families who celebrated life with music, song, dance, and story
   d)   All of the above
   Answer: d

A magical gypsy. An accidental angel. A peripatetic pilgrim. A few of the possibilities I yearned to manifest. No roots. No insurmountable impediments. No obligations. Live the gift of being able to go out and out and then to return to something else, to something more, to everything.

I still do that. Over and over. I venture out looking for something. I return with something else, something I didn't initially seek. Sometimes, I sense that I have not gone far enough or that I have come back too soon. Much too soon.

Maybe I'm destined (eventually) to become a nun and live in a cloistered convent with a beautiful garden and have a simple daily routine. When my life is going through a boring, demanding, or stressful time, I indulge in the achievable fantasy of a more interior-adventure or life.

Every day I wake up in a serene and pristine convent or monastery. I wash my face in cold water without looking in a tell-tale mirror. I pray. I eat breakfast in silence with my fellow monastics. I work joyfully in the vegetable garden and meditate and eat a silent noonday meal. I read and pray some more and maybe sing in the chapel and smile and feed the birds and assist in the refectory and think good thoughts and write an occasional uplifting poem and sleep peacefully and dream about the garden and... Could I ever be a supplicant?

Instead of choosing—or following—a pure and simple way of life, I chose a path filled with potholes, noise, risks, and an absence of quiet gardens. Perhaps "Hap-hazard" should be my middle name.

Like Kelly Gordon's lyrics to a Sinatra signature song: "I've been a puppet...a pauper...a poet...and a king." A pirate, too, no doubt!

It's also true that when I fall flat on my face, I always manage to get back in the race.

Following "The Fall of the House of Durham Gallery," I clung to an inner wobbly belief that before long I would be back on top again. Somehow, I thought I would find a new and fulfilling path or passion, or it would find me. The inoperative word was "somehow." I have spent my life looking for something else, something more: more than a respectable husband; more than healthy and successful children; more than a good or glamorous job; more than a great apartment, house, ranch, or mansion. Something more than New

York, Paris, Bangkok, or Santa Fe; more than the theatre; more than poetry, or politics, or sex, or fame. Something else enticed me, kept my heart beating, set my mind on fire. And, yes, I'm still searching for that more: contentment, satisfaction, completion, and true love. I'm still gliding through an apparent stillness in my moving search...wondering.

> [Wo]Men, go abroad to wonder at the heights of mountains, at the huge waves of the sea, at the long courses of the rivers, at the vast compass of the ocean, at the circular motions of the stars, and they pass by themselves without wondering.
>
> –Saint Augustine

When Acid Reigned

If you are serious about your religion, if you really wish to commit yourself to the spiritual quest, you must learn how to use psychochemicals. Drugs are the religion of the twenty-first century. Pursuing the religious life today without using psychedelic drugs is like studying astronomy with the naked eye because that's how they did it in the first century A.D., and, besides, telescopes are unnatural.

–TIMOTHY LEARY

The once and future superstar Lauren Hutton and I were invited to spend the weekend at the apartment of a charismatic and mysterious wannabe guru. Bob Williamson, a self-proclaimed expert in facilitating "trips" on the mind-altering drug LSD, offered us a professionally guided acid experience. He claimed to be part of Harvard University's Timothy Leary, Richard Alpert research group.

Lauren and I found his Manhattan apartment somewhere south of Houston Street. Bob served us a sugar cube laced with a two hundred microgram dose of Lysergic acid diethylamide dissolved in vodka. This was long before windowpane and all the other latter-day designer LSD variations that flooded streets, parties, and concerts.

We wait in comfortable chairs for the psychotropic effects of the "sugar cubes." Bob disappears. A few minutes later, he reappears with an orange, an ordinary orange. He begins to peel it. The perfect scent of this beautiful fruit fills the room. Tiny droplets of orange oil dance in the air as our host and guide slowly peels away its rind, revealing the inner flesh. He hands Lauren and me a section of this enchanted fruit. The taste is unbelievable. The essence of ambrosia. Never in my life—never, never before—have I tasted an orange. Not fully. Not until now.

Exotic and beautiful freshwater fish—red tail swordfish, angelfish, clown loaches, neon tetras, cardinal tetras, and one blunt-nose elephant fish—swim tranquilly around and through the rocks and grasses in Bob's sixty-gallon aquarium. Their exquisite perfection convinces me this night that only a God—to which I was previously not reconciled, or a God-ness out there somewhere beyond everything I can experience and comprehend—could be responsible for their creation. I feel incredibly safe and at peace, awed by all that my senses are experiencing.

Bob puts an LP on his record player: Bach's six cello suites, the Pablo Casals version. While he and Lauren retreat to the roof, I lie on a mostly maroon Persian carpet and sink into an utterly sublime connection with Bach and Casals. I am the cello, and Pablo and Johann are making love to me. My whole being responds to the beauty, the intimacy, the ecstasy. The sensations transport me to a place of profound wonder. I experience myself at the beginning, or end, of something unnamed, unnamable. Now. Forever. I am in tune with, and grateful for, the exquisite gifts I receive. I will always remember to be awed and thankful.

In the middle of those Greenwich Village years, in the middle of another acid trip, I "visited" a previously unexplored area in the depths of my mind. I stood in a cavernous warehouse with high ceilings and miles of aisles—a space that went on and on beyond my vision. The vastness of it amazed me. Row after row of huge filing cabinets filled the room, which I understood was my mind. Every piece of my history and everything I have ever learned or thought or seen or read or known or pondered was safely stored inside those endless filing cabinets. I had access to it all—everything. I could open a drawer, remove a file, review or re-discover and contemplate any moment, fact, insight, or emotion from throughout my timeline. And there were countless unused filing cabinets waiting to be filled. This soothed me.

It was the summer of 1967. Bart and I were hosting a Tibetan Full Moon Puja ceremony and picnic at our ranch in the high desert of New Mexico. The word was out. Counter-culture flower children from Taos, Truchas, Santa Fe, and other new havens for the recently relocated "tune in, turn on, drop out" society converged on our land, bringing homemade granola, cheap wine, homegrown grass, and apples from Dixon.

To feel more in tune with the moon, I dropped a tab of acid—or maybe half a tab. Early in the chanting and feasting, my nasal passages suddenly closed. Blowing my nose and sniffing really hard did nothing. It was as if someone poured cement into my nostrils and down the back of my throat, where it had hardened like igneous rock. No air could make its way along that usual corridor. Disturbed and utterly uncomfortable, I wandered away from the drums, dancing, and chanting and laid down beside a friendly tree. To calm my body, I closed my eyes, took a few deep mouth breaths, and urged air into my lungs. I was quiet. Still. I heard or felt a voice. A message filtered into my ears from somewhere...from God, I assumed: *Never take LSD again. Everything you needed to learn from this chemical, you have already learned.*

That full August moon marked the end of my "Acid Age."

"Bunny Jill," 1963
COURTESY OF EARLE DOUD

Little Annie Fanny and the "Ma-nipple-atled" Bunny

I have a Bunny tale to tell.

In the middle of my long-ago Bunny Jill years, Barbara Harrison, the director of public relations for Playboy International, asked me if I would be interested in doing a semi-nude photography shoot for Harvey Kurtzman, the founder of *MAD* magazine and the creator of the Little Annie Fanny cartoon that appeared periodically toward the back of *Playboy* magazine. She assured me that the pictures were for artists' reference only and would neither be published nor publicized. I needed that assurance. I had a daughterly concern that nude or semi-nude photos of me in a magazine (*Playboy* or *MAD*) would deeply embarrass my father, a foreman in a warehouse where centerfolds and pin-up pictures were the preferred lunchroom décor. The photo shoot paid sixty dollars an hour—an impressive amount in 1963. I said yes. Miss Harrison scheduled the shoot.

Several days later, right on time, I knocked at the door of Harvey Kurtzman's second-floor studio/office in an old brownstone on the Upper East Side. No one answered. I waited. I knocked and waited some more. Was I being stood up? I planned to stay long enough to be paid for my time, whether or not the photo shoot took place. I was nervous, inexperienced at modeling nude or semi-nude. I posed nude only once—on a deserted beach on Fire Island, in the off-season. And the photographer was a friend. I waited some more. As I was about to leave, I heard men's voices and footsteps on the stairs. Three men ascended.

"Hi. You must be Bunny Jill. I'm Harvey. Barbara pointed you out to me a few weeks ago in the Club. You were wearing a black Bunny costume. Very nice. Thanks for agreeing to help us out with this project."

Harvey introduced the photographer, but not the tall, sandy-haired man who stood somewhat apart with a distracted, glazed look. Was he the cartoonist?

I nodded. I had no words. I was about to get practically naked in front of these three men, all strangers.

The photographer unlocked the door, and the four of us entered an upscale studio: shiny floor, fancy furniture. Harvey kept talking.

"We ran into a problem with one of the drawings for a forthcoming Annie Fanny strip. We want to snap a few photos for our chief illustrator."

I found my unsure voice. "Barbara said this was just for reference, right? It isn't for publication, is it?"

"No, no. It's just as she indicated. Reference only."

"Will you give me a letter to that effect?"

"Sure."

The photographer set up his equipment. The Silent Man was silent.

Harvey showed me the so-called problem sketch of Annie: Little Miss Fanny was sitting on the lap of a handsome man. Her giant round breasts (outrageously out of proportion to the rest of her) with raspberry-colored nipples were fully exposed. Of course! I was aware, as I looked at the sketch, that my breasts were not nearly that round or that big, and my nipples were blush pink. This was starting to seem like a ridiculous, even suspicious, gig.

Little Annie Fanny's arms encircled the seated man's neck. Lovingly. Her legs, crossed daintily at the ankles, were in the air, pointing over the man's head. She wore spike heels.

"This is the pose we need. I'm sure you can duplicate it," Harvey said. "Shall we go ahead?"

"OK." *It didn't look difficult.*

Harvey gestured toward a small dressing room. I removed all my clothes except for my very high heels and my basic white cotton bikini panties. *Why didn't I wear pretty panties?* I took a deep breath and tiptoed back to the studio, noticeably shaky. I felt awkward and uncharacteristically shy. I didn't know where to look—certainly not at the three strange men. At the floor? At the clock? *The hands had barely moved.* I wondered what to do with my arms. I wasn't in any danger. I wasn't scared. I just felt very self-conscious. The men behaved matter-of-factly. They barely looked at me. *Maybe the clock had stopped.*

Harvey picked up a straight-backed chair from a spot next to his desk, carried it across the room, and placed it in front of a plain white wall. He paused for a few seconds and scanned the room. He seemed perplexed, like something was missing or not quite right. Then, he made a small eureka sound and gesture, suggesting that he had solved a temporarily perplexing issue. He turned to the Silent Man, who was standing at the far edge of the room, near the door to the hallway, gazing at the ceiling or into space.

"Hey Bud, would you mind helping out? Could you stand in for the man in the drawing?"

Without smiling, or nodding, or speaking, and with no particular eagerness or reluctance (maybe he even shrugged nonchalantly), he ambled across the room and sat in the chair. Harvey smiled at me and, with a sweep of his arm, beckoned me toward the Silent Man. I walked to the chair. My left eye twitched involuntarily. I sat on the Silent Man's lap and assumed (or approximated) the Annie Fanny position in the drawing. I let out a breath I didn't know I was holding.

"Can you turn a bit, honey, so your chest is facing straight out?" Harvey asked. Yes, I could. I did.

"Now, put your face a bit closer to him." Harvey called him "him." I put my face closer to "him."

"That's it, hon. That's perfect."

The photographer snapped a few pictures. I didn't know how many. The whole shoot was over in a few minutes. Harvey thanked me, and I scurried back to the dressing room to put on my street clothes. When I re-entered the studio, the photographer was putting away his lighting equipment, and Harvey was sitting at his desk. The Silent Man was looking out the window.

"Sixty dollars, right?" Harvey asked.

"Well, I was on time and you were late. So, actually, you owe me for two hours. Plus, I need the letter confirming that the pictures are not for publication."

"Fine," he agreed.

He typed a quick note on his letterhead and wrote me a check for one hundred and twenty dollars. The Silent Man continued to stare out the window, his back to us. He didn't turn or say goodbye when I left.

There I was, a girl in my early twenties, truly thinking I had been hired as a model to pose in my panties for a legitimate, professional purpose: for artist's reference. But wait! The cartoon was already drawn. And, although I didn't realize it at the time, cartoonists don't need real models to draw their cartoon figures. There was nothing about my body or my skillful ability to replicate a particular posture that would have aided the draughtsman in his rendering of—for God's sake—a two-dimensional cartoon. I didn't look like Little Annie Fanny. No woman on the planet looked like Little Annie Fanny. The newly created Barbie doll had a much more realistic figure than Annie. So, what was the real purpose of the shoot?

Maybe Harvey Kurtzman was fulfilling some sort of grown-up Make-a-Wish fantasy for the Silent Man. I now see how easy it was for *Playboy* executives and associates with power and money to exploit naïve young women. I thought I was in show business. That's what Playboy management told us when we were hired. Actually, I was just a glorified cocktail waitress, an inexperienced girl who was manipulated one afternoon for someone's prurient play. It took time to shed light on that shady afternoon.

Harvey Kurtzman, Hugh Hefner, and most of the men from the early days of *Playboy* magazine and the Clubs are now dead. But many of their long-covered-up stories lived on in the memories of countless young, not-so-young, and quite-old women. Unresolved incidents of shame, anger, or embarrassment ooze out of our collective closets. I don't know how many other co-eds, wannabe pin-ups, dancers, aspiring actors, or dreamers fell into those seedy and (most likely) lamentable encounters of sexploitation, tawdriness, or just plain bad judgment in exchange for a shot at fame or fortune. Too many.

The Playboy Club phenomenon did not travel well into the seventies or beyond. The world was changing. There was a war. The "Original Bunnies" were growing up. We were taking responsibility for our lives, becoming disenchanted, and disillusioned. Most of us moved on to other callings and careers. We completed our education, became professors, actors, politicians, artists, writers, mothers, gallery owners. We're retired now. We're grandmothers. We're on Medicare. Powerful men are less likely to exploit us for sexual favors or other manipulative reasons. Yet exploitation goes on.

By the time Playboy tycoon Hugh Hefner died in 2017, he had been exposed by millions as a cartoonish, bathrobe-clad, male chauvinist whose life was a raggedy compilation of a host of aspects of the good, bad, and ugly socio-sexual-political times that many of us can still see from the rearview mirrors of our moving-onward lives.

> I looked at my crying face in the broken mirror of the Cover Girl compact and said aloud, "I can have class. I can be a contender. I can be somebody."
>
> —Journal entry (undated)

Wreck-trospect (Beginnings, Middles, and Endings)

I was driving to the grocery store when a Crosby, Stills, Nash, and Young song came on the radio—the one about living in a very, very, very fine house, with cats in the yard, and everything is easy. I pulled off the road to listen, closed my eyes, and cried. Images flooded into that mysterious closed-eyes place inside of me. Tears couldn't wash away those pictures of a long-ago time of sweet family happiness in our very, very, very fine Durham-built house in the middle of a high-desert paradise, in the middle (or at the beginning, or near the end) of an idyllic family life. I knew Crosby, Stills, Nash, and Young didn't compose that song with the Durham family in mind. And yet, it so closely portrayed our family scene that I pretended the lyrics were about and for us. Lingering outside of time, I clearly saw Bart light the fire, while I arranged flowers or branches in vases or jars in the very first hours of the seventies.

Our son, Everett Andrew Durham, is three months old, and our daughter, Donna Lynn Durham, is not yet two. Bart's parents are about to arrive at our hand-built home in Cerrillos, New Mexico. They flew from New York to Chicago, then traveled by Amtrak's Southwest Chief across the midwestern plains to celebrate Christmas in the desert with us. Most importantly, they are coming to meet their first and only Durham grandson. Bart and Donna drive to pick them up at the train station in the small settlement of Lamy. I wait at home with baby Andrew, tending the fire, arranging the flowers, and making final preparations for this auspicious family occasion.

When I hear the car in the driveway, I wipe a smear of milk from my nursing baby's chin, bundle him up in a woolly blue blanket, and we go outside to greet Hortense and Hobart.

Grandpa doesn't look well. He's chalk-white, and he's staggering. Grandma is clearly concerned and confused.

Once we settle in the warmth of our cozy kitchen, both in-laws revive a bit. Grandma holds the baby, as Grandpa quietly stares at the littlest Durham's sleeping face. A boy! He was hoping for a boy. As we sit around the big kitchen table, Grandma explains that Grandpa became ill shortly before their departure, but he refused to go to the doctor, and he refused to postpone their trip. "It's just a touch of the bug," he dismissed. "And, he's barely eaten in four days," she tells us.

It's Christmas Eve, but no one, except little Donna and the baby, has any appetite. We sit for a while and talk about simple things. Grandpa listens. He leans back in the old brown leather chair that had once belonged to his Methodist minister father and gazes at his grandson, who is lying in a swinging cradle, intent on the fish in our big aquarium. Grandpa is struggling to breathe. I'm almost afraid to look at him. It's disconcerting to watch our family patriarch breathe with such labor as he witnesses the miracle before him: the existence and sheer perfection of the newborn son of his son. He instructs me on how to make a hot toddy (hot water, honey, lemon, and whiskey), and he sips it slowly. Before long, he and my mother-in-law retire to the makeshift guest quarters in Bart's laboratory. A good night's rest in the high desert will surely turn everything to right.

Bart and I put the children to bed and set about playing Santa Claus. We bring all the brightly wrapped presents out from their hiding places and arrange them beneath the big, gaily decorated Christmas tree. We fill the red felt stockings with holiday trinkets. Then we sit close together on the sofa, watching the fire. Eventually, Bart turns off the generator, and we settle in for a good winter's nap.

When the baby wakes up for his middle-of-the-night feeding, I'm delighted to discover that it's almost dawn. The world seems so peaceful, so perfect. In the stillness, I welcome the slowly rising December sun, while I nurse our precious child whose father sleeps deeply beside me. It is a beautiful Christmas morning.

Suddenly, Grandma opens our bedroom door and tiptoes into the room. "Bart?" she wails. Bart wakes up, startled. "It's Grandpa. I'm worried about him. He hasn't moved all night."

A succession of trance-like activities begins: Bart rushes to the guest quarters with his mother; Donna and Andrew wake up; I dress them in their Christmas morning clothes; Bart returns to the house, shaking, his words unnecessary. "He's dead."

Bart drives to the pay phone in the village to call for an ambulance. I sit in the living room with my mother-in-law. In shock, she's slumped in the big chair by the fireplace, staring into the middle distance, repeating over and over, "He was so cold. I couldn't get him warm." Baby Andrew nurses in my arms as Donna squeals with delight and alternately rocks in her fuzzy teddy bear chair and chases our big cat.

The ambulance arrives. The driver and emergency medical personnel inform us that they can't move the body because rigor mortis has set in. The coroner has to be summoned—another six-mile round-trip to the pay telephone. Minutes become hours. The grumpy coroner finally arrives, and they take my father-in-law's body to Santa Fe. Christmas afternoon, Bart and his mother drive to town to meet with the funeral director. I stay at home with the children. Friends stop by. Day becomes night. Grandma and Donna go to bed. It's very quiet.

Sitting on the sofa, encased in a bubble of wonder, my husband's head in my lap and my baby asleep in my arms, I see myself: a young, unfinished woman holding a brand-new life, comforting a man in his prime, remembering a man whose full and successful life has just ended. I stroke the forehead of the son of the remarkable man who died hours ago, having fulfilled a silent wish to rest his loving eyes on the face of the son of his son. Now, the son of his son rests sleepily at my breast.

I am a daughter, a wife, and a mother in the middle of the flow of the miracle that is life.

The image of that long-ago Christmas stayed in my heart as years dissolved into decades. Separations devolved into reparations. Rifts mended. Everything takes and took time. Time took everything.

In 2004, Bart died from pancreatic cancer. A brave death. On the afternoon of the day he died, he asked his fourth wife, Madeleine (whom in his delirium he called "Linda"), to cook a special meal for him. She called to ask me for help. I drove straight to the grocery store, bought the ingredients, went to their house, and prepared his favorite simple meal.

He was lying in a hospital bed in what had been their dining room. He was very weak, drifting in and out of morphine dreams. I fed him a small forkful of rare bone-in ribeye, heavily salted, fried with onions. I held his hand. He fell asleep. I kissed his forehead, said goodbye, and left.

Halfway home, my cell phone rang. It was Rocky. In a choked voice, he told me that his father, whom he and his sister loved so deeply, had died just minutes after I drove away.

I pulled to the side of the road, turned off the engine, and wept. Behind my closed eyes, I watched the movie of our life together.

Time is not linear. It can't be. Hobart Noble Durham's grandson—my baby, now grown to manhood—called me with the news, the devastating news, that his father had died. Time folded back on itself and filled me with unknowing.

> Listen, children:
> Your father is dead...
> Life must go on,
> Though good men die;
> Life must go on;
> I forget just why.
>   –Edna St. Vincent Millay

It's difficult to recall exactly when our picture-book family life disappeared. It's hard to fathom where all those years and all that happiness went.

During those years, I "played" Mother the way I thought a good Mother role should be played. The children and I read books together and laughed and cooked and kept pets (cats, rats, fish, guinea pigs, and raccoons). We made things. The kids had plenty of clothes and bedrooms full of toys and games. We went on road trips and wilderness adventures. Disney World. Summer camp. Good schools. Theirs—ours—was a rather normal, relatively privileged, middle-class American life. Or maybe it wasn't. Highlights obscure the conduits. By the time Daisy and Rocky were preteens, I was divorced, a single mother with a newborn gallery. Everything was different. Everything was full of change and tears and absence and abandonment. I became obsessed with the care and feeding of the gallery and its motley assortment of hungry ghosts.

Disappointment rose and subsided in my remorse-infested Mobius strip trip. I gathered in the good times, the sweet times, the reading-stories-and-playing-games times, the blissfully contented times. The making shirts for Bart times. Going camping and riding my horse times. Getting stoned times.

Glancing over my shoulder, I reviewed that stretch of my past to acknowledge the power and importance of those days and the power and importance of my children's father.

Following life's mysterious genetic code, Bart succumbed to various forms of addiction: alcohol, mainly. He functioned well during the day. At night, there was endless oblivion. We lost one another. I went to Al-Anon. It didn't help. I wanted the people in the group to tell me how to fix him. Instead, they tried to fix me. I didn't want to fix myself, to fix the marriage. Once I began working outside of the home, I slipped away from Bart and our easy family life in a quest to pacify my own addictions—to success, access, and to a different kind of excess.

As a child, I had looked across the ocean for a dream. That inborn curiosity and optimism accompanied me into adulthood. I overlooked or overcame the many real and imagined barriers I encountered and—lured by a call from my impetuous nature—set my sights on greener pastures, higher peaks, deeper seas. I bade farewell to traditional roles and safety nets and went in search of the *rest* of the world, a world I felt certain was waiting for me.

> But the bravest are surely those who have the clearest vision of what is before them, glory and danger alike, and yet notwithstanding go out to meet it.
>
> –Thucydides at (or about) the funeral of Pericles

Iraq: Been There, Undone by That

Over and again, decade after decade, instead of retreating to a world of safety, convention, and quiet contemplation, I chose to venture into dangerous or confrontational territory. In 2004, I went to Iraq.

I was a member of an international delegation of ten women that traveled to Baghdad to witness and report on the status of women and children under U.S. occupation. The trip was organized by CODE PINK, a peace and anti-war organization. The participants came from South Africa, India, Singapore, Washington, D.C., and California. Representing New Mexico's community of peacemakers, I set out curious and naïve.

Our Iraqi contacts met us at the airport in Amman, Jordan, with vans and drivers prepared to deliver us to Baghdad—across miles and miles of Jordanian and Iraqi desert and through the Sunni Triangle, an area of dangerous anti-U.S. resistance.

Kate, who joined our group at the last minute, had just been deported from Israel for her humanitarian efforts on behalf of the Palestinians in the West Bank. When our three vans reached the Jordanian/Iraqi border, guards took her incomplete travel documents and detained us for several hours before letting us all proceed. The delay meant we would be traveling through the unsafe Sunni Triangle at a most inauspicious time of day.

While three women slept in the back of our van with the blacked-out windows, I rode shotgun with our driver, Sadoun. Mile after mile, the three vans sped across the flat, dry desert, past incapacitated and decapitated power-line towers, their upper sections tipped sideways like clown hats. Sadoun and the other drivers played leap van at speeds in excess of 150 kilometers an hour, continually shuffling the caravan's order. I couldn't sleep.

"*Ali Baba! Ali Baba!*" (Arabic slang for bandits), shouted Sadoun as he swerved to the side of the road and braked hard to a halt. The women in the back seat cried out, "What's happening?"

With our necks craned, we could see through the windshield that one of our vans had been forced off the road by a menacing black Mercedes. Three men threatened the women and driver at gunpoint, demanded passports, money, and cameras, then rushed back to the Mercedes, and sped away. Shaken, but safe, our three-van band drove on.

Shortly before dark, we arrived at a small hotel in downtown Baghdad. Armed Iraqi guards flanked the front door. A loud explosion during the night woke us. At breakfast, we learned that insurgents bombed a small hotel not far from ours, leaving several people injured.

Our hosts, members of Baghdad's Occupation Watch, an Iraqi peace organization, were ready and eager to take us anywhere. We were taken to the Green Zone, where we met with one of two women members of the Interim Governing Council. I lost my small leather journal in the councilor's office, or somewhere in the compound, and, although I went back twice during the week to see if it had been found, it had not. My insightful (perhaps inciteful) jottings were lost forever or, in a more intriguing scenario, deciphered and pondered over by unknown Iraqi officials to no meaningful end.

Iraqis welcomed us in their homes. We visited schools, refugee relocation camps, and hospitals. At one of the heavily damaged hospitals, where there was no electricity, no running water, no access to the internet and insufficient medicines for the sick, an exhausted doctor met with us and delivered a heart-breaking report on the effects of the war on the very young: nightmares, bed-wetting, regression. Mothers wailed as they sat in dark rooms with their crying or listless children. In the dingy corridor, I embraced a distraught mother standing by an abandoned gurney where her lifeless infant lay.

I wept with her.

Our delegation marched in solidarity with Iraqi women and journalists who sought more freedom and participation in the political process. On a Sunday afternoon, my roommate, Leslie Hope, and I sat at an outdoor café and watched our fixers play dominos. An angry woman crossing the street noticed us and ranted hatefully about the United States and its infidels. She spat at us. She spat at me. I understood. It was not about me. She spat at a symbol of the cause of the devastation of her beloved and careworn and war-torn country. She spat at the loss of her way of life. I closed my eyes and clenched my fists. I heard the dominos slap hard on the wooden tabletop.

At a gathering in the dining room of our Baghdad hotel, Jodie Evans, CODE PINK co-founder, posed a question to a group of Iraqi citizens: "Which do you prefer: life under Saddam Hussein or life under the U.S. occupation?"

An English-speaking man stood. He was silent for a few seconds before speaking, "In our country, we have a saying: 'Same donkey, different blanket.'"

One afternoon, I asked Maher, a fixer and an observant Muslim, how he justified walking with me when the Qur'an prohibited interaction with Western infidels. "The Prophet of Allah says man is the guardian of his family. First, I have a responsibility to feed and dress my wife and children," he replied simply, honestly.

"Does your wife dress in the fully covered Shia Muslim way?

"Oh, yes, definitely. She is never uncovered out of the house and not even in front of my brothers."

"Does she ever complain about the heat?"

"Sometimes. Yes, she says she gets a rash around her neck."

"Suppose she didn't want to dress that way anymore?"

Maher answered without a pause. "Then she would not be my wife."

Our Iraqi fixers took us to a home in a modest neighborhood not far from our hotel. We were to meet a woman who had recently lost family during the current occupation. As we filed through a small patio and into the living room, a pretty young girl greeted and kissed each of us on both cheeks. Inside, an *abaya*-covered woman stood, holding a six-month-old baby boy. I stretched out my grandmother arms to receive the happy, willing, curly haired baby. We settled on upholstered benches that flanked both sides of the narrow room. A man appeared (an uncle, a brother?) with a tray of cool drinks.

With the help of our interpreter, the woman began to tell us her story. I held her baby while she spoke. Her teenage daughter stood at the far end of the room in front of a tall glass-fronted cabinet filled with family photographs. Gently and respectfully, sensitive to her tone and cadence, the interpreter conveyed her soft-spoken words.

"Last August, at about nine o'clock in the evening, a few minutes past the curfew..." she began. Everyone remained silent. She and her husband and their four children were returning home following a dinner with her parents. As they approached their neighborhood, they were stopped at a checkpoint. U.S. soldiers in big trucks drove out of the shadows, blocking the road, and forcing the family's car to a halt. She paused for a long breath. No one spoke or moved.

The soldiers shone searchlights at the car and pointed guns at the family.

The husband rolled down the window and shouted, "Don't shoot, please. Don't shoot. We are family...." The soldiers ignored his desperate plea. They began to shoot. They shot the husband. They shot both sons—one a high school student, the other a young man preparing to go to medical school in a few days. They shot the eight-year-old daughter. Then she told us that a female soldier reached into the car and took jewelry off the dying girl. The mother and the teen-age daughter screamed for help. There was no help. The husband, the two boys, and their eight-year-old sister died.

Breathe for a minute before continuing.

Our small peace delegation was speechless and weeping. The surviving daughter passed around photographs of the family during those days before the bombing, before the occupation—days in which they sat and stood together smiling. She repeated their names as she walked the length of the room, holding X-rays of the bullet-riddled skulls of her brothers, her sister, and her father. I held the beautiful curly haired baby—who had been present at the massacre, inside his mother's womb—on my lap. Tears flowed down my face, onto my jacket and onto the baby's little blue and white striped shirt.

"Collateral damage." "An unfortunate misunderstanding." "Lamentable," my government explained away the "unfortunate incident." "Justified under the circumstances." The U.S. government "compensated" this grieving widow—who could have been me in another time and another place—twenty-five thousand dollars for the loss of her husband, her two sons (one whose dream was to heal and save lives), her eight-year-old daughter, and her "future happiness."

At the crumbling former Iraqi Army officers' barracks-turned-refugee camp, a round woman with a warm smile embraced me. In animated pantomime, we discussed womanhood, motherhood, and marriage. She explained, with the help of a second woman who joined us, that they were both wives of the same man. They bore him eighteen children. The heavy-set woman took my hand and led me across an abandoned theatre proscenium and past the stage left wing, where a family had set up a small, makeshift living space.

Down a hallway and through a cluttered area, an elderly woman reclined on a few blankets in a corner. She raised her arm in a slow-motion wave and lowered her head as we walked by. We entered a square space that had once been two rooms—now divided by the remnants of a collapsed wall. A refrigerator domi-nated the space. My new friend opened it. It was empty. She pointed to a light fixture and indicated that there was no electricity. At the other end of the room, a stack of thin, brightly colored mattresses reached almost to the ceiling. In an inventive dancing pantomime, she showed me how the mattresses are spread across the floor at night. Her husband slept between his two wives.

One of the family's young sons entered the room. His mother gave him some quick instructions, and he darted away. He returned a few minutes later, holding a tray with a single glass of orange liquid. Probably Tang. He held the tray in front of me. His mother gestured that the beverage was for me. Please drink, his mother's eyes and smile said.

There was no running water in the camp. I noticed an open sewer near the officers' empty swimming pool. The water would not have come from a purified source. My health-conscious mind shouted, *do not drink their generous offering.* My heart told me not to refuse. I drank almost half.

The next day our delegation left Baghdad for the long drive to Amman. Along the way, I began to feel serious rumblings in my intestines. "I'm not feeling too well," I told my intrepid roommate, Leslie Hope, recounting the likely reason why. She gave me a dose of the strong antibiotic "Cipro" (Ciprofloxacin)—but not quite soon enough.

That evening, the pathogens were wreaking havoc on my digestive system. A few of us shared a room in an upscale hotel while we waited for our late-night and early morning flights. With good intent on not monopolizing our bathroom, I hurried downstairs to the lobby in search of a ladies' room.

An elaborate wedding reception was in progress. A beautiful bride and a procession of glamorous attendants and scores of finely dressed guests paraded through the lobby toward the staircase leading to the ballroom on the lower level. Smiling and hurrying, I rushed ahead of the crowd and found the powder room, not a minute too soon. From the seemingly forever isolation of my modern toilet cubicle, I watched fanciful high heels and the hems of beautiful gowns come and go. I listened to the gay, relaxed conversations of Arabic women as my body jettisoned all that the Tang-like drink had given me. It certainly wasn't life-saving like the water from Gunga Din: "It was crawlin' and it stunk, but of all the drinks I've drunk…" But it was a love-affirming drink.

I cherish those days in Iraq.

Lodged in a special mental file is a collection of powerful memories of that crumbling barracks—refuge for the desperately displaced: men, women, and children, smiling through the adversities and consequences of war. I can still feel the warmth of the mother and her son, who generously offered refreshment to a fair-skinned visitor from far away. I cherish their embraces and the mutual understanding of our shared humanity.

I treasure them for their kindnesses, for I had been a stranger in a strange and war-torn land.

> Sometime they'll give a war and nobody will come.
> –Carl Sandburg

I pray for that day.

Oh, My Gaza!

Five years after my time in Iraq, I joined my CODE PINK friends again and traveled to Gaza as a member of a peace mission to celebrate International Women's Day with the women and girls of that beleaguered strip of land between the Mediterranean Sea and Israel. Gaza has been called "the largest outdoor prison in the world."

Traveling under the auspices of the United Nations Relief Works Agency (UNRWA), our group of several dozen people entered Gaza through the Egyptian-controlled border. It was just a few months after Operation Cast Lead, the Israeli cross-border attack that killed more than thirteen hundred men, women, and children and destroyed much of Gaza's infrastructure, schools, homes, and farmland. The Human Rights Watch accused Israel's military of violating the international ban on "wanton destruction," a ban found in the Fourth Geneva Convention.

U.S. media gave the devastating incident scant press. Corroborating the aftermath and carnage in that sliver of land, I witnessed the tragedy and travesty of the shattered Palestinian territory and the unacceptable, ruinous conditions under which survivors lived: the constant short supply of food, construction materials, and medicines.

I cried with mothers, listened to students, and sang with children. Our group convened with professionals and officials. My anger grew as I listened in horror to three women who had been tortured physically and psychologically in an Israeli prison. Guards fastened foul-smelling bags of rotting garbage on their heads; yanked hair from their scalps; immersed stripped women in ice water, then in scalding water.

"We have become the victims of the victims," those we interviewed told us.

On the second day of our Gaza tour, I was one of three delegates assigned by UNRWA to visit the Rafah Community Center to observe a bread-making demonstration. Other members were assigned to libraries, schools, or hospitals, which I would have preferred. Not the bread-baking sort, I felt disappointed.

For a while, my well-traveled, compassionate, culture-loving self went missing, replaced by my misguided ego's arrogance and ignorance. My mind huffed. I felt certain it would be boring.

Several women, holding flowers, stood outside the unpretentious building on a short street in the settlement of Rafah, near the border with Egypt. They ushered us inside, where seventy-five women surrounded the three of us, applauded warmly, smiled, hugged, and kissed us. Unbridled joy pulsed through the room. Sisters meeting sisters. In minutes, we were sincerely united on International Women's Day.

The greetings and introductions accomplished, a small, old woman with an unselfconscious, missing-tooth grin, took me by the hand. She led me to a courtyard where nine or ten women were gathered around a metal-dome-covered campfire in the sand next to a rusty swing set. I sat in the sand by the fire. Someone handed me a glass of hot, sweet tea.

Is this the bread-making demonstration?

A woman in a dark blue abaya and a flowered headscarf rolled out dough in round disks. She tossed one disk onto the hot dome and quickly flipped it.

When it was my turn to roll out a ball of dough, I created an uneven oval instead of the desired circle. I tossed the egg-shaped dough onto the hot surface. "Oops!" It landed in wrinkles. My patient teacher flattened it. Flipping it, I singed my fingers—just a bit. My sisters' amusement was kind, and we laughed and shared the ovoid bread I made. *Making bread and breaking bread—together.*

Later, in the big community room, I gave an impromptu speech of appreciation. One of the teenage girls translated for me. It went something like this:

On this special International Women's Day, in honor of all women everywhere in the world, I acknowledge our bond of understanding—as daughters, sisters, wives, mothers, and grandmothers. I am so glad to be with you today to celebrate and share the power and joy of all that we are. I know that we all desire and deserve the same basic things—safety, shelter, nourishing food, clean water, health care, access to information and education, and the right and opportunity to worship and celebrate as we choose. May we find ways to bring these things to our communities, our families, and the world. Thank you for welcoming us. My heart is full of love for each one of you.

It was the women's turn. They had written, rehearsed, and prepared a deliberately hilarious play about Gaza home life to perform for an unknown group of American women who might or might not have succeeded in getting across the closed border with Egypt, and who might or might not have been able to share International Women's Day with them. Three of our fifty-eight-person CODE

PINK delegation shared that honor—the joy of being their audience, of laughing and dancing away an afternoon of female solidarity.

Later, at the Gaza City Hotel lobby, I wrote in my journal:

> This day was worth the whole trip. It was unlike anything I have experienced in my past; unlike my family gatherings; unlike long-ago, middle-school girls' groups; unlike gatherings in various workplaces, or in dance classes, or in conscious-ness-raising groups. Never. Nowhere. Today's communion with the generous and loving women of Rafah has helped to steer me through a neglected section of my ever-opening, never-closing heart and mind.

There is a candle in your heart, ready to be kindled. There is a void in your soul, ready to be filled. You feel it, don't you?

–Rumi

Yes, I feel it.

Two days later, twenty members of our delegation, escorted by the UNWRA staff, boarded a small bus for Jabaliya, a destroyed town in the northern part of Gaza.

Town officials and dozens of children, who matched our smiles with curiosity and eagerness, welcomed us. Little girls reached for me, held my hands, touched my clothes. I left the official gathering and followed a band of young boys and girls. They ushered me around rows of small tents that served as emergency shelters for the Jabaliya families after Israel's Cast Lead campaign turned their homes to rubble.

I loved being with these happy-seeming kids, laughing and singing in tempo-rary rejection of their ruined surroundings. Still, I was filled with helplessness. I wanted to help them. But how? In my small, green backpack, I had twenty painted ceramic animal beads on short leather straps. I purchased them in Santa Fe to give to children in Gaza. But I didn't have enough to give to the scores of girls and boys gathered around me. How could I give a small ceramic turtle or chipmunk to a few children and no ceramic rabbit or bear to others who shared the same horrific circumstances, who lived in the same collapsed buildings or temporary tent camps in the demolished remains of their town, and who survived the same rockets, bombs, tanks, and terrorism? None for all seemed (sadly) kinder than something for a few. The little gifts stayed in my backpack. It felt painful, regrettable, and real. I cursed my immediate helpless-ness. Although I had nothing tangible to leave with the beautiful children, I could smile, hold hands, and hug. And I could sing some cheerful songs, with amusing sounds:

"The moon belongs to everyone…"

"Getting to know you…"

"Zip-a-dee-doo-dah…"

"When the red, red robin comes bob-bob-bobbin' along…"

While I sang, the children laughed and mirrored my exaggerated gestures. And they sang back to me.

I "toured" devastated Jabaliya Refugee Camp guided by dozens of innocent children. I photographed them and their makeshift shelters and choked back tears as I walked with them through the devastation of their homes, their lives.

On the drive back to Gaza City, I gave the ceramic animal charms to one of the guides. He promised to find a place and a fair way to distribute them.

Until [man] has become fully human, until he learns to conduct himself as a member of the earth, he will continue to create gods who will destroy him. The tragedy of Greece lies not in the destruction of a great culture, but in the abortion of a great vision.

–Henry Miller, *The Colossus of Maroussi*

The Other *Audacity of Hope*

In the winter of 2011, I received an email invitation to apply to be a passenger on the U.S. Boat to Gaza, part of an International Peace Flotilla with the ambitious mission of ending the Israeli blockade on Gaza and bringing greater awareness to the plight of Palestinians living and struggling in the strip.

The five-page application listed my qualifications, references, considerations, reasons, and viewpoint. In February, two organizers interviewed me by telephone and contacted my references. In March, they notified me that I had been selected to be a passenger on *The Audacity of Hope*.

I felt honored to sail with other Americans who had become disappointed with the politics and provocations that created such an ongoing and untenable environment for the men, women, and children trapped in that embattled region—which I had visited not long ago.

Again, I am choosing to put my body, my eyes, and my abiding vision for peace at the epicenter of this conflict. Discontent has been festering here (and elsewhere) for far too long. It is clear to me that the anger, hatred, retribution, and continued bullying and retaliating of the ongoing Israeli/Palestinian conflict cannot continue unabated. It brings fear and tragedy to all who live in the region–it brings death to many. If our voices can be heard, and if our true intentions can be felt and understood, then, perhaps, a new and better dialogue will begin. Perhaps, the energy and insistent (but always non-violent) voices of the many engaged peace activists might (just might) move the stalled and disruptive dialogue a step closer to resolution, reconciliation, celebration. I know, I know. Many have tried and many have failed. Still, I go with Pulitzer Prize-winning author and social activist Alice Walker; activist and CODE PINK co-founder, Medea Benjamin; former CIA officer and analyst Ray McGovern; peace activist Kathy Kelly; octogenarian Holocaust survivor Hedy Epstein; and other committed passengers and crew as we embark on a historic initiative, and as we walk our talk and sail our tale. I am excited to be part of this bold mission of peace.

–Journal entry, June 2011

With the disturbing experiences of my 2009 Gaza trip still fresh in my mind, I arranged to fly to Greece to rejoin friends from the International Women's Day Delegation, along with other fellow peace and justice passengers on the U.S. *Audacity of Hope.*

Our boat, with its cargo of boxes of drawings, cards, and letters written by American school children and peace groups, was one of a number of vessels that formed the International Flotilla. Small boats from France, Spain, Ireland, Canada, and other countries joined in this humanitarian mission.

> Whatever you can do or dream you can, begin it. Boldness has genius, power and magic in it.
>
> –Goethe

I copied that Goethe couplet onto the first page of my *Audacity of Hope* journal. Later, I added:

> We are a brilliant, intrepid, and motley band of humanitarians. We practically defy a basic principle of physics, asserting that one cannot be in more than one place at a time. We are all moving from our boat to various meetings in four or five locations, through the mazes of the Metro, along the ancient streets of Athens and Parama and Piraeus. We gather in windowless rooms. We march on boulevards. Simultaneously. We work, without stopping, to prepare our "glorified ferry" to sail to Gaza with the other member boats in the Flotilla. We are in Syntagma Square, in front of the Parliament Building, rallying with the people of Greece while, at the same time, we are with the "fasters" across from the United States Embassy, singing and chanting. Everything is happening so fast. Sparks of Revolution are everywhere.
>
> –Journal entry

A long, black banner streamed across the *Audacity's* starboard side. Its bold white letters read: TO GAZA WITH LOVE. After days of bureaucratic delays, the captain, crew, land support, and passengers grew doubtful that we would ever obtain legal permission to sail. Considerable political interference from Israel, as well as from our own country, thwarted our plans for a smooth departure. Two or more of the Freedom Flotilla boats had been sabotaged in the dead of night, causing increased concern for the safety of our boat. The Israeli government falsely and ludicrously declared that the human rights passengers onboard our vessel were carrying sulfuric acid to throw on their naval forces if they stopped us as we approached our Gaza destination.

If our humanitarian mission was to succeed, it became clear that we would have to "set sail" at an unannounced hour and without the requisite documents from the authorities in Athens. But even before our hopeful and audacious boat was out of the mouth of the harbor, sleek Greek Coast Guard vessels, manned by menacing armed commandos in black battle gear, like futuristic Ninja warriors, blocked us, forced us to stop, and threatened to board with weapons. After a lengthy but futile stand-off, they escorted our boat back to a Greek Naval port. It was impounded; the captain and crew were arrested.

The world was watching. In real time, independent journalist and former *Democracy Now* producer Aaron Maté filed his report with the program's host and executive producer, Amy Goodman, from onboard *The Audacity of Hope*.

Officials at the U.S. Embassy had given our delegation nervous, superficial, and impotent lip service when we first met to respectfully request a statement or letter of safe passage for our voyage. It was sad and disheartening to realize that human rights, peace, and justice are not the primary interests and issues of my government—nor of most governments. Money and Power—those are the issues that our embassies seem to protect, support, and export. These facts burned and turned into a revised mission on land: peaceful demonstrations.

We demonstrated for the release of Captain John Klusmire, an American citizen whom officials charged with embarking from the port without permission and for endangering the passengers on our boat. We made numerous requests for assistance to our Consulate. They went unanswered—or answered with a non-answer. Part of the mandate of the U.S. Consulate is to aid and protect Americans in distress abroad. Captain John was an American in distress. He remained in an Athens jail with no visit from anyone in our embassy.

We couldn't bear to stand by idly. We staged protests. We fasted and conducted a sit-in/sleep-in across the street from the side entrance to the U.S. Embassy. Late in the evening, after a day of non-violent chanting and sign holding, as we were preparing to sleep in a grassy area across from the embassy, a group of gentle and polite Greek policemen arrived and asked us to leave. We stayed. And we sang.

"Please, we're just following orders," they apologized as they gathered our belongings, loaded us into a van, and drove us to jail. While detained at police headquarters, we sang scores of songs and chatted with on-duty officers. Eventually, the chief released us. It was after 3 a.m. when I returned to my hotel.

The next day, there was still no help from the U.S. Embassy. Captain John remained in jail. We continued to demonstrate and fast. On July 3, I contacted my long-time friend United States Senator Tom Udall. He called U.S. Ambassador Daniel Smith in Athens to check on the arrest status of Captain John and inquire about his condition. By email, I learned that the ambassador conveyed to the senator that he was aware of the situation and that everything was being "handled."

Unfortunately, nothing was being handled. Captain John was still in jail, and no one from the embassy had been in touch with him. And so, a few of the fasters (and friends of fasters—for by now I was not a true faster, having been tempted by a Greek salad) decided to go to the ambassador's house.

It was the Fourth of July. Independence Day. There were six of us. We had a few small signs and an American flag. Four members sat quietly in a grassy park (filled with feral cats) across from the entrance to the U.S. Ambassador's compound. Ray McGovern, a retired CIA analyst and Vietnam veteran, and I held hands and crossed the street. We didn't speak with the military-garbed men in the small guardhouse adjacent to the big metal gates in front of the residence. We walked straight to the main door and rang the bell. Two Brinks guards wearing bullet-resistant vests met us at the gate.

"Good afternoon. I'm Linda Durham from Santa Fe, New Mexico, and this is Ray McGovern from Arlington, Virginia. We'd like to speak with Ambassador Smith."

"That is not possible." The guard stiffened and furrowed his bushy eyebrows.

"I believe he is expecting me to call on him. I received an email from Senator Udall, who spoke with the ambassador and mentioned that I was here in Athens."

"You must make an appointment at the Embassy."

"Yes, we tried that yesterday, unsuccessfully. But now, it's the Fourth of July, and the Embassy is closed. We're just requesting a few minutes of his time."

The volley went nowhere.

The four remaining members of our visiting party continued to sit in the park across from the residence, anchored by the bright orange *Audacity of Hope* life preserver ring that served as one of the props from the fasting site. They held up signs. LET FREEDOM RING. FREE GAZA.

The Brinks men knew the drill and unwaveringly kept us at bay. A large, black SUV with tinted windows approached the compound gates. The guards ordered us to step aside. Instead, Ray stepped toward the black backseat window.

"Is that you, Mr. Ambassador? May we please have a word with you?"

No response.

"Are you too cowardly to speak with us?" Ray challenged.

The police or secret service pounced on Ray, knocked him to the ground, and forced him to retreat across the street. Motionless, I remained near the doorbell at the closed gate while a guard checked around and under the SUV for explosives. A second set of inner courtyard gates—like emerging and retracting menacing metal claws—opened and revealed a beautiful garden and a winding driveway. The SUV drove out of sight.

I rang the bell again. Mean-looking men in black suits scurried back and forth between two windowless doors in the gated entrance, but they didn't acknowledge my presence.

Across the street, police and more men in dark clothes strong-armed Carol, Ridgely, Debra, Ken, and Ray toward a squadron of patrol cars. I started to dart across the street when two towering men grabbed me.

"OK, OK. I'm leaving. Let go of me. Ow! You're hurting me."

Another tall policeman came up from behind, squeezed my arms to my sides, and lifted me off the ground.

"Let me go…I didn't do anything…I'll leave…I'm a grandmother…!" I said a whole string of things in a plaintive voice, and then I began to cry.

Tears had no effect. Jammed into the patrol cars, we headed to the police station where the night before we had been perfunctorily arrested for our benign sleep-in outside the embassy.

This time, things were different. The police didn't speak to us in the patrol car. When we reached the station, they were gruff and hostile. They offered us no ice water, and we weren't invited to sit in the little office where our songfest had taken place the previous night. The officers who had been so pleasant, even cordial, ignored us when they walked past.

The ritual began: a patrolman collected passports and called us one by one into an office where they grilled us for parents' names and other useless information. Ridgely refused to reveal her father's name. I wished I hadn't divulged the names of my parents, Everett and Lenore, both of which the interrogators misspelled. They returned our passports.

We waited. I sat on a step in the vestibule and clicked off quick snapshots in defiance of the strict prohibition against them. As long as I was being held for civil disobedience, I might as well be civilly disobedient. Two more times officers demanded and returned our passports. Instead of answers to our questions, demanding to know why we were being held and having to disclose personal information, we received blank stares or silence.

"Just following orders," said a surly policewoman. Orders? From where? From whom? From Hillary Clinton? The ambassador? Netanyahu? Papandreou? We could only guess.

"Are we terrorists?" I questioned the handsome, fit member of an anti-terrorist task force who spoke perfect American English. He didn't seem American. His eyes locked onto mine, and he met my question with a silent semi-smirk.

"Are you Israeli?" I asked. He turned his back on me.

At last—perhaps because the international pressures to release us exceeded the reasons to retain us—officials returned our documents and let us go back to our impounded boat. We sought internet connections for world response and news from loved ones. We returned to Syntagma Square. It had grown into a vibrant tent city of young Greek activists.

We witnessed Goldman Sachs being hung in effigy in front of the Parliament. We stood in solidarity with protesters in the Greek people's movement who were fighting against the oppressive government and the austerity measures that had taken their money and put it in the pockets of the rich.

We went to Athens, the birthplace of democracy. We saw, but we did not conquer. Eventually, we came home.

I must not linger or languish in my comfortable life. I must not forget the children in Gaza. The refugees from Syria. The men and women from the Occupy Movement. The schoolgirls from Pakistan. The Rohingya from Myanmar. The sex slaves from India. The Homeless and the Hungry. I must envision a better, more peaceful, more forgiving, more understanding world. Sadly, my peace-waging efforts seem so tentative, so impotent. I get lost in confused, mundane chores and perceived priorities while the world continues to be blessed and plagued with a veritable alphabet of gifts and concerns. This is a World of reasons and excuses, of bridges and barriers, of optimism and pessimism, of destruction, renewal, and resurrection.

—Journal entry, July 20, 2011

I Make My Way to Southeast Asia
Part 1: Vietnam Views

The Vietnamese people are determined to complete, most satisfactorily, their revolutionary undertaking and, at the same time, fulfill their obligations to the revolutionary movement of the world's peoples. The Vietnamese people will surely win; the Indochinese peoples will surely win; and the World's peoples will surely win in the struggle for peace, national independence, democracy, and socialism.

–Excerpt, speech delivered by Premier Pham Van Dong,
May 3, 1973, Hanoi

In 1998, I made the decision to visit Vietnam, in part, because I had wanted to visit that country for decades. But the real impetus was a middle-of-the-night call from my son, Rocky, who was traveling in Southeast Asia with a friend.

"Hello?"

"Mom, I'm in Hanoi." Rocky's excited announcement took a moment to register.

"Mom, I'm in *Hanoi!*"

A few months later, I booked a flight to Vietnam.

At the arrival terminal in Hanoi, serious, officious airport authorities informed me that my visa photographs were not acceptable. A few hours later and regulation photos in hand, I was free to go. That bureaucratic procedure didn't annoy me in Hanoi as it would have in the U.S., because I was already attuned to my moment-by-moment Vietnam adventure. *Linda, you're in Hanoi!*

The Vietnam War signaled yet another uptick in my personal political awakening. It burst through a wall of my small preoccupations in those years of death and devastation in a virtually unknown and largely misunderstood land far, far away. The nightly news reports, with images of young soldiers returning to the States in body bags and coffins, woke me up and kept me awake. Friends and acquaintances who survived the shock and tragedy and horror of war in

Southeast Asia still bear the physical and emotional scars.

As I studied the airport baggage handlers, document inspectors, and concessionaires in the Hanoi airport, painful memories of the war churned in my head. *Agent Orange. Body bags. Flag-draped coffins. Protestors. My Lai.* Thin, preoccupied men passed in front of me. Were they the sons, grandsons, nephews of the Viet Cong our GIs fought during that "Second Indochina War"?

I wondered what the airport workers thought about this lone woman carrying an American passport. Years eased or erased the animosity. My war memories were mixed with the exoticism of Vietnamese culture gleaned from movies, books, art, and the stories of those who made it back alive or almost alive.

Marshall McLuhan was right. "Television brought the brutality of war into the comfort of the living room. Vietnam was lost in the living rooms of America—not on the battlefields of Vietnam." Everything I knew, thought, felt, or imagined about Vietnam and the Vietnamese people, I learned from network news. Truth and lies and confusing reports remained tangled in my mind. When I arrived in Hanoi, only one thing was clear: I knew nothing. At least I knew that.

The taxi ride gave me an exciting (life-threatening) introduction to the city as we bumped, honked, swerved, and screeched our way through erratic traffic and heavy, dirty, yellow smog. Bicycles, motorbikes, cars, trucks, and people vied for a bit of space to move forward. Everyone seemed intent on going somewhere or, perhaps, nowhere in particular. I loved the rush of it—the unpredictability.

We drove the length of Hoàn Kiêm, the lake in the middle of the city. The name translates to "Lake of the Returned (or Restored) Sword." As I marveled at the calm and gentle work and play activities along its banks, I renamed it "Lake of the Restored Peace." By the time the taxi pulled up to my neighborhood hotel, I was completely captivated by the pulse of this vibrant, familiar/unfamiliar culture and eager to explore it.

The big window in my hotel room overlooked a peaceful, green park where early every morning people gathered on the grass to practice tai chi. In my pajamas, I watched and swayed in awkward synchronicity with them, approximating their stance and the slow and focused rhythm of their movements. At breakfast each morning, I sat on a low, three-legged stool at a tiny plastic table and ate mysterious and delicious street food from one or another of the instant restaurants that appeared on the sidewalks at first light. I inhaled, heard, and devoured Hanoi's smells, sounds, and tastes. I embraced her. I tumbled inside of her, and she held me fast.

One afternoon, on a personal mission, I ventured into the hustle of vehicles and bustle of people.

"Where can I get a good manicure and pedicure?" I asked an English-speaking Russian woman married to the proprietor of a neighborhood art gallery. On a scrap of gray paper, she jotted down—in undecipherable Vietnamese script—the street address of the beauty shop she recommended. She pointed me in the right direction, and I set off with my ragged nails and the piece of paper.

Before long, I was lost. Several times I stopped, showed strangers the wrinkled paper, only to have them study it curiously for long seconds, shrug their shoulders, and hurry away. Others pointed me in opposite directions. I walked past pot and pan vendors and stalls that sold automotive supplies. I walked and walked. No beauty shops.

I approached one passerby and pantomimed painting my fingernails. To others, I gestured, "I'm lost" and "Where can I find…?"

I flashed the gray paper scrap for a sign of recognition. My efforts amused and confused the street laborers I approached. One "helpful" man directed me to a barber chair and salon equipment store. That was progress.

It was late afternoon when I finally found my destination: a single, garage-sized space with the fourth wall open to the busy street and passing audience. Hanoi's non-tourist, everyday-woman's beauty emporium featured manicures, pedicures, haircuts, laughter, and animated conversation. The appearance of this hot and tired raggedy-nailed foreigner hardly caused a blink among the staff and customers.

A sweet-faced young woman guided me to a yellow plastic chair on a low platform. Soon, my hands were soaking in a bowl of warm, soapy water, balanced precariously on my lap. A smiling nail technician sat on a miniature stool in front of me. She carefully placed my feet in a pink plastic basin of soapy water, balanced (also precariously) on her towel-draped lap. We smiled across the absence of a common spoken language. In so many parts of the world, smiles can signal the beginning of trust and understanding. Smiles helped this big foreigner (người nước ngoài) become part of the liveliness in that small neighborhood salon.

There are universal rituals that require no language and connect women across cultures. This was definitely one of them.

We watched a beautiful young girl model her new red outfit. The oohs and aahs from the other women were infectious. I oohed and aahed with them. The older women teased her good-naturedly. In the back of the shop, partly hidden behind a length of flowered cloth strung on a wire from wall to wall, a beautician washed a woman's hair. She commented on something that must have been hilarious because everyone erupted in laughter. Their laughter infected me. Another woman—apparently in response to the hilarious comment—performed an impromptu strutting dance and momentarily lost her balance, which prolonged the hilarity. There I was—half again as large as any of the petite and lovely women in the shop—a pedicure-seeking American who wandered through miles of business frenzy on the unfamiliar streets of Hanoi to join in the camaraderie of women being women.

I reveled in the good fortune of finding much more than a manicure and pedicure. I connected to my universal woman-self in an unforeseen "anyplace/no place," where the foreign and familiar met, overlapped; a place where a stranger entered and was befriended; a place where superficial differences—language, skin color, size, and age—dissolved in the realm of a deeper membership: Women.

On that perfect afternoon, I didn't spill the bowl of water in my lap. I didn't fall off the armless chair. I just floated in an air of timelessness in a place without boundaries.

Much later, I discovered a poem by a Vietnamese poet that reminded me of that afternoon:

Free the moon for its fullness,
Free the clouds for the wind,
Free the colour green for the grass.
I return to myself.

Free the gentle girls
To be unaffected;
Free people from suffering,
From competing for fame,
Free them all, free them all.
I return to myself.

Free teenage girls
From hiding away,
Free gray hair
To be white forever.

–Lam Thi My Da, "I return to myself"

I Make My Way to Southeast Asia
Part 2: Khmer Chimera

From Vietnam, I traveled through Thailand to Cambodia.

In 1992, UNESCO designated Angkor a World Heritage Site to protect it from unauthorized excavations, pillaging, and land mines. One of the largest archaeological sites in the world, it includes the famous temple of Angkor Wat. That place is dotted with the ruins of the Khmer Empire's various capitals from the ninth to the fifteenth century. By 2004, years after my visit, the organization's successful restoration campaign had preserved Angkor to the degree then possible, and it was removed from the list of endangered sites. The Archaeological Park contains approximately fifty Buddhist and Hindu temples.

> Kampuchea is the Khmer language name for Cambodia. I arrived here hours ago—after a short flight from Hanoi via Bangkok. I am staying at a small guest compound in the jungly outskirts of Siem Reap. I have catapulted myself here to experience Angkor Wat and other remarkable sites in this ancient part of the world and to continue my pursuit of adventure, mystery, and connection. My search for more of my life and its purpose is ongoing. I am full of the kind of emptiness that creates room for the unknown.
>
> —Journal entry, January 1999

The rain was torrential. The mud, inescapable. Having nothing to do and nowhere to go, I sat under a makeshift canopy at the outdoor reception area of the simple, locally owned travelers' hotel, eating a simple meal. Alone. There was no one to talk to. I had nothing to read. I had finished my last novel on the plane. I thought I would find a book or magazine to read when I landed at the airport in Siem Reap. No. I assumed there would be something (anything) to read at the hotel—something someone left behind, a paperback cast off by a backpacker. There was nothing to read. Sometimes, when there are no books or magazines, and I'm alone and not ready to sleep or meditate, I find a cereal box or a jar of some kind with words on it. *Ingredients*, for example. And I rearrange the letters to make new words of four or more letters: greed, diet, tense, renting, nest, ring, indent, string….That night, there was nothing to read but the thick Cambodian air. I wondered what to think about and how to think about nothing. I paid attention to the almost-violent rain.

The hotel proprietors busied themselves in the kitchen. The few other guests had already retired to their cabins. The night seemed devoid of everything but the sound of the furious rain. For a while, I sat in my emptiness and listened to the downpour. In time, I stepped carefully from one narrow wooden walkway to the next, through heavy underbrush and even heavier rain, and made my way to my cabin.

The RAIN. The wetness of Kampuchea saturated me. I draped my dripping clothes over the small rattan chair in the corner of the room, put on a dry t-shirt, and climbed into one of two very narrow beds in the very rustic room. The deafening, heart-pounding rain bellowed its fury through the closed wooden window slats. No glass separated the jungle from the room. With no lights and nothing to read, I urged myself to sleep. I called out to the night, to the air, to the rain, to God, and to whomever or whatever might be listening.

"Hello, I am here in Cambodia, in a rainstorm, and all is well. I am alone and safe, and just a bit unnerved, and now I lay me down to sleep…."

Someone or something is in my room, under my bed. I can smell it. My heart pounds. Adrenalin floods my limbs, but I can't move. It's not one but two angry creatures—monkeylike things from under the bed. They jump on top of me, stinking, grunting, drooling. They're strong and mean and with no hands they try to strangle me, to kill me. I struggle, but I can't escape them. I try to scream, but I can't find my voice. Suddenly, my small guttural sounds power into a grotesque noise that bursts out of me.

My terrified scream wakes me from my false awakening. Did it frighten the handless monkeys back into hiding? My head throbs. My heart beats fiercely. My muscles seize and spasm. I'm afraid to go back to sleep. It's so dark. And it's still pouring. I find my flashlight and turn on my micro tape recorder: "The monkey creatures…with no hands…they came from under the bed…they tried to kill me…."

Morning brought a soggy end to the rain and a promising hint of sunshine. The ark of my room survived. At breakfast in the vine-covered dining area, I shared a table with an older couple from London on their third trip to Southeast Asia. They wore matching red and blue sweatshirts. While he adjusted the camera strap around his neck and she returned binoculars to a small leather case, I mentioned the remarkable deluge. Between bites of sweet Khmer fruits, they assured me that it was nothing more than a typical seasonal storm. Still shaken, having survived the murderous midnight episode, I related my monkey monster nightmare.

"Oh, you must be taking Lariam, the antimalaria drug. It does that. It's practically banned in the UK. Too dangerous. Too powerful. It's been linked to a string of murders and suicides, you know."

As a matter of fact, I was taking Lariam. "Well, that explains it!" I said as a finale. Or did it?

After breakfast, at the suggestion of the proprietors, I hired a driver and a guide. The three of us headed to the remarkable heritage site ruins. We walked along the causeway to Angkor Wat, past scores of beggars with no legs or no hands *(no hands!)*. We climbed the steps of the main temple, and I marveled at its construction and reconstruction. On the short drive back to the inn, two monkeys *(two monkeys!)* leaped out of the jungle and knocked a young girl off her bicycle. She screamed like I had screamed in the night. My driver stopped the car. He and my guide darted at the monkeys, waving their umbrellas threateningly, scaring the attackers back into the bush. They picked up the frightened girl and helped her back onto her bicycle. She pedaled away shaken, but unharmed. In out-of-breath voices, the two men told me about a tourist who had been attacked by vicious monkeys the previous week. My driver rushed the injured traveler to the hospital, where nurses treated bites on his ear, arms, and hands.

"He almost lost a finger," my guide added.

The week passed. The handless monkey creatures never showed themselves again, although each night I sensed them under the bed, waiting to pounce.

On the eve of the last dawn of my days in the little cabin in the jungle, I programmed myself to wake up early to catch my short flight back to Bangkok. In the dim morning light, I opened my sleepy eyes and beheld—just inches from my head—a full-maned lion. I felt his warm breath. He watched me, close, protective, like a guardian angel. I blinked a few times. He was still there, gently looking me in the eye. I stared back, unafraid. Slowly, very slowly, he faded from view.

Une illumination soudaine semble parfois faire bifurquer une destinée. "A sudden illumination sometimes seems to turn a destiny."
–Antoine de Saint-Exupéry, *Flight to Arras*

Disturbing thoughts still bombard my quiet moments. Apprehension. There is a dark and powerful presence of anger, hate, and fear that pervades the atmosphere in Cambodia. It's impossible to erase the recurring visions of dozens and dozens of beggars lining the causeway leading to Angkor Wat: nameless, numberless victims of the horrendous landmine crimes whose lives or limbs were ripped away by evil. It was humbling to witness the aftermath.

The Bottom of the Top of the Bottom

Little by little, one walks far.
–Peruvian Proverb

Peru enfolded me. After days in Cuzco, Pisaq, and Ollantaytambo, I arrived at a small hotel near the awe-inspiring brink of Incan culture at Machu Picchu. In one of my hungry ego's searches for acceptance, recognition, fame, or personal power, I challenged myself to hike to the top of Huayna Picchu, the haunting emerald peak over Machu Picchu. The first time I saw a picture of that majestic crest looming over those mysterious ancient ruins, I gasped at the shape, the color, and the surroundings, and I yearned (or vowed) to be there. I fantasized about standing at the top of that verdant peak and looking out and over the vast Urubamba Valley.

At daybreak, I hiked alone through the fifteenth-century Incan city to the trailhead of Huayna Picchu. I signed my name in a soggy notebook at the makeshift kiosk. There was only one signature above mine. Overcast skies gave way to drizzle. The wet path became slick. Within minutes, I met the other hiker coming back down. The unstable weather and slippery trail derailed her climbing intention. Not mine. I was determined to stick it out.

I had Huayna Picchu entirely to myself. I trudged the mushy path toward the summit accompanied only by rain, the spirit of ancient peoples, and the impending sense of power and joy that I anticipated. Joy switched on and off. At one moment, I was cold, then hot, then soaked by the fierceness of a sudden torrent. At last, tired and wet, I scrambled through a cave-like opening and stood atop Huayna Picchu. I took a deep breath and stretched my arms as high over my head as they would go. I clenched and unclenched my fists and called out, "Thank you."

Then, I looked down. To nothing. I could barely see my feet. Clouds, mist, and fog beat me to the summit. The Urubamba Valley? Vanished. Nature overpowered me, thwarted my goal. I reached the top only to realize that I stood at the very bottom of the sky.

In a moment, my disappointment vaporized, like the world from this vantage point. Something filled me with unanticipated and much-needed wisdom. *I am here. And it is now. This is what "now" looks like. Breathtaking.*

I embraced the perfection of that now. After breathing in the majesty of this special point on my planet, and after experiencing the exhilaration of being in the clouds, I snapped a mental selfie once again and hiked down.

Questions to self: Why do I keep repeating patterns of remembering and forgetting? Will my life continue to revolve around or redound around scattered acts of gathering and discarding pieces of evolving truth? It seems that initial goals are rarely ultimate goals. What is my quest? That's a good question. What's wrong with continuing to twirl in the unknown? This climb toward truth is precipitous. The truth needs grasping. I'm searching for something more meaningful and satisfying in myself than the mere fleeting glee of completing one ego-set goal after another. I think or hope (pray?) that I will connect with the vulnerable and true part of myself that lies hidden in the deeper recesses of my heart. Dormant. I don't want my life to be (simply) about climbing up and looking down. That is no life purpose!

−Journal entry

In memoriam: Having Huayna Picchu to oneself is no longer possible today. Four hundred ticketed people, in groups of two hundred, climb to the summit daily. I'm thankful again and again for the gift of that rainy-day climb.

Driven by a Word—Patagonia

Patagonia. I first encountered the word and world of Patagonia years ago, while reading *Up into The Singing Mountain*, a sequel to Richard Llewellyn's novel *How Green Was My Valley*. The story relates the trials and tribulations of a small group who survived a mining disaster in Wales and moved to Patagonia in southern Argentina to begin new lives.

Patagonia replaced Timbuktu as my favorite go-to, fun-to-say, remote place in the world. I liked creating sentences using (or misusing) the word: *That's as remote as Patagonia!*

Pat a Gonia: It won't bite!

Two bibliophile friends and I were browsing in a Denver used-book store. Jim was looking for Revolutionary War material. Jan and I were hunting valuable mispriced books. The proprietor, an old man with a shiny, mostly bald head, asked if he could help me find something.

In a tongue-in-cheek (or smart ass) manner, I responded. "Yes, where is your Patagonia section?" I expected him to say, "What?" or "Huh?"

Instead, he replied, "It's right over here."

I touched each of the seven or so Patagonia titles on a shelf of miscellaneous South American volumes and selected an 1853 personal narrative by Benjamin Franklin Bourne, *The Captive in Patagonia: Or, Life Among the Giants*. I loved the beguiling title. The book became my first "Patagoniana" purchase. Over the years, I found and purchased dozens of rare and not-so-rare books, maps, and prints of and about Patagonia.

My fascination with the word became a fascination with the place—a remote windswept region at the bottom of the South American continent. Perhaps in Patagonia I might uncover yet another piece of the incomplete, ever-unfolding puzzle of my life's purpose. I didn't yearn to go there to meet the tall, mysterious Patagonians. The last of the true Patagonians became extinct long ago—slaughtered by Magellan and others—as some unverifiable stories go.

No, I just wanted to go there and be there and then return, filled with the magic and power of having been there, breathed there.

In the mid-1980s, I purchased a "fly anywhere in Argentina" ticket. After a few days in beautiful Buenos Aires, where I ran into artist friends who lived in the colorful La Boca neighborhood, I boarded a flight for Ushuaia, the southern-most city in the world. The Aerolíneas Argentinas plane bumped and bounced in the notoriously dangerous South American atmosphere. Throughout the flight, I gripped the armrests and told myself over and over that planes are made to withstand this kind of turbulence, and that the highly experienced pilots in the cockpit were trained to deal with even more violent buffeting than we fright-ened, airsick passengers were currently experiencing.

I closed my eyes and imagined that I was on a rickety bus on firm ground. This calming visualization made me feel safer than the disquieting reality of being on a bucking plane at thirty-six thousand feet. I pushed away thoughts of crashes like the one I read about in *Alive: The Story of the Andes Survivors*, in which members of the Uruguayan rugby team who survived a crash in the rugged Andes resorted to cannibalism in their desperate hopes for survival. After a pretend eternity, we landed bumpily on the tarmac. Everyone clapped. The plane taxied into a corrugated metal hangar before allowing the well-shaken passengers to disembark. A wiry old gentleman in a wrinkled brown suit kneeled and kissed the concrete. *Terra firma*—what a concept. I survived the most frightening flight of my life.

Days later, before dawn, we set off by truck on the long drive from Comodoro Rivadavia to El Calafate and the Perito Moreno Glacier. My traveling compan-ions were two men: Jorge, a local driver who came highly recommended by business friends from Buenos Aires; and Peter, an occasional traveling partner and future husband who joined me in Ushuaia.

Jorge knew the region and the road well. Peter (bless his handsome, well-traveled, Harvard-educated soul) spoke fluent Spanish. The faces of the Argentine people lit up whenever he began to speak. His conversations with shopkeepers, executives, street vendors, and Jorge went on and on. Everyone, it seemed, was delighted to listen to him and engage him in lengthy discourse; everyone except me. I spoke only emergency Spanish and frequently felt left out and frustrated.

Whenever possible, I wandered off on my own. When that wasn't possible, I wandered off in my mind and inhaled the mysteries and rugged beauty of this country. As Peter and Jorge chattered on, I quietly accessed my repertoire of songs and poems that celebrate wilderness and nature. Under my breath, I whisper-sang words about the love of wandering, of wearing a knapsack on my back while intoning a "la-la-la…ha, ha, ha," or humming a favorite old folksong about leaving home, taking a train, and traveling hundreds of miles away.

In those moments, mentally alone, I had time to recall Henry David Thoreau's affirmation: "In wildness is the preservation of the world." And the preservation of the soul, I would add. I thought about John Muir's thirst for exploration: "The world's big, and I want to have a good look at it before it gets dark." I agreed with John. My goal, too, was to have a good look at the world, have a good feel for it. As Omar Khayyam mused, "Oh, Wilderness, were Paradise enow!"

Hmm. What is enough?

Daybreak. We headed west in front of the light. Mile after hour, we drove through the majestic wildness of Patagonia, tamed only by flocks of grazing sheep. Such magnificent landscape, vast and unspoiled, dense with emptiness.

Just as Jorge's truck began to cough for lack of gas, we rolled into the small settlement of Esperanza. Nothing more than a truckers' way station, Esperanza lay quietly in a flat, featureless stretch of road, empty of human sound and full of the fury of the wind. The outpost consisted of three or four ramshackle buildings, among them a shabby wooden restaurant—our intended destination. The fierce wind hurried us across the dusty expanse.

We stepped into the dim and dirty café. In an alcove to the left of the door, three men with scruffy beards and rough clothes slouched on mismatched stools, talking, drinking, and smoking. They turned to size up the strangers in their midst: two tall, clean-shaven Anglo men and a shapely, young-enough woman with golden hair.

We chose a wobbly table in the middle of the room. The place turned quiet. We waited. Soon, a woman appeared through a curtained doorway. Her appearance stunned me. She could have been my age, or much older, or much younger. Her clothes were dirty, her hair disheveled. Her eyes seemed dead, but they brightened a bit when she saw us. We ordered three coffees.

"¿Por favor, donde esta el baño?" I asked in my emergency Spanish.

This woman with soot on her face directed me through the curtained threshold, down a dingy hallway, and past a few stall-like sleeping compartments to a toilet room. It was the second most disgusting "bathroom" I ever had the misfortune to need. Still, I was thankful for it. I had my period and had been riding in a bumpy truck for hours.

When I returned to the table, Peter and Jorge were discussing something in mile-a-minute Spanish. The men at the bar kept staring at us. The woman returned, balancing three mismatched mugs on a crusty, greasy oven tray, which she held with a kind of vestigial elegance. She placed a small, folded flowered cloth in front of me, along with the prettiest of the three mugs. We smiled at each other. Time disappeared from her face.

The men at the bar called her over and began pawing her. As we prepared to leave, she wrenched herself away from the filthy men, and our eyes met once again in a silent exchange of understanding—woman-to-woman.

Once we arranged ourselves in the truck cab, Jorge and Peter exchanged cynical remarks about the absence of elegance in the Esperanza whorehouse. A whorehouse? It hadn't occurred to me that it was a whorehouse. I thought it was just a funky café.

Two days later, on the way back to Comodoro Rivadavia, we stopped again in Esperanza. This time, at night. The cantina was noisy and crowded with a motley assortment of rough cross-country truckers. Again, all eyes turned toward the Anglos. The same woman presided over the bar. That night, she wore a shiny red dress, and her hair was brushed to the side and fastened with a silvery metal clip. Bright crimson lipstick accentuated her downturned mouth. She smiled when she saw me. I smiled back.

Peter and Jorge sat a table against the wall. I headed toward the curtained-off hallway to the filthy bathroom. From the corner of my eye, I noticed a grimy man get up from his barstool and start toward me. The woman yelled something at him in a commanding voice. Other men laughed as he shuffled back to the bar. My protectress gestured for me to wait. From a narrow shelf near the bar alcove, she removed a flickering red candle, took my hand, and led me down the lightless hallway, past the cubicles (now with curtains drawn) to the toilet. She handed the candle to me. In the soft rosy glow, I couldn't see the filth I knew was there. My silent lady friend waited outside the door in the dark. When I came out, she took the candle and my hand and escorted me back to our table. She smiled and squeezed my hand. Or did I squeeze hers?

Somewhere, inside my mind or soul, I felt a bond with that woman, a kind of "there but for the grace of God go I" sensation. I knew her. I could have been that woman in the shiny red dress.

As we pulled away from this lonely place in the middle of nowhere, I spoke aloud, *La señora de la esperanza.*

Peter overheard me and added his commentary: "*La señora sin esperanza.*" Both men laughed. I fell silent.

¿Sin esperanza? Without hope?

Por favor, Madre Maria de Dios, que bendiga el ángel.

From time to time, my thoughts catapult me back to that far away shabby shack, and I see my eternal sister in her shiny red dress. I see her smile. And I smile back, across the miles and years and fate. *Buena suerte, mi hermana....*

Studying the antique maps and prints of Patagonia in my collection sparked a specific fantasy goal for my trip: to stand at the southernmost point of South America, that final patch of *terra firma*, and to feel the power and energy of the entire western hemisphere at my back. Quirky passion brought me to Land's End, to Finisterra, to Ushuaia, in far southern Argentina.

A trusty Fuegian guide led me through a pristine forest. He plucked something off a tree trunk and told me to eat it. Like Alice in Wonderland, I bit into it. I felt a tapping at my temples. My mind expanded. Or shrunk.

We hiked for nearly half an hour through a cold and isolated terrain of scattered rocks, muddy patches, splashing eddies and rivulets all jumbled together until we approached the not-quite-solid bottom of the continent. I stopped and gasped. I stood for a long time looking toward and beyond the expansive clearing—wide, vague, and broken. Where was the sharp, definitive point of land, the destination my imagination created? The reality in front of me was at odds with my fantasy. Instead of arriving at a geographic point, I reached an interior point, and I began to understand the pointlessness of striving to conquer pinnacles, goals, and singular achievements.

It was enough to savor the expansive majesty of everything—everything before me, around me, behind me: land, trees, rocks, glaciers, rivers, wind, pampas, sheep, villages, mountains, hillsides, towns, buildings, people, countries, continents, years, centuries....

The experiences themselves merged into a vast and timeless beyond-all-imagination moment of enlightenment. As I stood looking out over the wind-whipped waves of the impatient Beagle Channel, I felt supported by the solidity behind me. I was wonderstruck by the fluidity in front of me. I sensed the beginning of so much more beyond the edges of this ragged end.

It is good to have an end to journey toward; but it is the journey that matters, in the end.
–Ursula K Le Guin, *The Left Hand of Darkness*

Pacific Ghost of a Chance

"Don't wait for me," the comet said, "you'll be gone before I'm back!"

Intent on observing Halley's Comet from the most ideal location on the planet, my traveling companion and I booked passage on a small explorer ship out of Tahiti. In addition to forty or so adventurous, comet-seeking passengers, also onboard were a renowned oceanographer, a world-famous ornithologist, and two professional astronomers.

Our first evening at sea, during an extravagant banquet, the captain announced that there might be an opportunity to view the comet late that night. Those who were eager to get a first view of the celestial celebrity could request a 2 a.m. cabin call. Most of the sated and sleepy passengers chose to skip the (possible) middle-of-the-night sighting in favor of a restful sleep. "It's a long cruise, and I need time to find my sea legs," said a portly gentleman at our dinner table of stuffed and sleepy passengers. I signed up.

A buzzer and scratchy intercom voice woke me from a deep food- and alcohol-induced sleep: "The comet is visible." I dressed quickly and joined the eight or so people already topside: several groggy crew members; two wide-awake astronomers; and a thin, elderly woman who had seen the comet in 1910.

My tired eyes focused through one of the telescopes that the astronomers aimed at the celestial phenomenon. *I see it, I see it! Halley's Comet!*

It looked like a big, fuzzy star wearing a dunce cap—not at all what I imagined—nothing like the images in astronomy books. There was no long curving tail, no "Star of Bethlehem" head. Still, here was Halley's Comet zooming past our little planet Earth, back for a brief time from its seventy-six-year Mobius strip journey. In awe, I imagined where this comet had been, what it had seen, and where it was going.

The frail, elderly woman who was seeing the comet for the second time, broke into tears. In a halting voice, she described to the assembled comet-gazers how her father had awakened her in the middle of the night, bundled her up, and carried her out into the cold Nebraska prairie to show her the comet.

"He held me in his arms and pointed to the comet and…" she said, pausing. I held my breath.

"He said, 'Remember this night, Little One, and…'"

Her voice became a whisper. No one stirred or coughed.

"'Be a good girl and take good care of yourself and…you might get to see this comet again.'"

And she did.

Mesmerized, I raised my gaze to the sky, to the stars, to the fuzzy comet phenomenon and to the vastness of all my human eyes could see, knowing that beyond the beyond there was more and more and more still unseen. I held the small hand of this once-little prairie girl who, in 1910, was encouraged and inspired by a thoughtful parent to travel carefully and wisely through seven decades to reach this magical long-held goal. And in 1986, somewhere in the vast Pacific Ocean, I watched as she cast her gentle eighty-one-year-old eyes skyward and beheld her father's timeless gift again.

The next day, heavy clouds blanketed the South Pacific—and the next day, and the next. There were no more opportunities to see Halley's Comet on that South Pacific cruise.

Life admits not of delays; when pleasure can be had, it is fit to catch it.

–Samuel Johnson

Another Escape and Escapade

Not too long ago, with barely enough denial energy to keep my recurring financial disappointments and existential loneliness (more or less) at bay, and with signs of the (personally) dreaded Hallowe'en season on every corner, I decided to escape from true money woes and false cheerfulness and go on a solo road trip.

I planned no plan—just drive somewhere, anywhere, and lose myself in an unfamiliar location. In the solitude of my car, I'd listen to Eminem, or Queen, or Carole King. Or the conversations in my wandering mind. Or to the sound of silence.

I would mask out all the resident problems if they refused to stay home. I chose a Deep South drive-about: Texas, Louisiana, Arkansas, Mississippi, Alabama. To give the road trip a theme, I planned to offer printed "Wonder postcards" to people I met along the way. I affixed to each postcard a pretty stamp and the mailing address of my recently created Wonder Institute. On the verso were the words "I wonder…" with plenty of space to write. I would invite random people to accept a card and, when they had a private moment or two, write whatever they wondered about and drop the postcard in a convenient mailbox.

I didn't ask for names and addresses, or religious affiliations, or political preferences. I didn't want to know how old the participants were, or whether they smoked, or what kind of car they drove, or if they were married, divorced, or single, or even if they rented or owned their home. I just wanted to know what they wondered about. The responses would be posted on my website.

The first day, as I drove southeast on my way to nowhere in particular, my mind was empty and full. Ideas, memories, and discoveries floated across my consciousness in a delightfully random fashion. I hit the delete button on business concerns and trick-or-treats in favor of dreams of past and future travel destinations. With each mile, I felt more relaxed, relieved, and unburdened. The Dixie Chicks kept me company as I settled into travel mode. Yes, I, too, was taking "The Long Way Around." That seems to be my way: the long way. I might settle down someday, but not now. Now, I'm traveling the long way to somewhere.

In Corsicana, Texas, on Day Two, a funky-looking café just off the main street looked like a great place to take a break from the road. I strolled through its tunnel-like cellar of dark and gloomy rooms. Customers lounged in corners against the rock walls, reading, writing, and chatting. Two women in flowered dresses huddled in a nook, knitted, and whispered. I browsed through old yard-sale books and out-of-date magazines scattered across a wobbly late-Victorian table.

"A low-fat latte," I said, striking up a conversation with the friendly barista, owner of the café. I showed him the Wonder postcards, which triggered a brief conversation about Corsicana and the probable, or possible, wonderings of its population.

"You can leave a few of those on the counter, by the jar of chocolate chip cookies." I thanked him and took my latte into the back room, settled into an old, overstuffed chair upholstered in worn, green, cut velvet, and wrote in a little blue journal.

It's good to be gone—to be where no one can find me—where whatever is going on at home is off my itinerary, off my plate, and out of my mind. If something is amiss back in my everyday life—and it very well might be—it will have to right itself, or solve itself, without me. Someone else will have to deal with it. Maybe it's irresponsible to disappear like this. Maybe, but I reframe this absence from all home and work life as necessary to my personal welfare. Essential. This is how I stay healthy and balanced. This is where I figure things out. Here, in a private nowhere between two somewheres. My Subaru waits outside with Chet Baker, Leonard Cohen, and other remarkable, spirit-comforting music friends who have been entertaining me for years. Soothing me, restoring my soul. The voice and words of Amy Winehouse waft through me: "They tried to make me go to rehab...."

Two days past Corsicana, I drove into deserted-looking Pass Christian, Mississippi, cruised along the gulf road, and up and down a few streets in search of a motel or a guest house where I might spend a night or two. It was not long after hurricane season, and everything seemed closed for repair, or for the season, or for forever.

In the middle of a block of neat ranch houses, an elderly man in a red plaid bathrobe stood in his driveway. I parked in front of his house, grabbed a Wonder postcard, and walked toward him. He looked startled and perplexed as he watched me approach. I paused on the sidewalk.

"Good afternoon, sir. Could you please tell me where I might find a motel or guest house?"

"What?" he barked.

"I'm looking for someplace to spend the night. A motel? Is there one nearby?" I smiled in a polite and friendly way.

His stern face softened a bit as he shouted, "I'm deaf. Come closer so I can hear you."

I moved closer. In a few words, I mentioned The Wonder Institute and my Postcard Project. I handed him a postcard. He studied it closely, then turned to me with powerful, glassy eyes.

"You want to know what I wonder about?"

I nodded.

"I'll tell you what I wonder about." He took a slow, deep breath, turned his head a bit, and squinted into a private middle distance. I followed his gaze, but where his focus was, I could not see.

"I wonder about my wife. That's what I wonder about. I wonder what she's thinking. She has Alzheimer's. I had to put her in a long-term care place."

His face quivered, and he swallowed hard several times. I waited, perfectly still, and stared at the pattern of his plaid bathrobe, at the left shoulder where the lines didn't align.

"Every day I visit her," he said. "Every day I take her ice cream. My wife loves ice cream. She always loved ice cream. And every day she asks me, 'Who are you?' And I tell her, 'I'm your husband, dear. We have three children together.' Then she smiles at me and eats the ice cream. She loves ice cream."

He closed his eyes and shuffled his slippered feet.

"She is still so beautiful to me. You know, she was a Mardi Gras Queen for two years in a row." Silence. "Do you want to come inside? I'll show you her picture and…Would you like a cold root beer?"

"Yes. Thank you."

A large photograph of his Mississippi beauty queen, in her satiny full-length gown and sparkling tiara, graced the wall across from the front door of his very neat living room. I admired the picture effusively and sat on the brown Early American sofa. He excused himself to retrieve two hearing aids from another room, then padded into the kitchen for two icy bottles of root beer.

Once settled on the ladderback chair across from me, he began to recount the high points of his ordinary and extraordinary life. He started with his boyhood in Pass Christian and then his years in the Army during the Second World War and how he attended college on the G.I. Bill.

He paused, bowed his head, and took a slow sideways glance at the picture of his Mardi Gras Queen. He spoke to a motionless audience of two—his wife's portrait and me.

Through starts and stops, he mentioned teaching high school and becoming the principal of the school that gave him his basic education. He spoke about the joy of meeting and marrying his beautiful wife. He looked at me, then turned to look again at his beloved beauty queen.

"I'm ninety-four. I have a nice house, three grown children, some grand-kids…." He stopped and bowed his head. We sipped our root beers in frozen silence.

Everything this lonely husband had wanted to say, he had said. A self-conscious stillness moved me to stand. I put the half-finished bottle of root beer on the cork coaster on the coffee table.

"I'm very glad to meet you," he said, taking my hand in both of his. "I'll fill out your wondering card." His eyes glistened with memories. I felt the hot sting of my own tears as I gathered his stories into my heart. My throat closed.

"Thank you for the root beer and, most especially, for telling me about your wife."

"I miss her. I visit her every day. In my eyes, she is still the most beautiful woman in the world. She doesn't recognize me anymore, after all our years together and our children. She doesn't even remember that she has children. She does love the ice cream I take her…."

I walked down the driveway very slowly. When I reached my car, I turned and looked back at his house and saw a lonely ninety-four-year-old man in a plaid bathrobe, standing in the doorway of his life.

As I put the key in the ignition, I spoke to the woman in the rearview mirror with the aging, tear-streaked face. "Hello there, my friend. Let's keep driving for a while; let's drive to Alabama."

I punched the button for the CD player.

"Hello, darkness, my old friend…."

I never received a Wonder postcard from Pass Christian.

My Brother: Seeds and Pollen of a Priest

The morning before Thanksgiving 2004 was unusually overcast for New Mexico fall. I had just started a fire in the kitchen wood stove and was feeding my dog and cats when I heard a car door close outside my Galisteo house. From the window, I watched my son, Rocky, walking across the courtyard. Even with his head low, I could see his sullen face. We met at the door.

"Your brother died." Those few words, and then a long, silent embrace.

"Your sister's been trying to reach you since last night. The phone lines are down in this part of the county."

My brother is dead.

The cells in my body gushed with unfamiliar physical sensations and difficult emotions. I felt dizzy and confused and remorseful and relieved. I hardly knew him, didn't like him, never trusted him. Now he was dead. The end. Not the end.

Stanwood Eugene Graves II and I disagreed on almost everything: religion, politics, music, family. We were the unacknowledged alpha and omega of the Graves Family. He was mysterious, controversial, manipulative, powerful, confused. He called me mysterious, controversial, manipulative, powerful, confused. He never leveled with me about his lies, secrets, and obsessions, much less his fears and dreams. Now, I would never know him.

By the time I turned ten, Stan was an Army enlisted man on active duty in Korea. That's where he met the Archbishop of Canterbury, and that's when he decided to become a priest. After a general discharge, he enrolled in college, met a nice Tennessee debutante named Sandy, graduated, and entered the seminary.

When he was ordained deacon, he and Sandy married. It was an old-fashioned Southern wedding. Sandy joined Stan at the altar in virgin white satin with an antique lace veil from the antebellum attic of an antique cousin. Bridesmaids in lavender organdy dresses and sunbonnets carried beribboned bouquets of lilies of the valley. Guests sipped mint juleps in sterling silver cups. White-linen-covered tables displayed lovely presents from well-wishing friends and family:

Waterford crystal goblets; an ornate sterling silver tea service; an equally ornate silver ice bucket; flowery bone china place settings with matching gravy boat and soup tureen; and a plethora of genteel gifts traditionally presented to bright, conservative couples about to embark on happily-ever-after marriages.

Within two years, Stan abandoned the Episcopal Church and its (initially) supportive congregation. The official story was that the Church excommunicated him for his outspoken—some said violent—opposition to the ordination of women and changes in the liturgy. Father Graves found sanctuary as an Anglican priest in the Church of England, assigned to a parish in Clarence Town, Long Island, Bahamas. He and Sandy moved their Victorian furniture, crystal, fine wedding silver, and linens to a small rectory on a low hill overlooking the Atlantic Ocean.

In 1971, my husband, Bart, and I visited Sandy and Stan and their tropical congregation. My brother renamed himself "Father Michael," in homage to his favorite angel. Parishioners called Sandy "the Father's wife."

One balmy evening, when the men were "up island," Sandy and I sat on the rectory porch, lingering over a casual dinner of conch fritters, coleslaw, and chilled white wine. Sandy seemed uncomfortable, distracted. She kept twisting a dainty flowered handkerchief around her wedding ring finger and staring beyond me at the tamarisk tree.

"I...uh...um...your brother and I..."

She picked up her wine glass and held it close to her lips as if to silence the words before she could speak them. *Were she and my brother getting divorced?* I said nothing.

"He and I have...we...uh...well...we..."

"Yes, you and he have...?" I coaxed.

"He and I have never consummated our marriage." *How strange that Sandy never referred to my brother by name.*

"What? You just said you and Stan never consummated your marriage?"

"That's right."

"But I don't understand, Sandy. You've been married for years. How can that be?"

"Well," she hesitated and sighed heavily. "On our wedding night, we were so tired, we just went to sleep. The next night we were traveling, and...well, the night after that, I asked him when we were going to...uh, make love. And...well, he turned away and told me, 'You just have a fairy tale idea of what marriage is about.' Then he told me never to mention the subject ever again...and I didn't."

"Never?"

"Never."

"But, Sandy, didn't you have some idea of this before you were married? I mean, you were together for five years before the wedding."

"I know," she said in her soft, sugary drawl. "I just thought he was a gentleman. I thought he was being polite, respectful. Don't say anything. Please. Not ever."

Two years after her confession, my innocent Christian, Southern Belle sister-in-law was diagnosed with uterine cancer. She died. Everyone who knew her was devastated. My brother was inconsolable. Her secret and the tragic irony weighed on me. She couldn't grow a baby. Instead, she grew an inoperable tumor.

Not long after Sandy's death, Stan abandoned the Anglican Church, became a Greek Orthodox priest, and relocated to Haiti. He was no longer Father Graves, no longer Father Michael. He became Pére Michel, a self-described servant of God. He lived in Haiti for eighteen years and devoted himself to various good works and semi-Godlike enterprises. He became both a beloved and detested spiritual leader with a flock of followers and a gang of detractors. He built a chapel, a school, and a clinic in the picturesque mountain town of Pétion-Ville, a suburb of Port-au-Prince.

He turned the rectory compound into a haven for young homeless boys—at least, that's what we read in the monthly newsletters he wrote in which he implored his readers and stateside followers to send money for the poor and hungry orphans. From time to time, I did.

My brother was a paradoxical man: sinner/saint, greedy/generous, nice/nasty, intelligent/ignorant. Strange that news of his death brought him more alive to me than he had been for years. Père Michel, the larger-than-life orthodox paradox, was dead on the island of Hispaniola. I made arrangements to fly to "La Perle des Antilles."

On Thanksgiving Day, I met my sister in Fort Lauderdale, and we gave thanks for a steam table turkey dinner in the lobby of a travelers' hotel. The next morning, we caught a flight to Port-au-Prince to claim the brother we could not know: Stanwood, Stan, Father Graves, Father Michael, Père Michel?

I had been to Haiti several times in the quite-distant past—even before my brother moved there to carve out his priestly life in the hills above the capital. I loved the Haitian culture—so rich, and yet so impoverished, so magical, and yet so bedeviled by nature and the wretched neglect of her neighbors. I vividly remembered riding deep into the countryside on a colorful "tap-tap" to meet a group of underground revolutionaries and drink homemade wine from a shared bottle. I remembered hiking to the top of the Citadel in Cap-Haïtien where, long ago, "brave men served their country well," as Harry Belafonte's old song told us.

In 1984, I traveled to Haiti to experience "Haitian Defile Kanaval" with its Mardi Gras parades, feasts, lavish costumes, music, and days and nights of dancing frenzy. I joined hundreds of university students in a noisy drumming march through the dark streets of Port-au-Prince. It was well past midnight when I returned to the hotel and fell asleep under the spell of the intoxicating rhythm that altered the beat of my heart.

The next morning, the spell continued as I became an entranced spectator at the Shrove Tuesday Carnival parade. I stood and shouted and clapped with the crowd as the wild floats, colorfully costumed groups, stilt-walkers, and giggling schoolchildren moved to the music of popular Haitian bands: Scorpio, DP Express.

Late that afternoon, I accepted an artist's invitation to experience a real cockfight deep in the mountainous countryside near his home in Jacmel. Behind the makeshift arena, a group of women cooked smoke-scented Haitian food on open fires. Inside the fight pit, men drank, made bets, and strutted around with their cocks. I witnessed very little fighting—mainly flying feathers and ear-piercing squawks.

In the middle of the night, sharp back pain woke me: probably a pinched nerve from the twisting and turning of the day's adventures. Sitting and lying down were excruciating. Moving helped. I considered cutting my trip short and flying to Florida for medical relief.

Instead, I delayed that plan in favor of a hike through the enormous Port-au-Prince cemetery with a befriended taxi driver. We walked along dusty dirt paths, past open concrete tombs where families rented space to place the bodies of their recently deceased relatives. Once the corpse had been reduced to bones by rats and birds and atmosphere, the family would remove the bones, and the tomb would be rented again to other relatives of a newly dearly departed. Rats as big as cats scrambled from behind tombstones and scurried across untended paths of rocks, papers, weeds, and containers filled with flowers, some as dead as the person they had been placed there to honor.

After an hour of wandering through the city of the dead, we came upon a solitary Voodoo priest. He was performing a private incantation in front of a tall obelisk honoring Baron Samedi, an important Haitian spirit, an intermediary between earthly life and God. We stood in silence and listened to his deep, low utterings. When he became aware of us, he mumbled something to the taxi driver in the local patois. He offered to contact a dead relative of mine.

"You must tell him the name of your dead relative, and you must pay him," the driver instructed. I gave the priest a handful of money and asked to have the blessing directed to my paternal Grandmother Graves, a stately, late-Victorian woman with a wicked sense of humor. "Bertha May Treat," I said. Her birth name always sounded like a short and generous declarative sentence. She would surely appreciate a call from Haiti. The Voodoo priest instructed us to close our eyes, and he began a raspy chant. I thought it would do no harm—through the good offices of Baron Samedi and the kindness of this representative—to tack on an additional spontaneous request.

"Would you please remove this back pain?" I asked in silence as the incantation continued.

The taxi driver translated the priest's words. It was comforting to learn that my late and truly great Grandmother Graves was able to assure me of a long life from her unknown location in the Beyond. The priest told us that she laughed when she learned that her favorite granddaughter was in a cemetery in Haiti, hanging out with a Voodoo priest. Just like her. Good to know there was laughter in the hereafter. When the chants were over, we retreated through the cemetery the way we had entered. My back pain was somewhere behind me. It was gone.

Early accounts indicated that my brother had been murdered. Poisoned. Voodoo. Facts were fuzzy and destined to remain fuzzy—like the facts of his mysterious life.

The year before Stan died, he told the family that he had been interviewed by some men from the CIA regarding his association with former President Aristide, with whom he professed to have had a close friendship. Several U.S. officials took him to dinner at an upscale restaurant in Pétion-Ville and drugged him. He awoke the next morning, naked, in a strange hotel room, with the door locked from the outside. My brother was frequently a magnet for strange encounters. Maybe it was a CIA plot. Or maybe it was a prelude of what was to come.

I'm in Pétion-Ville with my sister. We are here to comfort the grieving and the aggrieved, to assuage the angry, the manipulative, the confused, the sinister, the misinformed, the greedy, the destitute, the deceivers, and the deceived.... There are tangled webs to unweave, bank accounts and documents to uncover, rents to pay (if any money can be found). In a locked closet, we found dozens of religious icons and hundreds of ornate vestments. What shall we do with them? And what about the poor homeless "boys"? It is clear that the fifteen or more homeless and hungry "boys" in the compound are not boys…. They're men—big men—in their twenties and thirties. Under the dark and evil influence of Rosemont, a suspicious-acting man of great size and mystery, these "boys" have stolen my brother's cash, vehicle, and pet beagle, as well as some of his correspondences and documents. They have trashed the rectory. They have threatened Father Randall, the priest from Port-au-Prince who assisted my sister and me. He has fled back to the capital. We are in danger. The landlady hired private armed guards to protect the houses in the compound from Rosemont. The private guards are afraid. They told us, "When our bullets are gone, we're dead." The police cannot help. They are totally corrupt. I arrived here with an open and generous heart—with every intention of solving problems, comforting those who were saddened by the loss of Père Michel—their protector and teacher. I can comfort no one. There is no way to solve all the issues and accusations that are hurled at me. I am his sister, but I hardly knew him. Among his many documents, my sister and I found incriminating notes and letters, and we are removing them. Stan was smart, corrupt, and disturbed…a closet homosexual and most probably a lifelong pedophile….Sad word "pedophile."

Here he is, my big brother, lying on a slab in a small stone cell in the subterranean mortuary in downtown Port-au-Prince. I am standing by his head while a Matron and the Deacon from the church wash and dress his body. I look away when they uncover his nakedness to pull on his underpants. I am very still. I study his face—all composed and serene and at peace with his secrets. I touch his silvery hair….It is very soft.

—Journal, December 2004

Tropical Reflections

Bart, the children, and I are spending a few months in Clarence Town, Long Island, one of the Out Islands in the Bahamas, where we own a small and totally unpretentious house. By unpretentious, I mean no electricity, no telephone, no running water. Behind the house, there is a shallow brackish-water well, and beyond that a dilapidated outhouse. Inside our little island cabana, there are three small rooms separated by turquoise-painted tongue-and-groove walls that have been eaten by termites and then abandoned so that there is almost more paint than wood on the partitions that do not go all the way to the ceiling. There is a sitting area with a table and a few mismatched chairs and a narrow corridor barely big enough to accommodate two canvas camp cots for the children.

The third section of our island habitat functions as a combination kitchen/master bed-room. The rickety double bed takes up half the room. A red kerosene-fueled refrigerator (a luxury, to be sure) and a counter with a two-burner gas stove and a makeshift plastic sink complete the household amenities. The real amenities are the ocean and the birds and the fish and the fruit and the Bahamian people.

Our closest neighbor is Euterpie Straughn. Born on this undeveloped island, she's lived in the same one-room cottage as far back as she can remember. She doesn't know her exact age. She must be at least seventy, which seems ancient to me. Euterpie spends every day singing unfamiliar or made-up church songs in her loud, monotonous, off-key voice as she plaits sheaves of straw into long thin strips. She sells these to the mailboat captain who, in turn, sells them to women in Nassau, who fashion the straw strips into tourist-favored handbags and hats. I love to visit Euterpie and listen while she shares her songs and thoughts about whatever is on her mind. Mostly, she talks about Jesus.

"Jesus, He my friend. He comin' to get me one day. Ye'as, tha's right. He gone come an take me straight up to heaven." And she laughs an unselfconscious belly laugh.

Euterpie also likes to talk about Nassau, which she has visited twice in her life.

"In Nassau, they got lights stay on all night. Tha's right, all night long—eight o'clock, nine o'clock—all night." With a tone of incredulity, she adds, "and they got a store sells nuthin' but shoes. Shoes, shoes. Tha's right. Nuthin' but shoes."

She laughs some more—a loud, happy, infectious laugh.

Her third favorite topic is her health.

"Oh, I'm feelin' poorly this mornin'."

"Really, 'Terpie, what's wrong?"

"Oh, I got the wind and the gas."

"The wind and the gas? Oh, my."

"Tha's right. Wouldn't be so bad if I had the wind on the bottom and the gas on top… but I got the gas on the bottom and the wind on top…and ooh-eee…I feel mighty, mighty baaad! Uh, huh."

I'm sitting on the floor of her tiny house, watching her hands twist strands of straw into flat braids, when she starts a sentence with her frequent prelude to something prophetic.

"Mmm-hmm, all right, I tell you. If you got good manners, uh-huh, ain't no place you can't go. Yes ma'am, good manners…they gonna carry you all over the world. All over. That's right. Nassau, Baltimore…all over. Ain't no place you can't go if you got good manners. Yes, ma'am, uh-huh."

Then she sings to me—a song she made up about Jesus.

During one of our long stays in the Bahamas, two-and-a-half-year-old Daisy was not feeling well. She was listless, didn't want to play, and didn't want me to read to her. She just wanted to sleep. Her fever frightened me. Loquacious and irrepressible Daisy wasn't talking. The only doctor on the island, a British expat, was in Stella Maris, almost a hundred miles away. Via "the jungle telegraph," the constable contacted him.

When he arrived, Daisy was lying on her little cot, not moving, not responding, not even when he peered down at her with his big glasses and stranger face. He was definitely concerned.

"Does she have a hearing problem?"

"No," I said. "No, she's perfect." I thought I might faint. I stood by the red refrigerator and bargained with God.

"If you just let her live, God, I'll spend the rest of my life taking care of her, reading to her….I won't ask for anything else, ever, ever, until the end of time. Please, please, let my precious daughter be okay."

"She's severely dehydrated," the doctor said and prescribed a carbonated drink.

Dehydration? An inexperienced mother, I was unaware of the dangers. Daisy drank a sugary 7-Up and almost immediately began to recover. She wasn't going to die. She wasn't deaf. She was my precious and healthy little girl. *Thank you, God.*

For years, I read to her almost every day. And I took excellent care of her— though not to the exclusion of the rest of my life, my other life, my "What's it all about/Who am I/How do I look?" life. And, of course, I did make other emergency requests of God. So, in addition to letting God down, I let Daisy down.

Once, teenage Daisy hurled an ugly epithet my way.

"You're the Queen of All Narcissists," she said with a look that speared me as deeply as her words.

First, I cried—which probably lent credibility to her point of view. Then, I made a joke, acknowledging, "Perhaps I might be a Princess of Narcissism or a Narcissistic Lady-in-Waiting, but surely not the Queen, not the Queen of All Narcissists! I have no way to quantify my position in the League of Royal Narcissists. Unquestionably, I've a place on that list!"

For most of my life, I've been oblivious to the extent of my nar…narcis… narcissm…my brain and fingers have trouble even spelling it: narcissism. There it is. Narcissism. Melville regarded it as "the image of the ungraspable phantom of life." I acknowledged Melville's insight and took the Mayo Clinic's Narcissistic Behavioral Disorder test online. I scored twenty. Not over the top, but too high for one who would aspire to an NBD rating of eleven—or possibly twelve. My therapist told me that I'm an "enlightened narcissist." That helped. I reflected. Cracked mirrors. Smoky mirrors. I rejected my reflection.

Eventually, I realized that my uncomfortable conflict with Daisy was less about her few hurtful words and more about some inadequately explored or unresolved conflicts with myself. Although I set out to be the kind of mother I would have chosen for myself, I may not have been the kind of mother my children would have chosen—or dreamed of having—"if wishes were horses."

I bonded with my unborn babies from their first life-affirming kicks. The bonds stayed strong through all the stings and barbs we weathered together during the years that I nurtured them, molded them, and they molded me. It may not have looked or felt like "enough" to them, but it was everything I had, everything I had to give.

In the trusty vault that holds my fragile, irregularly pumping heart, I harbor a collection of insecurities about my parenting shortcomings. I close my eyes against a fear that I might become no more than an unhinged appendix, drifting at the periphery of my children's lives.

I'm an unfinished woman living in a world of doubt, and yet…*dubito ergo sum!*

Perhaps I read Descartes and the existentialists too early. And, perhaps, I didn't understand them. Are my calls to God antithetical? Can an off-and-on atheist call upon God for aid and comfort and expect to get either? Is "atheist" just a fallback position for a self-conscious intellectual who can't solve for G = T? (God = Truth.) For much of my life, I embraced the belief that I was and am alone; that my essence came from nowhere.

But where is nowhere? I find myself deposited on this strange yet familiar earth with the not-so-simple task of figuring things out for myself. Whom can I count on if not myself? God? I've long wondered if I've been talking and praying to a made-up notion of what God might be.

I listen. I interpret signs. I think of the ravens.

That unfettered narcissism, propelled by my relentless search for an unknowable, yet inevitable destiny, lured me away from safe choices toward chance encounters with Life's offerings and awakened and sharpened my creative problem-solving sense. It catapulted me into near and far arcs in the world. It altered our family life and created chaos and heartbreak. I want and need to believe that my thoughtful or impulsive choices also created opportunity, strength, and the seemingly contradictory interdependent independence in all of us.

I've continued to build a road toward that inevitable destiny. I'm going for it, whatever "it" is. Where there's a will, I reason, there's an inheritance. That inheritance must be the "Now."

As for me, I am tormented with an everlasting itch for things remote. I love to sail forbidden seas, and land on barbarous coasts.

Herman Melville, *Moby Dick*

Carousel and Carousels of Courage

A layer of loneliness and anxiety is washing over my usual sense of optimism and fearlessness this morning. My "I can handle it" bravado is yielding to a wave of reluctant depression. I am continuing to struggle to keep my public head high by wrapping myself in an everything-is-OK cover-up. I smile. I direct my attention to the needs of others. Some days nothing erases that free-floating anxiety, that depression. Hugging my dog helps—but only for a minute. I make my bed. I read my emails. I take some deep breaths....

–Journal entry, 2013

This April day, I linger in a particularly dejected and disconnected mood. I brew a cup of tea and sip it, watching the clouds outside the kitchen window turn from sheep to wolves, from rabbits to rowboats. As my afternoon of free-floating ennui wanes, I teeter on despair before a wall of books, searching for an uplifting memoir or a collection of essays to raise my spirits and resurrect my hibernating sense of optimism: writings by or about mystics, perhaps. Or poems by Wisława Szymborska, Pablo Neruda, or Mary Oliver. Or, maybe, a few passages from a favorite French novel.

Instead, I turn on the television. Just for a minute. Maybe I can catch up on the depressing news to remind me that there but for the grace of God—or whomever, whatever—go I. I'm not expecting anything. I've become uncomfortably comfortable in my drifting, low-energy place. This, too, will pass. What's the rush?

By accident (or is it?), the remote-control lands on Channel 2: The New York Philharmonic Orchestra, Live from Lincoln Center. Rodgers and Hammerstein's magical musical *Carousel* is just beginning. It is the beginning of a small, personal miracle.

Oscar Hammerstein, who wrote the lyrics to Richard Rodgers' beautiful score for this 1940s Broadway show, has been my special mentor and angel since I was a teenager and an inspiration for all the decades that followed. His wisdom and philosophy remain a subtle presence in the "backlot" of my life's play.

I fall into its romantic spell. "If I loved you, time and again I would try to say..." And Billy Bigelow's remarkable soliloquy: "My boy Bill...my little girl..."

I first saw *Carousel* when I was fifteen, while working as a wardrobe apprentice at the Camden County Music Fair, a professional summer stock theatre in New Jersey. At the end of every performance, I sat in the dark, at the back of the theatre-in-the-round tent, and cried—not just because Billy Bigelow dies, or because in the afterlife he redeems himself, or because his spirit gives encouragement to the daughter he never got to meet on Earth, but because the unfolding of a parent's soulful redemption is so painfully beautiful. *Carousel* gave me hope and courage then. It gives me hope and courage today... to walk on, to have my dreams tossed and blown, to walk alone or never to walk alone....

A framed letter from Oscar Hammerstein hangs on a wall in my house. Mr. Hammerstein wrote it about me in 1960. It is a letter of recommendation to Boston University. He wrote:

> *I do not know this girl very well, but I have seen her in action, and I have had reports on her from people who have worked in the same companies. The theatre is a place not only for dreamers but for people tough enough to translate their dreams into practical achievement. I have a strong feeling that this girl is made of the right stuff for the theatre.*

This most remarkable, gentle humanitarian, a giant in the world of literature and theatre, not only took the time to respond to my request for a reference but he also had recalled that summer encounter with a stage-struck, earnest teenager who he believed had "the right stuff for the theatre."

I imagined myself on a brightly painted carousel horse, or on a silver and gold unicorn, riding around and around on a Mobius strip, looking.

Maybe courage is a gift. Maybe it's a muscle that one can develop. Maybe courage comes from Angels. Or maybe Angels are a gift that comes with courage. I hope so.

—Journal entry

Bunny Clouds

My friend Norma Cross called to tell me that our mutual friend Bunny Conlon, who was in a small residential home for people with Alzheimer's, Parkinson's, or dementia, was "fading fast." I knew what "fading fast" meant. It meant that Bunny was going to die soon. I visited her the next day.

The receptionist on duty buzzes me in and escorts me through a labyrinth of narrow halls to Bunny's room, a cell-like space with a single bed, a small chair, and a bedside table. A glamorous photograph of Bunny's mother, taken in the forties, I assume, hangs high on a wall by the door.

Bunny struggles to sit up. She seems barely aware of me. I perch on the edge of the bed and put my arms around her frail body. I stroke her hair. I search my memory and use my best concentration skills to superimpose the beautiful woman that Bunny had been over the fragile, gray form in my arms. Bunny was always enviably thin, tall, and graceful, and I want to add "willowy," because willowy is such a wonderful word that perfectly describes this remarkable woman I met more than forty years ago.

While I hold my disappearing friend and gently rock her, she mumbles words I cannot understand in a calm and faraway voice. She responds with garbled syllables to my impromptu monologue of stories from our long social and business history together: tales of the artists we have loved and the lovers we have shared. I feel her relax in my arms. I compliment her emerald-green shirt that complements her moss-green eyes—eyes that are focused far beyond the small room in which we sit and slowly rock.

Years disappeared in a flash. They collapsed into incidents: parties, people, conversations, places....Even long, full years of friendship collapsed into imperfect memories that appeared and faded. It's not possible to stretch out memories into real time. So much real time has gone.

Bunny and I were confidantes and colleagues in the Santa Fe art-gallery world. Long before our gallery years, we were part of the big escape from conventional life that brought so many of us to the mountains and high desert of New Mexico in the sixties and seventies. We came from all over, and we knew one another by first names or nicknames. Bunny and I must have met at one of the big, informal bring-a-dish gatherings, where there was always plenty of pot, too many watermelons, and not enough homemade banana nut bread. And there was always music. Lots and lots of music.

Bunny, a stunning widow, lived with her young son in the remote, rugged, not-too-friendly-to-outsiders mountain village of Truchas along the High Road to Taos. I was an ex-glamour girl from New York who lived off the grid with my scientist husband and two toddlers in a hand-built house on a rough expanse of desert and sandstone south of Santa Fe.

Most of the people we knew in those long-ago days were some combination of misfit, adventurer, hippie, anthropologist, artist, drifter, and draft-dodger. Many of us had abandoned—or narrowly escaped—the middle-class lives of our parents when we gravitated to "the Land of Enchantment" in search of aspects of ourselves that couldn't swim in the mainstream.

As the free-spirit years passed, and our children became adults, and the world changed, we changed. We got straight jobs; we went back to graduate school; we moved away; we died. Before we ever thought about dying, we lived, we laughed, we made love.

Bunny and I loved artists, perhaps even more than we loved art. We discovered ourselves and our abiding passions at right and wrong places, in right and wrong times. We created galleries where people came and drank our wine and looked at our exhibitions and bought the paintings, drawings, and sculptures we showed. We did this way before most everyone who does it now did it. And now we don't do it anymore. Now, what do we do?

Bunny is drifting, dreaming, sliding through her last days. Attendants in red attendant uniforms lift her into a wheelchair, put her feet into rubber slippers, straighten her legs. I wheel her down the narrow hallways and into the dayroom, where two residents ("We don't call them 'residents' here," a supervisor corrected. "We call them 'elders'; it's more respectful."), excuse me, where two elders are sitting in front of a big-screen TV, singing along with a sing-along DVD, "...just direct your feet to the sunny side of the street...." We claim a position near the big picture window and look out at the blue sky and the clouds.

"Clouds," Bunny whispers. I think that's what she says. I hold a straw and a glass of juice to her lips. She takes a sip. I take her hand, and we look out the window past the gated pen with two little goats eating something out of a red metal bucket, past the fence, past the parking lot, past the...

"Clouds," she says again, softly.

But Bunny didn't "fade fast." She retreated into a faraway place for more than a year. Her strong heart kept beating and beating. Toward the end of her breathing days, her son and his compassionate girlfriend moved her into their home. With love and gentleness, they fed her and turned her and bathed her until she was gone.

The last time I visited her, she was propped up in a proper hospital chair, holding a small stuffed bunny, staring at a TV animal documentary with the sound turned off. I held her soft hand and sang to her, and to myself. I sang about finding ourselves in times of trouble and Mother Mary comes—to comfort, "speaking words of wisdom." Then I closed my eyes and felt the soulfulness of life and...

Let it be.

Rick Dillingham in his studio, 1987
© HERBERT LOTZ / NEW MEXICO HISTORY MUSEUM-PALACE OF THE GOVERNORS

Limitlessness

My friends are dying. We're coming of age: The Age of Dying. I know I'm going to die at some point, and I can't begin to understand that phenomenon. I take a break to reread Philip Larkin's haunting poem "Aubade." Years ago, I memorized it so I could recite it to a friend who mailed it to me along with a hastily scrawled note, "I can't imagine the world without this poem." Now, neither can I.

> …Unresting death, a whole day nearer now,
> Making all thought impossible but how
> And where and when I shall myself die.
> Arid interrogation: yet the dread
> Of dying, and being dead,
> Flashes afresh to hold and horrify….

It's natural that we lose one another, but it feels unnatural. We lose people through neglect, preoccupation, misunderstanding, accident, and relocation. We lose track, direction, interest, and control while we're running, slogging, skipping, crawling, and bounding through days and decades. We find time, opportunity, inspiration. We find things we've lost. And we lose things we can never find again. Times change, and time changes us. Birth. Death. People die.

Here, in the friendship part of my life and heart, artists and writers and art collectors and gallery luminaries die.

One of the most tragic and untimely deaths during my thirty-three years as a gallerist was the death in 1994 of Rick Dillingham, a profoundly gifted ceramic sculptor whose work my gallery was honored to represent. AIDS killed Rick at the height of his career and at the height of the insidious pandemic—but not without a righteous fight. He battled AIDS for years, with courage, grace, style, and genius. Rick's death was a painful loss for so many in the art community. He was not only a highly accomplished artist and an excellent businessman, but also a remarkable scholar, a generous philanthropist, and an amazing friend. It's the friendship part that most defined him for me.

Among the hundreds of magnificent vessels that Rick made, his four black, cast bronze (not clay) AIDS gas cans with the slight silver leaf linings at the edges of the rims are most dear to my heart. He created them near the edge, the rim of his too-short life. They were neither easy artworks to love at first sight, nor were they easy to sell. The gas cans existed/exist on that thin but exquisite line between beautiful and ugly. They were and are simple and powerful, unbreakable, yet, to me, heartbreaking. I loved them then. I love them now. Most collectors coveted his elegant ceramic bowls and open vessels in bright oranges, reds, yellows, and golds rather than those dark, foreboding, yet strangely optimistic pieces.

During his final creative burst, Rick identified three big goals he wanted to achieve before he died. He wanted to fly to Europe on the Concorde. He did that. He wanted to ride his motorcycle to the Sturgis Rally in South Dakota. He did that with the help of a gravity-fed contraption attached to his bike that dripped his four-hour infusion of an HIV-fighting drug through an opening in his chest. His third wish was to hear Barbra Streisand sing at her New Year's Eve show in Las Vegas. He did that, too. And then he came home. And he went to bed. Not long after that, he died.

There was an amazing wake at his house. I arrived early to act as an informal host. Herb Lotz, a well-respected photographer and close friend of Rick's, greeted me. He put his arm around my shoulder and took me aside. I was shaky and full of tears. I knew that Rick's body was in the next room.

"Have you ever seen a dead body before?" Herb asked in a soft voice.

"Not for years." At that time, I had seen only two dead bodies: my Grandfather Graves, who died when I was nine, and a schoolmate who died of cancer when we were in the sixth grade.

"Well, he'll look a little different." Herb described what I would see when I entered Rick's bedroom.

"He's lying on his bed and…" I deeply appreciated his simple kindness.

Rick looked beautiful, peaceful. A few of his friends had dressed him in a blue and white kimono. They had covered the walls with white sheets and placed fresh boughs of evergreen around the room. Forest scents. The scent of nearby pueblo fires: Santa Clara, San Ildefonso, Cochiti…

I sensed Rick's presence—and his profound absence.

His final words were printed on a card placed at the foot of his bed.

this plane is singularly
the worst piece of shit with
all of the yayas
and bimbo parties with
no warning for us

so, get another ticket.

I want to go
into
the
water.

–Rick Dillingham, 1/16/94

All stories, if continued far enough, end in death, and he is no true-story teller who would keep that from you.

–Ernest Hemingway, *Death in the Afternoon*

Terry Lazin and the accidental iPhone photo of me, Santa Fe, 2014

My Opposite Twin

Terry Lazin and I met in the waning days of Linda Durham Contemporary Art—a bit before it was clear that the days of the gallery were, in fact, waning, and a bit before I knew that Terry was dying.

One morning, Tracey, my gallery director, took a call from Terry, who was inquiring about the paintings of James Havard, a prominent artist whose work we represented. Tracey handled the preliminary work of sending images of available paintings to Terry's home in Arizona. After a couple of telephone conversations, Terry's seemingly endless questions and protracted indecision annoyed her.

"That woman will never buy anything," she huffed.

On a quiet Saturday a few weeks later, when I was alone in the gallery, this woman, whom Tracey had dismissed as a waste of her time, appeared with two chic Italian friends. She looked incredibly stylish with her quite short hair, her casual yet elegant clothes, and her straight-forward and eager demeanor. I liked her instantly. She seemed to like me instantly as well. That afternoon she purchased two paintings.

A friendship began, one that quickly grew into a powerful bond between two women as different as there are ways to cubbyhole others. She—a wealthy, dog-obsessed Jewish Republican lawyer, and wildly successful business-woman—with Stage 4 ovarian cancer. Me—an almost-broke-with-serious-debt cat lover, unaffiliated with any religion, left of a Yellow-Dog Democrat, gallery owner sliding close to foreclosure—in excellent health. In other words, two quite diametrically opposed types of women—who adored one another. We called ourselves "The Opposite Twins."

Over time, Terry and I acknowledged that some of our opposites blurred. As I jumped the highest of my financial hurdles, I began to see I wouldn't lose my house. Grievously, it became ever clearer that Terry would lose her greatest treasure: her life.

Toward the end of her battle with cancer, Terry sent an open letter to close friends and family.

There are two days that no one gets to control—yesterday and tomorrow. One only has TODAY to take action, get involved, and make yourself and your actions matter. I don't fear dying."

As her Stage 4 cancer continued (there is no Stage 5), she wrote:

I am grasping onto life as hard as I can and squeezing every delicious drop out. I still believe that my cancer has brought me many more gifts than it ever could have taken away. Yes, indeed, I am a lucky girl and wouldn't trade places with anyone in the world for this exceptional journey. I'm happy, and I'll keep fighting for one more day. I love you all.

My overnight bag was packed and leaning against the front door. I was gulping the last of my latte, ready to jump into my trusty Outback and drive to Terry's side, when the phone rang.

That early spring day, so full of promise, Terry died in a luxurious hospice room that she had reserved months in advance, her three beloved dogs by her side. I loved knowing that the day before, Terry had a manicure, pedicure, facial, and Botox injections. Beautiful, completely splendid—for all tomorrows.

I drove to Scottsdale to attend the memorial service at a fancy resort hotel that, in the weeks before she died, Terry had directed and designed down to the last detail. Uplifting, contemporary music set the tone. Celebrators of her life gave eulogies; everyone clapped as Pharrell Williams sang what Terry knew so well: "Happiness is the truth." Wonderful episodes of Terry's remarkable life—as a lawyer, an event planner for the NFL, and founder of a no-kill dog shelter—flashed across an eight-foot screen.

Terry had even chosen the elegantly presented trays of lox, bagels, and fruit. Friends and family gathered in the lush garden, introduced themselves, hugged, shared stories, and sipped mimosas. I didn't know anyone, didn't feel like meeting anyone, or hugging anyone, or eating a bagel, or a peach.

I changed out of my simple black dress, checked out of my fancy room, and—without saying goodbye to anyone and without standing in line to sign the guestbook—I headed home.

In the emptiness of Arizona's beautiful, minimalist landscape, I pulled over and wept.

"Clap along…if you know…if you feel…if it's what you want to do…"

Much later, while deleting old or uninteresting images from my iPhone, I came across a most miraculous photograph. On a blustery afternoon, I had driven a very weak Terry to the Santa Fe Ski Basin. We stopped at a scenic overlook. Buffeted by fierce wind, I struggled to shoot a picture of Terry against that spectacular landscape and dropped my iPhone. As it fell, the shutter snapped.

An accidental shot, a throw-away image. I studied it. The photo that took itself captured the side of my head looking at the ground, my hair blowing, and Terry looking down at me. Celestial cumulus clouds with glowing edges filled much of the deep-blue sky behind her. It was as if Terry was looking down at me from Heaven, where she surely must be. I had the blurred photograph blown up and restored somewhat. It hangs in my dressing room, above my head—Terry, my Guardian Angel.

> …in the end, the most interesting people always leave.
>
> –Paul Coelo

Lessons for the Duration / for the Journey

GOOD INTENTION / BAD RESULT

Almost two decades into this new millennium, and through a fifty-year lens, I'm surveying the long-gone days of my unabashedly free-spirited life. I'm capturing a few salient points from the not fully assimilated lessons learned while traveling this winding road, replete with sex, drugs, and rock and roll. And, finding—even through loss—truth, beauty, and redemption. The shallowness and callowness of a maze of youthful choices and challenges neither shocks nor embarrasses me. I'm grateful for them.

The 1960s "Bunny Jill" is a shadow. Every now and then, her apparition appears and whispers gentle reminders of major or minor transformations, lest I forget. I admire the way that pre-woman lived in the city of her dreams, made enough money to pay for an apartment in Greenwich Village, buy new clothes, get her hair done, treat her friends to dinner, and take an occasional exotic vacation. And I like that she grew into a thoughtful, responsible (yet still wild and risk-taking) woman of the world. Early East Coast experiences collapsed over these decades into a few stories that continue to resonate.

I'm a daydreaming Day Bunny. At nineteen, I'm not old enough to serve liquor at the Club after 8 p.m. It's a municipal regulation of some kind. This is incredibly disappointing because it prevents me from participating in the sexy glamour of the Playboy night life.

On the rung of Playboy hierarchy, Day Bunnies are nearest the bottom, but I've adjusted and carved out a successful place for myself in the lunchtime and happy-hour shifts, serving cocktails and simple platters of roast beef or filet mignon to bankers and corporate businessmen, some of whom are generous, steady customers.

The arrangement leaves me footloose and fancy-free to socialize with my Bohemian friends in Lower Manhattan and Harlem's cafés, studios, and jazz clubs.

Five mornings a week, I take the subway to 60th Street and Fifth Avenue. I walk one block south past the Sherry-Netherland Hotel, turn east, stroll a few yards past the hotel's service entrance, and enter the Club at 5 East 59th Street.

A dreadfully disfigured man stands at the hotel's service door. Huge bumps the size of jawbreakers cover his face, neck, and hands. He has the kind of unfortunate face that would cause most anyone to turn away. The first time I see him, I turn away. And the second time, too. But the third time, a surge of compassion sweeps over me, and I turn, smile, and give in to the compulsive urge to blurt "Hello!" The next time, almost by instinct, I add a few more words—nothing much, nothing provocative, just a friendly "good morning, lovely day." In time, we exchange names.

Before long, Duncan knows my schedule and anticipates my daily, almost clockwork arrival around that corner. He is so pleased to see me and to exchange a cordial sentence or two. It feels good to offer a bit of warmth to someone most people avoid.

Craving a few days in the sun, I take a welcome break to Puerto Rico. When I return a week later and round the corner onto 59th Street, Duncan is there. As I approach, his once-frightening face explodes into a monstrous grin of recognition and joy. He bounds forward and throws his arms around me.

I automatically recoil. I don't mean to.

"Are you okay?" asks the observant Playboy Club doorman as I reach the employees' entrance. I close my eyes briefly.

"I am," I tell him, nodding, although I nervously wipe my cheek and neck. The unexpected and unwanted hug shocks and repulses me.

"Please don't touch the Bunnies." Untouchable Bunnies hear and repeat this commandment almost daily. No one is allowed to touch us, especially a man with a horrible skin disease. Suppose he has leprosy?

The doorman informs the Club manager who reports the incident to the hotel powers-that-be.

Duncan is relieved of his job at the service entrance of the Sherry-Netherland Hotel. I never see Duncan again.

Dear Duncan,

I'm so sorry. I have never forgotten you. In a way, you have lived in an unsettled part of my heart for all these years. I have imagined your loneliness and how the Fates separated you from so many common pleasures. I hope you had people in your life who loved you and took care of you. It seems that even kindness can be cruel, and well-intended attempts at friendship can turn painful.

Love,
Bunny Jill

FIRST LESSON/LAST LESSON

"One person's first lesson is another person's last lesson," my wild friend Silver announced to me. She wagged her finger in my face, piercing my know-it-all attitude with her eyes. Those nine words were her definitive response to a judgmental admonition I threw her way.

"You shouldn't smoke." I shook my finger at her as I watched her light up yet another Chesterfield.

Having said something I needed to say, Silver responded to my sisterly scolding with something she needed me to hear and understand. "One person's first lesson is another person's last lesson."

Silver, a gifted horse whisperer, serious drinker, chain smoker, and handsome renegade woman, died more than a decade ago. Friends and family watched her galloping, stumbling, and tumbling at highest speeds into a gully of thorny consequences. Posterity surely watched her racing toward difficulties and destruction. Alcohol, tobacco, and drugs eclipsed her stellar spiritual center—or maybe alcohol, tobacco, and drugs defined her center, her spirit.

Silver introduced me to the Self-Realization Fellowship philosophy. I still order the Fellowship's annual calendars. I read Paramahansa Yogananda's quotes under each glorious, uplifting photograph. As far as I know, Yogananda never said, "One person's first lesson is another person's last lesson." No, Silver said that. Now I say it, but I always give her credit.

I'm not sure what my first lessons were, and I have no idea what my last lesson will be. But I'm paying attention to some of the important lessons that I'm learning in between.

BAD INTENTION/GOOD RESULT

ON NOT BECOMING A BULLY—WHEW!

In elementary school, I was the class clown, the trickster, the dreamer, the kid who interrupted. I was the kid who looked for exceptions to the rules, who whispered and joked at inappropriate moments. I was never the teacher's pet, never the pupil who always turned in homework on time, never the student who obeyed all the classroom regulations.

My fourth-grade teacher, Mrs. Condit, wore wire-rimmed glasses, practical shoes, and frumpy crepe dresses (navy, purple, and brown) like my Grandmother Graves and her two elderly sisters.

Most days, after geography, arithmetic, or reading, when it wasn't raining or snowing too hard during recess, the class would go outside to play softball or dodgeball. Every classmate had an opportunity to be a team captain and choose a team.

Today Mrs. Condit chooses Richard Cella and me to be team captains. Richard and I stand on opposite sides of the room, getting ready to choose our team members. We glance around at the class. There is Katherine, the best artist, and Joyce, who can throw a ball better than the boys. There is Edward, who is clumsy and confused, and there is Bill with the funny teeth. I have a crush on Bill. And there is Jane.

Jane is very, very fat. She can't wear normal clothes. She can't fit in a regular desk chair. She can't run. When the nurse comes to the classroom to weigh and measure us, she weighs and measures Jane privately. Most of the kids ignore her. Team captains always pick Jane last, because whatever team she's on is the losing team.

Today, I get to choose first. I know! I'll choose Jane first. All my friends will laugh. It'll be a total surprise. What a funny joke!

"Jane," I call out.

Jane gets out of her oversized desk on the very last row, waddles up to the front of the room, and stands next to me near the pencil sharpener by the big bulletin board. My friends and I stifle our secret smiles and laughs, so we don't get in trouble.

The choosing continues. Then the two teams go to the softball field to play a few innings. Our team loses, of course, because of Jane, who can't hit the ball, or catch it, or run.

Later, while the class is reading quietly, Mrs. Condit comes up to me.

"Linda, may I see you out in the hall, please?"

Uh, oh! A feeling of dread encircles me.

The hall smells like wax and disinfectant. Voices echo. Mrs. Condit looks at me over her glasses. She is very serious. I look at my shoes.

"Please give this note to your mother," she says, handing me a small blue envelope.

Uh, oh! I'm in trouble again.

"That was a very kind and thoughtful thing you did today, Linda, choosing Jane first. You made her feel special. You gave her a chance to feel included. It was a mature and lovely gesture. It meant a great deal to Jane and to me. I'm proud of you. You taught the whole class a lesson about kindness and good citizenship."

Kindness? Good citizenship? Mrs. Condit doesn't know it was a joke.

"Be sure to take this note home. I want your mother to know what a very generous thing you did for one of your classmates who is having a difficult time. You made Jane feel like a welcomed part of the class."

A sense of shame at being praised for my thoughtless act blanketed me. The next time we chose playground teams, Mrs. Condit picked Jane to be a captain.

Jane chose me first. It took me a long time to understand what it would be like to be so different, so handicapped, so lonely. And it took me even longer to recognize that I covered my own loneliness and insecurity with brazenness and jokes.

Recently, through the magic of cyberspace, I located Jane. She's a retired minister living in New England. I called her. She remembered me. She didn't remember the fourth-grade incident that I never forgot.

But what she did remember is something I had forgotten: the afternoon club my mother created for the girls in my class to teach us how to become "young ladies." Mother called it *Les Chansonettes*. She organized dress-up teas and taught us how to set a proper table. She showed us how to go through a receiving line and to RSVP to a formal invitation. Jane was *une Chansonette*. My mother insisted on it—every girl in my class had to be included. She recognized and cared about the struggles of the little fat girl.

Sixty years later, Jane's remembrance sparked insights deep within the angry daughter that I had been. Her words challenged me to see my mother not as good or bad, conscious or unconscious, but simply as unabashedly human, and to find balance in my long-corroded view of this mother-daughter bond.

During our one telephone conversation, Jane and I talked about bullying and pain and life and growing up and God and figuring things out. She told me that she still weighs the same as she did in grade school. She sent me this email:

Linda,

It was surprising and interesting to talk with you the other day. I had so much "bullying," as they now call it, that I was totally unaware of the incident you spoke about. What you probably don't know is that I endured that at home from mother, father, and sister as well. It became normal for me. By the time I was 30, I was a mess and working with a psychiatrist who helped me a great deal, although I still have some residue of feeling unworthy. Fortunately, God was a deep part of my life from the age of 9 when I asked to serve him after reading Matthew 7:7. It took many years for the repair work to be done, and so it was in my 50s that I was able to serve as a pastor, attend seminary, graduate, and be ordained. After 23 years in my church, I'm now freelancing in what is called supply preaching, which entails a small summer church at a lake from May through October.

Forgiveness is something God through Jesus gave to us, so forgive yourself. You've carried this burden long enough, and I certainly forgive you. Jesus *told us to forgive one another 70 x 70 times, so if we follow Him sincerely, what else can we do? Your phone call and the whole story would make excellent sermon material for a message on forgiveness. I hope this brings you peace.*

So, Reverend Jane forgave me. And I forgave myself.

A Wiff of Princeton

"Guess what?" I blurted to my classmate Jeanette over the phone. "This boy named Dennis just invited me to a tea dance at Princeton. He's the son of one of my mother's friends. I barely know him…he isn't very tall…I mean…he's not even as tall as I am…and he's very pretentious…he uses Greek and Latin phrases when plain old English would make more sense…I don't know why he asked me…probably no college girl would go with him…or maybe his mother made him ask me."

From the moment he called and I accepted his invitation, my mother began instructing me on her version of the behavioral dos and don'ts at a college tea dance. I don't know where she acquired all that dated information about gloves and hats and calling cards. Her formal education ended in the eighth or ninth grade. I think she enjoyed bragging to her friends that her daughter was "dating" a Princeton man. I was pretty sure she wished she had married an Ivy League man instead of my father, a regular guy who was kicked out of two New England boarding schools and who never went to college. Clearly, she was far more excited about this date than I was. My excitement centered around her promise to buy me a new dress.

She took me to a fancy dress shop in Haddonfield—the fanciest town in all of Camden County. A chic woman in a stylish navy-blue suit greeted us.

"We're looking for a dress for my daughter to wear to a spring tea dance at Princeton University," my mother said in an unusually refined tone. While we followed the saleswoman to the formal dress section of the store, my mother whispered to me that all the saleswomen at this snooty boutique (snooty for this part of New Jersey) were required to wear stylish navy-blue dresses or suits. I don't know how she knew this. She never shopped there. They didn't carry her size 20½.

I tried on several dresses in the expansive private dressing room with royal-blue carpeting and an upholstered fainting couch. My mother and the saleswoman studied and discussed the appropriateness and fit of each dress as I modeled one ballerina-length frock after another and posed self-consciously in front of a three-sided, full-length mirror. They finally decided on the pale aqua dress with the fluffy ruffled skirt. "It's demure and elegant," said the saleswoman. "Yes," my mother echoed, "very elegant, very demure."

I liked the pink dress more, but my mother said that pink was unbecoming to redheads.

While my mother was paying for the dress and talking with the stylish saleswoman, I noticed the skinny girl with mousy brown hair who worked behind the counter. She was about my age. She wore a uniform from Camden Catholic High School: a gray jumper with a white, starched blouse. The blouse had a brownish stain on one sleeve. The skinny girl started to wrap my dress. I was certain she overheard my mother talking (bragging) about my Princeton date. I guess I was a bit puffed up about it, myself. Maybe it was the perfumed atmosphere.

Funny, I thought. It wasn't like, "Oh, I have a date with a boy named Dennis." It was more like, "Oh, I'm going to Princeton University on a date." Anyway, I confess. I was feeling very smug. *I am a customer buying a fancy dress in a fancy store, and she's just a stringy-haired shop girl. I am Ivy League material. I am destined for, for…I don't know, for STARDOM, no doubt, and for unimaginable success. I will be out of this nowhere place before long, and she, my uniformed Catholic school counterpart, will probably never even leave New Jersey.*

While I stood there in my pseudo-privileged self-importance, I watched this uniformed school girl carefully prepare the box, and I compared her day with mine.

She held my dress in front of her and looked at it approvingly before laying it out on the wrapping counter next to the big dress box. She took pale pink tissue paper and crushed it a bit and stuffed it carefully into the bodice of the dress. She folded several more pieces of tissue and eased them into the body of the dress. She zipped the zipper to the top. Then she placed neat layers of the pink tissue in the empty dress box before carefully folding the dress, lengthwise, and placing the skirt of the dress in the gray and pink box. Then she added more tissue and gently, gently folded the top of the dress in the box so the pretty bodice was showing. Slowly and carefully, she blanketed layers of the pink tissue over my pale aqua tea dance dress. I watched her put the cover on the box and tie it with a wide, cranberry-colored ribbon, making sure the store logo was visible: Lillian Albus. She picked up the box, came out from behind the counter, handed it to me, and smiled.

"Enjoy your beautiful new dress. And enjoy the dance."

"Thanks," I said, accepting the dress box and smiling in her direction. I cast my eyes at the floor, at my scuffed school shoes and hers. Felled by an awareness of the difference between pride and pridefulness, I walked toward the door where my mother waited.

I still remember the girl in the shop. I don't remember the tea dance.

I'm nobody! Who are you?
Are you – Nobody – too?

—Emily Dickinson

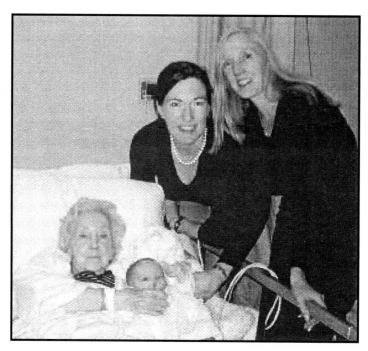

Audrey Claire Durham with her mother, grandmother,
and great-grandmother, 2003

The Incredible Rightness of Forgiveness

The weak can never forgive. Forgiveness is the attribute of the strong.

–Mahatma Gandhi

I believed I could never forgive my mother for a variety of real and exaggerated abuses. I was wrong. I forgave her over and again in the past few decades. Still, from time to time, I revisit the years preceding that forgiveness, years when I held on to my resentment as a way of avoiding looking at the truth. It took a long time to get to a place where I had room in my heart to consider the harshness, criticism, tragedies, and abuse she must have suffered as a child. What did her father do or not do that made her hate him so much?

I was four years old. My Grandfather Bailey and his Las Vegas showgirl companion made a once-in-a-lifetime visit to our house in Philadelphia. To me, Grandpa's showgirl looked like a fairy princess with her long blond hair and bright red lipstick. She was very tall—taller than my father. The showgirl gave me a big fancy doll in a blue satin gown with lace and sparkles and shiny white slippers. The doll's golden hair felt real. No one ever gave me a doll so beautiful. When my grandfather and his showgirl left, my mother took the doll from me and threw it in the big trash bin in the alley behind the house. I cried.

My mother's vicious denouncement of my decision to divorce my first husband and pursue a relationship with the man who eventually became the father of my children was a hurtful indictment of me—one that lasted until she died.

"No decent people will ever respect you." She hurled her curse at me. "Nothing good will ever become of you."

Perhaps her private hurt, confusion, and sadness were so enormous that she had no room to comfort me in my hurt, confusion, and sadness. From my perspective, it appeared that she simply didn't like me and didn't approve of my lifestyle.

"Your shameful behavior has damaged our family's reputation. Your father and I will have to move to another community."

And they did—but surely not because I divorced a man whose post-marriage decisions would have forced me to embrace a life that was counter to all our premarital dreams and intentions, counter to my free-spirited truth.

When I married Craig Campbell Mac Nab at nineteen—a marriage destined not to last—I thought I had succeeded in escaping my mother's daily admonitions and interferences, if not the deep sense of sadness that her never-ending judgment chiseled in my heart. I recall her disappointment as she studied the freckled face of her kindergarten daughter.

I'm sorry I have freckles, Mommy.

"When I was a little girl your age, my skin was like pale ivory silk. People would stop my mother on the street to compliment her little 'princess doll.'"

I'm sorry no one compliments you about me, Mommy.

"In Ireland, they put urine on freckles to make them go away. Perhaps we can put urine on your face. What would you think about that?"

Please don't put urine on my face, Mommy.

The last time I saw my mother alive, she was in a rehabilitation hospital, recuperating from a minor injury, a dislocated arm, I think. I agreed to join the three other generations of Graves family females to pose for a photograph— for posterity. I didn't care about the posterity part; I just wanted to please my daughter. And so, while on business in New York, I carved out a day, jumped on a bus at the Port Authority Terminal, and traveled to South Jersey. My sister, daughter, and baby granddaughter met me there, and we drove straight to the hospital.

Mother seemed fine. Her eyes were sharp; her mind, clear. She had a small bow in her hair, and she wore a bit of pink lipstick and maybe some rouge.

I smiled for the camera, my arm around the woman from whom I had been estranged for most of my life. I was wearing Christian Louboutin heels and the most chic and expensive article of clothing I had ever owned: a Gianni Versace jacket that I purchased in Milan for many thousands of *lire*—not quite understanding the exchange rate. I felt her disapproval.

I stood at the foot of my mother's bed, feeling stylish and very tall. She looked very small. Fragile. Harmless. Sweet, almost. I was aware of an invisible shield

surrounding me, protecting me. Protecting me from what? I knew I would probably never see my mother again, and I thought I could say, "I love you, Mother."
But I couldn't. I didn't want to. I just wanted to say goodbye and leave. And
that's what I did.

It was the last time I saw my mother alive. A few days later, she died. I returned
to New Jersey again for her funeral.

An artificial fire gives artificial warmth to the reception hall in the spacious funeral
home. Next to a brown leather chair is a mahogany sideboard. On the sideboard is a
bowl of individually wrapped oversized Life Savers. I note the unintended irony. I put a
Life Saver in my jacket pocket. I take a few deep breaths and enter the chapel and make
my way down the empty aisle to the casket in which my mother's body lies. Although I
saw her just the week before, she no longer looks familiar. The morticians fixed her hair
in an unfamiliar style. They positioned her head at an unnatural angle, giving her a regal
look in death that she never had in life.

I finger the Life Saver in my pocket. Time passes or stands still….I don't know which.
Thinking, or not thinking, I remove the little ruby friendship ring that my Burmese family
gave me years ago. I ease it onto the ring finger of my mother's stiff right hand. And I stand
over her permanent stillness, swaying, slowly, moving to a soundless rhythm deep inside.
I search for my tears and don't find them. A lifetime of repressed memories flows into an
all-encompassing pause. I whisper: "This is a forgiveness ring, Mother. I offer it with love.
May it be a conduit from my heart to your heart. I love you. I forgive you. Please forgive me."

…and we ourselves shall be loved for a while and forgotten. But the love will have been
enough; all those impulses of love return to the love that made them. Even memory is
not necessary for love. There is a land of the living and a land of the dead and the bridge
is love, the only survival, the only meaning.

–Thornton Wilder, *The Bridge of San Luis Rey*

Lucinda Rabbit

A giant, fluffy, white rabbit suit hangs in the back of my closet. I bought it years ago from a costume shop that was selling off excess holiday inventory. The outfit consists of a one-piece faux-fur suit, a fuzzy head bonnet with tall pink satin-lined ears, furry white booties that can fit over shoes—up to men's size 13, white mittens, an oversized yellow, gold, and white plaid vest, and a big, padded, yellow satin bowtie. It's a one-size-fits-every-conceivable-big-person disguise.

I put on the outfit and stared in the looking-glass on the back of my bathroom door. Linda disappeared. I took on the persona of Lucinda Rabbit. I smiled at the free and ageless character smiling back at me. Occasionally, Lucinda appeared at children's birthday parties. She crouched down low, so her size didn't frighten them. Once they warmed to her giant rabbitness, Lucinda sang and danced around, played rabbit games, and ate birthday cake with them. Her other responsibilities centered around visiting hospitals, nursing homes, and senior care centers.

It's just before lunch Easter Sunday. I hop into my Lucinda Rabbit persona and drive to a Santa Fe nursing home. Most residents are playing cards with other residents in the cheerful community room or visiting with relatives. Some are dozing or drifting off in big-people highchairs amid party-store decorations.

"Hello, everyone. Happy Easter!" I chirp in my cartoonish rabbit voice. Bony, blue-veined and brown-speckled hands reach for the sweet, squishy white rabbits and the marshmallowy yellow "Peeps" that I offer from my Easter basket. I dance and sing around the room. Everyone smiles.

Linda would feel foolish dancing around in this bunny suit, but Lucinda is in her element. I feel the freedom of stepping out of my grown-up persona and into a character who loves all these people: the drooling ones; the old, old women with whiskers on their chins; the ones who stare blankly. Lucinda hugs them, lights up their faces, and makes most of them smile.

From the Day Room, I wander down the halls to visit the people who are in their rooms—confined, sleeping, or with visitors. At the end of one hallway, two attendants stop me. They know Lucinda.

"Don't go in that room!" they warn.

"Why?"

"Because that woman is really mean."

Mean? How mean can an old lady in a nursing home be? And aren't I an imposing— but friendly—giant white rabbit on a sunny Easter Sunday, carrying a basket of jellybeans, marshmallow chickens, and spongy bunnies?

As soon as the attendants are out of sight, I step across the threshold of the "mean" lady's room, strike a pose just inside the doorway, and utter a Lucinda greeting.

"Hello there, Happy Easter!"

The tiny old lady stares at me with dark, deep-set eyes under bushy black-and-white eyebrows. Whiskers fringe her cheeks and chin.

"Happy Easter!" Lucinda Rabbit hums again.

"Come here," she commands without a note of surprise at my appearance.

I step closer.

"Would you like a marshmallow bunny?"

"Come closer!" Such a gruff voice from a birdlike woman in a hospital bed takes me aback.

"It's a beautiful Easter Day, isn't it?" I step closer, look into her fierce eyes.

"Closer!"

I'm at her bed.

"C-c-candy?" I force a smile.

She grabs my floppy vest.

"A little yellow p-p-peep?" I chirp.

She yanks me to her with a strength that belies her size.

"S-s-some jellybeans?"

She looks into Lucinda Rabbit's soul and with a gruff raspy voice commands, "Get me out of here!"

Life would be tragic if it weren't funny.

—Stephen Hawking

Relativity Comes of Age, or Age is Relative

What is an adult? A child blown up by age.
—Simon de Beauvoir

As I sit by the window in my dentist's waiting room, reading a day-old newspaper, a fragile, old woman with wispy white hair struggles with the front door handle. I contrast her bright pink jacket, flowered pedal-pushers, and purple beret to my black jeans and dull gray sweater with a split seam on the right shoulder. I can't resist spying over the top of the paper as she navigates across the room, walking sticks in both hands. She stops to steady herself in front of a long, waist-high table full of magazines and dental advertising brochures.

Propping up her walking sticks, she pulls a zippered, see-through makeup case from her handbag. She dabs a little pinkish foundation on her forehead, chin, and nose. Bringing her small compact mirror close to her wrinkled face, she traces a dark arc of Maybelline pencil over her nearly invisible eyebrows, then sweeps a mascara brush over her invisible eyelashes. With her finger, she smears two circles of lipstick on her cheeks, then redraws her pale lips a fiery red. She checks the results in her mirror.

I smile to myself.

How strange and sweet that such an old woman fusses to make herself "look pretty" before she faces her dentist.

By extension, something else occurs to me. A basic tenet of womanship (for most women, I believe) is the desire to put our "best face forward"—whatever that means to each of us—when we venture out to meet the world. That may mean hiding that which we don't want strangers, friends, or dentists to notice.

I wonder what self-conscious fear this elderly lady covers with those two ruby-red, baby doll circles on her wrinkling cheeks. I feel a sudden and unexpected connection with her—a rush of love. Her desire to prolong lingering beauty nudges a gentle reconsideration: my initial judgment was wrong. I see beyond my newspaper barrier to an awareness and compassion, bordering on unexpected awe, not just for this woman, but for all women, including me.

I think about my own aging transits: a growing preoccupation with concerns about wrinkles and waist thickening and knee stiffening. From my peekaboo intrusion into this woman's preparation for a routine teeth cleaning or examination, I see her as more than an old woman in colorful clothes. I recognize her as a messenger angel, showing up in my life not a moment too soon.

Her makeup process complete, my angel picks up her walking sticks, glides her now-ready "self" to the leather couch, and smiles at me.

We speak a few words the way waiting people do in a waiting room. Today is her eighty-eighth birthday. I tell her I'm seventy-two.

"Oh! You're so young."

"And you, you're so beautiful…and your beauty inspires me."

Her eyes twinkle. The dental hygienist calls my angel and escorts her out of the waiting room. I examine the seventy-two-year-old face in my Cover Girl mirror and wipe away mascara that has seeped into an endearing new rivulet beneath my left eye.

I consider my countless attempts to make myself look better for someone, or for some occasion, or for myself. I have hidden myself in plain sight. Head-turner clothes, facials, haircuts, skin treatments, positive thinking, meditations. I realize I always wish I had taller genes. Or a different nose. Or longer eyelashes. Or better skin. My investigations into the realms of inner satisfaction do not hold. Long before I reach eighty-eight, I want to have reconciled all my insecurities about the outward-appearing me. I want to have found the truth in the truth that I have always been beautiful.

I'm ready for my own dental close-up.

> …How many loved your moments of glad grace,
> And loved your beauty with love false or true,
> But one man loved the pilgrim Soul in you,
> And loved the sorrows of your changing face…
>
> —William Butler Yeats, "When You Are Old"

My Life in the (Inevitable) Denouement Lane

There is something comforting about the passage of time, about aging, about entering a phase of life known by various names that I'm learning to embrace. Most ageist euphemisms still make me cringe. Senior citizen. Crone. Old. Elderly. Hag. Twilight years.

To find comfort in the debatable concept that time moves forward and, in my case, has moved quite far, I practice a private and uplifting process that brings hopeful optimism to my septuagenarian self. I imagine that I'm a healthy, life-loving, eighty-eight-year-old, like the peddle-pusher-wearing woman in the dentist's office:

In the privacy of my boudoir, I close my eyes. I become very still. I relax. I'm quiet. I imagine being eighty-eight years old. I take time to experience my body. I see my late octogenarian self. I walk, but with a bit less bounce in my step. I wear practical shoes—no Jimmy Choos. I have an ACE Bandage on one knee and a bottle of prune juice in my refrigerator. With closed eyes, my hands survey the map that is my face. I feel its rivers, valleys, mountains, furrowed fields. Several pairs of glasses are strategically positioned around my house. Yesterday, I called my granddaughter by my daughter's name. I have a growing fear of falling. I have lost my passion for trekking alone in exotic countries.

And then, from that eighty-eight-year-old consciousness, I consider my former seventy-something self. That whippersnapper's foolishness is laughable. She thought herself so old too soon. If only she had known at seventy what she knows now.

I relax, open my eyes, and celebrate that I do know now what a less-contemplative seventyish woman might have failed to know about the importance and opportunities that are around me, before me….Still.

"May you stay forever young." I sing aloud Joan Baez's version of Dylan's song in my seventy-something voice.

Revolutionary Travel

All travel is revolutionary—if one is open. I am. I embrace the philosophy to which William James ascribed in his 1897 text *The Will to Believe*:

> All the higher, more penetrating ideals are revolutionary. They present themselves far less in the guise of effects of past experience than in that of probable causes of future experience.

To past and future experiences, I would include those in the present. How enlightening, how empowering, to travel through one's today and tomorrows— including those inevitable mundane days of errands and routine—with a sense of opportunity and a conscious spirit of adventure. I see it as traveling with the heart and mind of a revolutionary.

Revolutionary travel is about waking up (in all senses), engaging, and paying attention to one's world, one's environment. It's about being alert to the wonders of one's life. It's about traveling consciously and audaciously through jungles (in all their metaphors), deserts, beaches, cities, farms, parks, malls with sponta- neity, optimism, and truth. Albert Camus perfectly expresses my truth:

> The only way to deal with an unfree world is to be so absolutely free that your very life is an act of rebellion.

In that context, late one Saturday afternoon in the spring of 2013, to shake off a bit of ennui, I made a last-minute decision to attend that evening's banquet for a former U.S. Ambassador to the Middle East. I called the Santa Fe Council on International Relations, secured the last ticket, dressed in banquet style, and arrived in time for pre-event cocktails. I schmoozed with Santa Fe acquaintances, many of whom I met as a member of the Board of Directors of the CIR and The World Affairs Forum.

My table was one away from the ambassador's table. All through dinner, my charming nonagenarian tablemate, Edward Aldsworth, and I chatted about art, local politics, love, and literature. Just before the formal program began, Mr. Aldsworth turned to me.

"I know a very nice man just your age," he said out of the blue. "I think you would like each other. He's an intelligent, well-traveled man who worked for a humanitarian organization. Like you, he's writing a book."

"Perhaps you can tell him to call me."

"Oh, no!" He patted my hand. "I would never do that. I prefer to arrange a luncheon."

Our conversation ended abruptly with a glass-tapping signal from the podium.

Ten minutes into the ambassador's speech on official U.S. policy in the Middle East, it was clear that my beliefs were antithetical to his expressed beliefs. I have developed a low tolerance for cautious State Department speak. Although I'm reluctant to appear impolite, his matter-of-fact and toe-the-line viewpoint triggered my strong urge to leave. I whispered goodnight to my tablemates, rose, and walked out while the address was in process. I didn't look back. I didn't wave to anyone or feign a headache. I just walked out because my humanitarian soul ached. I felt spiritually ill.

My government's propaganda surrounding Iraq and other countries that have experienced the devastating effects of U.S. invasions and occupation left me cold. I was angry at the contrived information fed to the mainstream media that flows back out and poisons or confuses the minds and rational reasoning of millions of everyday people. There is no doubt that my government assaulted and killed innocent people—men, women, children—and its policies and invasive extraction of natural resources put an end to ancient cultures, including in Iraq, the location, scholars believe, of the original Garden of Eden.

My love and compassion for the Iraqi people, the heartbreak I experienced at their country's war-torn hospitals, orphanages, and refugee camps, set me at odds with the ambassador's endorsements of U.S. foreign policy.

At the meet-and-greet portion of the banquet, I zipped my lip when a retired undersecretary-of-something, in a dismissive tone, blustered, "Anecdotal" to a statement I made about an experience in the Green Zone in Baghdad.

"Not anecdotal. Firsthand and meaningful," I replied before zipping. Alone, on the drive home, I told that old guy a thing or two—that his knowledge of Iraq and foreign policy was probably ancient, dusty, and as fictitious as *Gulliver's Travels.*

At noon on many Fridays, I stood at a major intersection in Santa Fe, in peaceful sign-holding solidarity with a motley group of veterans, peaceniks from the Unitarian Universalist Church, and members of CODE PINK. We waved PEACE NOW, NO WAR IN IRAQ, and FREE GAZA signs. Drivers honked and passengers waved support. Some hurled expletives and made rude gestures. And still, we held our signs and waved.

In those public condemnations of national policy, I felt the stirrings of revolution—a revolution of spirit, awareness, peace. Perhaps I was mistaken. Perhaps there was only the outward agreement among a small group of discontents—people of social conscience—who understood that the real revolution was inward and could never be televised.

> ...The revolution will not be right back after a message
> About a white tornado, white lightning, or white people
> You will not have to worry about a Dove in your
> Bedroom, a tiger in your tank, or the giant in your toilet bowl
> The revolution will not go better with Coke
> The revolution will not fight the germs that may cause bad breath
> The revolution will not put you in the driver's seat
>
> The revolution will not be televised, will not be televised
> Will not be televised, will not be televised
> The revolution will be no re-run brothers;
> The revolution will be live.
>
> –Gil Scott-Heron, "The Revolution Will Not Be Televised"

I'm still standing, waiting, and moving toward a clearer understanding of my life's purpose—if, in fact, I truly have one. Certainly, I'm not waiting for a blind luncheon date with an old man and a gentleman my age who is also writing a book. Still...

Opening night at the Santa Fe Opera, tailgating
with François-Marie Patorni, 2018

Love in the Age of Wrinkles

Mr. Aldsworth came through. He arranged a luncheon with his writer friend, and we met at one of Santa Fe's fancier restaurants, The Compound. The attractive gentleman in a navy-blue cashmere blazer and a Hermes ascot, who spoke with a strong French accent, had worked for an international aid organization. He had old-school manners and serious green eyes, like a man with a meaningful secret.

Two days later, Mr. Conservative-looking invited me to dinner at a charming French bistro where he knew the owner and the chef. Our evening conversation flowed pleasantly from one mutually interesting topic to another: environmental issues, local politics, Madagascar, Patagonia, Paris, writing. Lingering over a second glass of wine at a table in the garden, he said that we had met before.

Really? We met at a show at my gallery? I had no memory of meeting him.

The concept of the exhibition was the brilliant idea of my artist/tattooist friend Dawn Purnell. The special tattoo exhibition that the gallery mounted was a benefit for St. Elizabeth's Homeless Shelter. Dawn's framed drawings and paintings filled the main gallery walls. The night of the *vernissage*, however, the *tableau vivant* highlighted ten or twelve of Dawn's heavily tattooed clients, each a complex expression of Dawn's ink.

Two women sat facing each other, playing mahjong, dressed to expose the exquisite ink designs from their necks to their waists. A beautiful couple embraced on a loveseat—their fully inked arms and legs entwined. A man in short shorts sat on a bench and softly strummed a guitar, his chest, arms, and legs a nod to the creativity of the tattoo culture. Yet another man—in Samurai regalia and mask, his arms and legs intricately inked with classic Japanese symbols like tigers and dragons—strolled around the gallery.

"Who is he?" I asked Dawn.

"One of my best clients," she said. "He wanted to hide his identity because his conservative friends don't know about his tattoos."

He and I had a brief and cordial conversation, and then I forgot about him.

Toward the end of an almost perfect evening, my soft-spoken, cashmere-jacket-wearing date, who loves animals (especially dogs and donkeys), who was writing a book on the history of the French in New Mexico, and who spent his career with United Nations agencies in Africa, India, and other hotspots around the world, admitted that he had a confession to make. Shyly, he asked if I remembered the man in the Samurai outfit the night of the tattoo show, because he was that man.

While I took a very deep breath, my mind filled with the fine silence that accompanies the absence of thought or words. How extraordinarily disconcerting it was to consider the two disparate aspects of this man. I touched his arm, pulled up his jacket sleeve, unbuttoned and pushed up the cuff of his blue linen shirt. There—just above his wrist—the telltale ink began.

Late that night, I struggled to reconcile the seemingly conflicting aspects of this disarming Frenchman. I thought about the journal entry I had written in Johannesburg, wondering, as I have done before, if I would ever meet a compatible mate in the age of wrinkles.

As I settled into my cozy, yet lonely bed, I ticked off my mate/lover's requisite characteristics and qualities. Intelligent. Kind. My age. Well-traveled. I drifted, contemplating the powers that exist where opposites meet and are joined, or where they collide. Conservative and wild. Secretive and forthcoming. Foreign and familiar. Linda and François-Marie.

Over the years, he and I have become quite bonded to one another. Travels, philosophical agreements and disagreements, world politics, and "sacred lunches" kept us moving forward together as we studied the differences and similarities of our similarities and differences.

In addition to his professional portfolio, François-Marie modestly calls himself an "amateur" astronomer. Yet, that hardly seems fitting. He wonders daily, sometimes hourly, about the vastness of the universes that exist at distances that cannot be fathomed by the human mind. He is aware of every coming conjunction of the planets, and every special (or not-that-special) comet sighting, eclipse, partial eclipse, and solar flare. Astronomical wonders frequently occupy vast portions of our dinner table and bedtime conversations. He explains, with numbers, graphs, and models, the sizes and distances from one heavenly body to another. I think of the distance from his heavenly body to mine, and I measure it not only in inches and miles but also by ethereal, emotional, and experiential yardsticks.

My One and Only Physical Circumnavigation
of the Earth (So Far)

I did it! For seventy days, in celebration of my seventieth birthday, I breathed my way around the world. Finally! I started out from my house in Santa Fe early on a cold December morning and headed east: first by car, then by plane, and, eventually, by foot, boat, bus, van, bicycle, and taxi. And I kept going. I propelled myself around the world in pursuit of life, trailed by life, fueled by life. By March 2013, I found myself back at the point of my eastern embarkation.

Mindset, perception, and time had shifted the reality of that dreadful year—2011—when I had no clear vision of who I would or could become following the loss of my beloved gallery. At this mystical peripatetic pilgrim's homecoming, my thoughts once again springboarded to William James' poignant insights about reality, abstraction, and possibility.

In returning to the disparate tangible and intangible artifacts gathered over my life, I saw them afresh, intertwined with the silver cord of reconciliation—a union and reunion with self and others. "It is as if the opposites of the world, whose contradictoriness and conflict make all our difficulties and troubles, were melted into unity." Yes, William James. One's attitudes do "open a region," though finding the map is up to the explorer.

I stand in my kitchen and study an aerial photograph of my neighborhood taped to the inside of the back door. I take a pencil and draw an arrow to my house. Along the margin, I scrawl, "You Are Here." The feeling of home—where the hearth is, where the art is, where the heart is—makes me smile.

My black lab, Ruby, follows me as I wander from room to room. My two semi-feral cats, Spooky and Cassie, eye me from a distance. In the courtyard garden, towhees, house finches, juncos, doves, and jays feast on peanuts, millet, and sunflower seeds.

The view from my bedroom window looks peaceful. Dry. Spring seems reluctant to show up. I study the paintings on the walls. They hang exactly where they hung on the day that I set out on this journey. The dozen or so travel books are still where I left them—on the desk, in the study: *The Art of Pilgrimage, Without a Guide, A Winter in Arabia, Nothing to Declare*...so many. Everything seems the same in the house. Even in the cold garage, there—piled and stacked impatiently, neglected—lie the remains of my gallery life.

Yet, everything is different. Inside of me, everything is different. I am different. I welcome myself back to my starting square. I close my eyes and travel at memory speed: from here to the boys in Soweto; to David and the orphaned children in Lesotho; to Manatera and the Grandidier baobabs in Madagascar; to the sprawl and hustle of Bangkok; to the gentle artists and dancers of Myanmar; to the mystical spurting volcano in Hawaii; to the rush and chaos at LAX; to the moment I landed in Albuquerque and exclaimed to my seat partner (a handsome stranger), "I've been around the fucking world"; to this moment, here, in my strange and familiar kitchen.

Breathe, I tell myself—or maybe my inner guides whisper it. Perhaps it's an angel who reassures me: "Leave your suitcase and backpack on the bedroom floor. No rush to unpack. You don't have to call anyone tonight. You're not hungry. You have no schedule to meet, no other place to go. You are here. Just 'be' for a few minutes. Just 'be here.' Be still. Everything is unfolding on time—including you."

Gratitude fills me. I'll be grateful forever for the will and ability to manifest my dream, for the thrill of the voyage, for the wonder of the arrival—every arrival and return.

This moment, I'm thankful simply to...be...here...now.

> I will drink life to the lees...
> Much have I seen and known; cities of men
> And manners, climates, councils, governments,
> Myself not least, but honored of them all...
> Far on the ringing plains of windy Troy.
> I am part of all that I have met;
> Yet all experience is an arch wherethro'
> Gleams that untraveled world...
>
> –Alfred Lord Tennyson, *Ulysses*

Reveries Revive Me

For now, home and peace. Soon, I'll become restless again. My days will begin to seem stagnant, unchallenging. I'll begin again to yearn for a new world-travel adventure. I've never been to Tasmania, or to Finland, or to Bulgaria. I've never taken a paddle-boat trip down the Mississippi River. I've never even been to Graceland. No, I've only been *near* Graceland. I dream of returning to Myanmar and Madagascar and Patagonia.

In my past, restlessness often preceded recklessness. It signaled a move that could jeopardize or compromise something secure in exchange for something obscure. Often, when this restlessness overpowered my contentedness, I scratched it raw. I followed an impulse in search of my real life, my real calling, whatever I thought that might be.

Again and again, I have taken flight in search of the ever-elusive life's purpose. I escaped the trappings of feeling trapped. By whom? By what? I corralled the Earth. Like the old woman in the nursing home, I asked the Universe to "Get me out of Here," to "Get me to There." A recurrent inner calling to search *out there* inevitably delivers me *in here*. How long it has taken me to discover that the faraway place called "there" is actually right "here."

Circumnavigating the Earth, I briefly circumvented my discovery: going from here to somewhere does not necessarily mean abandoning, rejecting, or renouncing that which has gone before—nor does it mean disowning my connections to the past, or to the future.

> I am not alone;
> Not abandoned by the sky.
> We move in synchronicity,
> The clouds, the wind, and I.
> I sing in concert with the birds.
> I keep my counsel with the sun.
> The restless moon consoles me.
> I am guided by the stars.

My desire is to feel free, to be free, to come (untethered) and go (unfettered). Over and again, my wandering nature captures me. I have discovered and abandoned and rediscovered and lost and embraced—over time or in an instant—the fathomless distance from inclination to realization and the measureless proximity of the lost to the found.

To live is to create one's own world as a scene of personal happiness.

–Thomas Merton

I'm approaching the end of my story, although it is not the end of my journey. This is just a pause before the forthcoming beginning.

"There is no real ending," Frank Herbert wrote. "It's just the place where you stop the story."

I close my eyes and see myself on the never-ending Mobius strip. I imagine myself skipping along it.

I'm a skinny girl with crooked teeth and tangled red hair.

I'm a young woman with slightly awkward pin-up looks.

I'm a mother with two perfect children.

I'm a lover, a leaver, a loner, moving through days, ideas, places…looking.

I'm moving toward more answers, more questions, more quests.

I'm a November woman in a lonely month, wondering, smiling, reading to myself.

I'm gazing out the window of a house, a plane, a train, a bus.

I'm walking in a city, a village, a meadow.

At some long-ago now point, I come upon a little girl with bright rust freckles, crooked teeth, tangled hair. She's sitting in the dirt under a tree. She's taping two ends of a long paper strip that her father twisted only once. She's singing, "the moon belongs to everyone…."

I sing with her.

A journey of a thousand miles must begin with a single step.

–Lao-tzu

And it must end with a single step. And each step takes us closer to the beginning.

Not so near THE END

Epilogue

I am still moving along the path of *What Can Be*, sauntering past the junction of *What Has Been* and *What's Ahead*. As the road widens and narrows and widens again, I revel in the opportunities for renewal.

Crystalized from my permanent and ephemeral archives are a few maxims that have gotten me through challenging phases, mazes, and days. Trust your instincts. Be original. Pay attention. Dream big. Be curious. Have no (lasting) regrets. Be grateful and forgiving. Tell the truth. Listen to music. Dance. Live with courage, compassion, and grace.

There is so much to make out of life. Make friends. Make amends. Make time. Make discoveries. Make love. Make a joyful noise! Make peace with yourself and the world.

And, until that last breath…remember this: as long as you don't give up when you encounter Life's inevitable, surmountable barriers, you're still moving.

Every beginning is only a sequel, after all, and the book of events is always open half-way through.

–Wisława Szymborska

With Bart at the Durham Ranch, Cerrillos, NM, 1967

Acknowledgments

If my beloved business hadn't failed, and if I hadn't thrown all caution to the proverbial wind and used creatively raised funds to embark on a trip around the world, this book would not exist. And there would be no one to thank.

However, serendipity, mystery, magic, time, and happenstance conspired to set me on a path that led to this memoir-writing chapter of my life. Inevitable or pre-ordained? Who knows how this pick-yourself-up person started all over again and landed here, with the opportunity to acknowledge, salute, and thank the many people who stood, sat, walked, talked, sweat, cried, or laughed with me through the long adventure of birthing *Still Moving*.

Early, valuable coaching support came from the following: Tanya Taylor Rubenstein, who collaborated with me on "Mobius Strip Tease," the one-woman show that was a precursor to this book; JoAnne O'Brien Levin, who helped me see the theatrical play, wonder, and potential of the book; Carlos Beuth, who transcribed rough drafts and journal scribblings and urged me to keep writing; and Aline Brandauer, who read a too-flawed-for-prime-time version of the manuscript and warned me about potential lawsuits. I am grateful for sage advice from Weston DeWalt, Dana Newmann, and Douglas Preston, who read closer-to-prime-time versions of the manuscript and encouraged me to take time to assess and reassess my work.

Loving thanks to Judyth Hill, teacher, poet, coach, and friend who rescued the raggedy chapters of my work-in-progress, shuffled and re-shuffled pages, and helped me find ways to tell the stories of a lifetime in a workable and wildly non-sequential way.

Several fine writers, working on their own projects, shared their words, ideas, passion, projects, tears, successes, and failures with me: Heloise Jones, whose valuable coaching and comments (mainly at my kitchen table over tea) convinced me that I was a real-life storyteller; Jonelle Maison, a gifted poet whose steady mind and uplifting spirit boosted my confidence; Marsha Pincus Rosenzweig, whose deep commitment to pedagogy and sound political consciousness inspired me; and Joan Brooks Baker, whose memoir-writing years paralleled mine. Thank you.

Many close friends endured countless soliloquys about my writing without ever seeing tangible evidence of a book: Marjolein Brugman, a remarkable combination of beauty, brains, heart, and soul with whom I've shared years of friendship through tough and terrific times; Richard Berman, a fine artist, trusted buddy, and world-class mensch; Sandra Filippucci, Joan of Arc scholar, inspired artist, and go-to confidante and cheerleader; Shen Robinson, a worldly intellect whose deep, active, and ongoing care and concern for the imperiled humans in our near and far worlds is tireless; Daniel Martinez, my brilliant creative brother from another mother; Cynthia Whitney-Ward, photojournalist extraordinaire; Lynda Braun, a consummate artist whose exquisite "eye" and immense talent I admire, as Agnes Martin did. Thank you, thank you.

Love and gratitude are deservedly bestowed upon my grace-filled friend and author Laura Davis Hays, my co-conspirator on a variety of social and literary projects. I'm thankful for our intellectual, emotional, and spiritual connection and for the many wine-enhanced conversations that supported me through the highs and lows of writing this book.

For more than forty years, Jill Cooper Udall, Romona Scholder, Ellen Bradbury Reid, and I have met every month to share the unfolding stories of our similar and disparate lives. Through weddings and divorces, births and deaths, successes and failures, we have supported one another's dreams. I am so grateful.

I extend mountains of love and awe to my remarkable children, Daisy and Rocky, who have been present and tolerant and supportive through it all and who have had the most lasting and profound impact on this unfinished woman and flawed—I mustn't forget flawed—mother.

When I was at the very most dejected place in the years of writing and abandoning this project, an editor, teacher, angel came out of the ethers, stayed with me, and guided me through hundreds and hundreds of changes, mistakes, glitches, clichés, misunderstandings, conversations, arguments....To Charlotte Meares, I owe an enormous pallet of gratitude. Her knowledge, integrity, energy, above-and-beyond tolerance and patience merit a special precious metal medal.

Lastly and firstly, I am blessed with the constant love, care, and companionship of my dear and patient partner, François-Marie Patorni, who means the world to me.

About the Author

Linda Durham's professional and personal life centers on art, artists, global travel, and humanitarian causes. She is the founder and director of Santa Fe's Wonder Institute, which sponsors art exhibitions, lectures, workshops, and salons focused on discovering and implementing creative solutions to contemporary social and cultural issues. For more than three decades, Durham promoted New Mexico-based artists as the hands-on owner of a contemporary art gallery with seven exhibition locations through the years: six in Santa Fe, and one in New York. In 2012, the New Mexico Museum of Art acquired her extensive gallery archives. A prolific writer and speaker, she has been guest lecturer or workshop presenter at Brigham Young University, the University of Wisconsin, Ohio Wesleyan University, Yale University, the Sundance Institute, the College of Santa Fe, Santa Fe Community College, and the New Mexico Museum of Art. For her seventieth birthday, Durham circumnavigated the world in seventy days, meeting Indigenous women, educators, artists, entrepreneurs, and peace activists, and planting "Seeds of Peace" in gardens, schoolyards, and parks in South Africa, Lesotho, Madagascar, Thailand, Myanmar, and Hawaii.

The Wonder Institute Postcard Project, 2012
COURTESY OF JERRY WELLMAN AND MATTHEW CHASE-DANIEL,
E PLURIBUS UNUM PROJECT, AXLE CONTEMPORARY, SANTA FE, NM